The Politics of Direct Democracy

Referendums in Global Perspective

LAWRENCE LEDUC

broadview press

National Library of Canada Cataloguing in Publication

LeDuc, Lawrence
    The politics of direct democracy : referendums in global perspective / Lawrence LeDuc

Includes bibliographical references and index.
ISBN 1-55111-433-X

    1. Referendum.   2. Direct Democracy.   I. Title.

JF491.L43 2003   328.2'3   C2003-904353-3

Broadview Press, Ltd. is an independent, international publishing house, incorporated in 1985.

North America	UK, Ireland, and Continental Europe	Australia and New Zealand
Post Office Box 1243,	Plymbridge	UNIREPS
Peterborough, Ontario,	Distributors, Ltd.	University of
Canada K9J 7H5	Estover Road	New South Wales
Tel: (705) 743-8990	Plymouth PL6 7PY	Sydney, NSW, 2052
Fax: (705) 743-8353	UK	Tel: + 61 2 96640999
	Tel: (01752) 202301	Fax: + 61 2 96645420
3576 California Road,	Fax: (01752) 202333	info.press@unsw.edu.au
Orchard Park, New York	orders@plymbridge.com	
USA 14127		

Broadview believes in shared ownership, both with its employees and with the general public; since the year 2000 Broadview shares have traded publicly on the Toronto Venture Exchange under the symbol BDP.

We welcome any comments and suggestions regarding any aspect of our publications—please feel free to contact us at the addresses below, or at broadview@broadviewpress.com / customerservice@broadviewpress.com / www.broadviewpress.com

Broadview Press Ltd. gratefully acknowledges the financial support of the Government of Canada through the Book Publishing Industry Development Program for our publishing activities.

Cover design and typeset by Zack Taylor, www.zacktaylor.com.

 This book is printed on acid-free paper containing 30% post-consumer fibre.

Printed in Canada

Eco-Logo Certified.
30% Post.

In memory of Donald E. Stokes

Contents

Tables and Figures

Tables

Figures

Acknowledgments

This project began as a Research Opportunity Seminar sponsored by the Faculty of Arts and Science at the University of Toronto. I am indebted to the undergraduate students in that seminar for their enthusiastic participation in the project and particularly to Josh Koziebrocki and Helder Marcos, who continued to work on it in various capacities long after the seminar was completed, and who contributed to it in various ways. I am also grateful to Michael Harvey, who served as senior research assistant for the seminar and also on the larger Comparative Referendums Project, from which some of the material contained in this volume is drawn.

The support of the Social Sciences and Humanities Research Council of Canada (grant no. 410-98-4161) for the Comparative Referendums Project is gratefully acknowledged. Some of the work in this volume was also completed under the auspices of the Democratic Education Project, organized by the Centre for the Study of Democracy at Queen's University. I am particularly indebted to its director, Professor George Perlin, for his support of the project and for his permission to use material published in Ukrainian as part of the Democratic Education Series in this volume. I would also like to thank Professor Michael Marsh of Trinity College, Dublin, Professor Palle Svensson of the Institute for Political Science, University of Aarhus, and Professor Ian McAllister of the Research School of Social Sciences, Australian National University, who provided me with access to research materials and facilities at their respective institutions. Finally, I am grateful to Michael Harrison of Broadview Press for his encouragement and support of this volume.

Introduction
Understanding
Referendums

This book is intended to provide a broadly comparative, empirically based introduction to the institutions of direct democracy as they exist in the world today. As the first chapter of the book establishes, the use of devices such as initiatives, referendums, and other types of direct votes has increased substantially over the past two decades. In Britain, where these institutions were long considered to be largely incompatible with traditional forms of parliamentary government, there have been no fewer than seven important referendums since 1975, including landmark votes on issues such as European Union (EU) membership, Scottish and Welsh devolution, and Northern Ireland governance. Other European countries such as Ireland and Denmark, which have long had referendum provisions in their national constitutions or on the statute books, seem to be using these mechanisms more frequently. In Chapter 1 of this book I discuss some of the reasons for this widespread recent growth in the use of instruments of direct democracy. For various reasons the referendum seems to fulfil a need of both governments and citizens in many contemporary democratic societies.

Referendums are relatively rare events in the politics of most democratic nations. In only a few countries is the referendum a long-established and frequently used device for obtaining popular consent on major public questions. Switzerland, as discussed in Chapter 6 of this book, uses the referendum as an integral part of its process of government, and Australia (Chapter 3) does so for all constitutional changes. Instruments of direct democracy are also widely employed in many American states, although there has never been a nationwide referendum in the United States. In a few other instances, notably Italy and Ireland, the referendum is a more frequently used, but still far from routine, part of the political process. Irish referendums on divorce (1986, 1995) and abortion (1983, 1992, 2002), for example, and the referendums in several European countries dealing with European Union issues are important cases that can help to illustrate several attributes of the referendum as a device for dealing with complex and contentious public issues.

In Canada there is increasing discussion at all levels of government about the potential of the referendum as a device for improving the quality of democracy and reducing the perceived "democratic deficit." The two Quebec sovereignty referendums, as well as the 1992 federal constitutional referendum on the Charlottetown Accord, were events of major national significance. Yet the overall Canadian experience with referendums, particularly at the federal level, has been both modest and controversial. The three federal votes that have taken place over our history—the prohibition plebiscite of 1898, the conscription plebiscite of 1942, and the referendum of 1992—all singularly failed to resolve the particular political problem that each was intended to address. At the provincial level, referendums or plebiscites have been used somewhat more often, but they are still far from commonplace. Newfoundland used a two-stage referendum in 1948 in its decision to enter Confederation, and votes in the Northwest Territories in 1982 and 1992 prepared the way for the creation of Nunavut. However, with a political culture firmly rooted in the British parliamentary tradition, Canadians generally tend to look at the California style of politics with a sense of both fascination and trepidation.

Considering the extent to which the referendum has been used in modern democratic politics and considering that both practitioners and theorists are increasingly advocating its use, as a political institution the referendum remains much understudied by political scientists. In North America particularly, advocates of the referendum tend to idealize it as a democratic device, while at the same time knowing relatively little about the actual behaviour of voters during referendums that have actually taken place. While referendums can appear on one level to be the ultimate expression of democratic values, they can also be manipulated by elites. Voters may have imperfect information, and turnout may be low. The argument that referendums are a superior device for democratic citizen participation depends heavily on the assumption that institutions and rules can be created to guarantee high levels of knowledge and participation. In

Switzerland, where referendums are more commonplace, voter turnout is often well below 50 per cent, although it may rise to higher levels when a particular issue engages wider interest. Referendums often provide a more volatile electoral environment than do ordinary elections. Such was the case in the 1992 referendum on the Charlottetown Accord, when voting intentions shifted dramatically over the course of the campaign. However, these aspects of voting and participation in referendums might be expected to vary considerably from one case to another, because each referendum is unique, and the political context can differ widely. The goal of this book, therefore, is to provide a more nuanced understanding of the referendum as a device for democratic citizen participation. Our understanding needs to be empirical as well as theoretical. By studying actual examples of referendums, rather than merely the arguments commonly advanced in support of or in opposition to them, we may be able to arrive at a more realistic appraisal of their potential to enhance the quality of modern democratic life.

Plan of the Book

I begin this analysis by considering a broadly inclusive set of referendums in thirty-nine countries that took place between 1975 and 2000 (Table 1.1, Chapter 1). Because referendums are rare in the political life of most countries, this comparative approach provides a way to identify and consider the many legal forms and variations of the devices that I refer to here under the generic label of "referendums." I examine both the theoretical and the practical arguments that are commonly advanced concerning instruments of direct democracy and the manner in which they engage various actors in the political process, including citizens, groups, governments, and political parties.

As will become evident from the initial broad survey of examples of referendums drawn from a number of countries, the subject matter of referendums varies widely. In many countries, the process is reserved for major constitutional changes or exceptionally important issues on which public consultation seems essential. European Union membership, changes in the electoral system, secession, and major changes in the form of governance are obvious examples. Because referendums are often limited to such issues in many countries, they are rarely used there. Yet citizens of

Switzerland and of California are often called upon to vote on issues that seem trivial by comparison. Among the subjects of recent referendums in Switzerland have been matters such as highway speed limits, the length of the workweek, casino gambling, and the creation of a new federal holiday. Term limits, environmental measures, and tax limitation proposals have been the subject of direct votes in a number of American states. In spite of this diversity, it is possible to discern some distinct patterns in the issues on which citizens are asked to vote. Referendums most commonly take place on *constitutional* issues, *international agreements* and *treaties*, questions of *sovereignty* or self-determination, and other more general matters of *public policy*. These four categories will be used to classify the various referendums discussed in Chapters 3 to 6 of this book.

Within each of these respective categories, I examine several specific cases. In Chapter 3, I consider referendums on major constitutional questions that took place in Canada, Russia, New Zealand, and Australia over the last decade. Chapter 4 examines cases involving treaties and international agreements, including the 1986 Spanish referendum on NATO membership, the French vote on the Maastricht Treaty, the referendums in Norway, Sweden, and Finland on European Union membership, and the vote in 2000 in Denmark on participation in the European Monetary Union. In Chapter 5, I consider referendums that have involved issues of sovereignty, including the two Quebec referendums, Ukraine's independence referendum of 1991, the Scottish and Welsh devolution referendums, and the three votes on statehood that have taken place in the US Commonwealth of Puerto Rico. Finally, in Chapter 6 I examine votes on various public policy questions, including a 1980 vote in Sweden on the issue of nuclear power, the Irish referendums on divorce and abortion, and the wide-ranging set of issues on which there have been direct votes in California and in Switzerland.

By exploring in detail a diversity of cases and contexts, I hope to achieve a better empirical understanding of the contribution that referendums and similar instruments can make to democratic political life. In Chapter 7, I consider what this broad comparative analysis of cases can teach us about the activities of key actors, such as political parties, in referendum campaigns and about the behaviour of voters when they are called upon to make the kinds of complex political choices that are often presented to them in a referendum. In the concluding chapter, I assess the contribution of direct democratic processes to modern political life and consider whether such institutions are in fact capable of delivering on their implied promise to improve the quality of our democracy. This book aims to provide students and others with a comprehensive, up-to-date survey of direct democratic institutions and devices as they have developed both in the thinking of modern political theorists and in the actual political practice of democratic states.

1
Referendums in Democratic Societies

The condition of democracy in the world today is cause for both optimism and concern. On the one hand, democracy flourishes in more places than ever before. The transition to democracy in the nations of the former Soviet Union and Eastern Europe, parts of Africa, and much of Central and South America brought about what Samuel Huntington (1991) has called a "third wave" of democratization around the globe. Yet not all citizens of the newly democratized nations of the world see their experiment with democratic political institutions as an unqualified success. In many instances, democracy has not delivered better living standards, economic prosperity, or even political stability and genuine reform. While democratic institutions and norms have consolidated in countries such as Spain, Poland, and South Korea, they remain fragile in many other nations. In the longer term, the survival of democracy in some of these new environments will depend on the performance of democratic institutions and processes and on their citizens' ultimate evaluation of that performance.

Although democratic political institutions themselves are under no threat in the more established democracies of the West, many citizens express varying degrees of dissatisfaction with the quality of their democracy. The concept of a *democratic deficit* first found political expression in Europe when control over many areas of political life seemed to be passing from national governments to the more remote and centralized (and inherently less democratic) institutions of the new Europe. Subsequently, protests against "globalization" became commonplace in many of the developed countries of Europe and North America, reflecting a perception on the part of many citizens that new economic regimes had brought with them a serious decline in the effectiveness of traditional processes of democratic accountability. Steadily lower voting turnout in recent elections in many countries provides additional hard evidence that all is not well with democracy in the world today.[1]

Public opinion surveys in recent years have identified at least part of the explanation for this democratic malaise. They disclose a widespread feeling among citizens that governments have become disengaged and remote and that elections alone cannot guarantee sufficient choice or accountability. Elected officials are often seen as unresponsive and out of touch, even in many countries with long-established and seemingly well-functioning democratic regimes. Ordinary citizens feel an increasing sense of political powerlessness and express little trust in the ability of existing political institutions to address their concerns.[2] But most critics of existing political institutions and practices seek to improve democracy, not to replace it. They demand political processes that might allow for greater participation by the people and a sense that governments can be made more responsive and accountable to the electorate.

In seeking ways to reduce these feelings of dissatisfaction and malaise, many reformers have begun to look favourably on political institutions that were once associated with an earlier, simpler vision of democracy. Various devices, such as term limits, recall of elected politicians, citizen initiatives, and referendums, have generated renewed interest in numerous countries, states, provinces, and municipalities. In particular, the referendum, a long-established but sparingly used method of deciding important and contentious political issues, has found new favour.[3] Giving citizens the chance to express their views directly on important political questions or providing them with additional opportunities to intervene in the sometimes impenetrable processes of political decision making seems an obvious remedy for the present democratic malaise. While the referendum may not be capable of resolving all of democracy's problems, it does respond to at least some of the concerns expressed by many citizens in contemporary democratic societies. This new interest in an old institution of direct democracy reflects the mood of the times.

Indeed, there is little doubt that a once-radical view associated with a more populist form of democracy has found new favour throughout the world today. Referendums of a number of different types have been used much more frequently in recent years. Many countries or jurisdictions that previously had no legal provision for referendums have adopted new initiative or referendum legislation.[4] Other countries that have long had ref-

Figure 1.1

Worldwide Use of the Referendum in the Twentieth Century

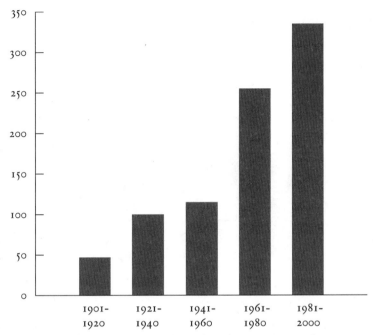

Sources: Butler and Ranney (1994); *Electoral Studies*; University of Geneva Center for the Study of Direct Democracy (http://c2d.unige.ch/); *Keesing's Record of World Events.* National referendums only.

erendum provisions in their national constitutions or on the statute books seem to be using such mechanisms more frequently.[5] Ireland, for example, has conducted referendums on a number of issues related to the European Union (1972, 1987, 1992, 1998, 2001, 2002), on the contentious issues of divorce (1986, 1995) and abortion (1983, 1992, 2002), and on the Northern Ireland peace agreement (1998), as well as on various other constitutional issues. Denmark has conducted no fewer than five referendums on various European issues and treaties since it joined the EU in 1973.

The data displayed in Figure 1.1 show the extent to which the various nations of the world have embraced ideas of direct democracy in the latter part of the twentieth century, particularly in the period after 1960. These data reflect national usage of initiatives or referendums only and do not include referendums conducted below the national level. In the

Figure 1.2

US State Initiatives and Referendums in the Twentieth Century

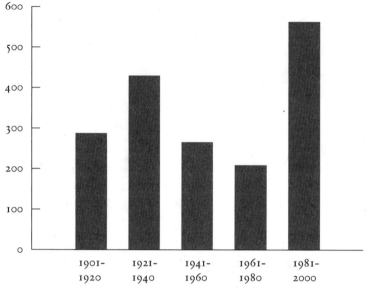

Sources: Initiative and Referendum Institute (http://www.iandrinstitute.org); Magleby (1994).

United States, for example, these devices are employed in many states and localities, even though there has never been a national referendum in that country. All states except Delaware provide for amendments to their state constitutions to be submitted to a popular vote, and most also permit the legislature to place other types of issues on the ballot. Twenty-four have provisions for citizen initiatives.[6] Several Western US states, such as California, Oregon, Colorado, and North Dakota have used instruments of direct democracy extensively and with dramatically increased frequency in recent years. In many of the states, such institutions were first adopted during the Progressive Era in the early part of the twentieth century. Populist traditions were stronger in the Western US states than in the older states of the East—a pattern that still largely holds today. Following a period of gradual decline in the postwar period, the use of initiative and referendum procedures in the American states exploded during the 1980s and 1990s (Figure 1.2). On the day of the November 2000 presidential election in the

Table 1.1
Referendums in Fifty-eight Democracies, 1975–2000

Country	Number	Date	Subject	Number of Items	Yes (%)	Turnout (%)
Argentina	1	1984 11 25	Treaty with Chile	1	81	73
Australia	4	1977 05 21	Constitutional amendments/national song	5	*	92
		1984 12 01	Constitutional amendments	2	*	94
		1988 09 03	Constitutional amendments	4	*	92
		1999 11 06	Republic/constitutional preamble	2	*	95
Austria	2	1978 11 05	Nuclear power	1	49	64
		1994 06 12	EU membership	1	67	81
Bangladesh	3	1977 05 30	Constitution	1	99	85
		1985 03 21	Presidential term	1	95	72
		1991 09 15	Parliamentary regime	1	84	42
Benin	1	1990 12 02	Constitution	1	73	63
Belgium	0					
Bolivia	0					
Brazil	1	1993 04 21	Form of government	2	*	80
Bulgaria	0					
Chile	4	1978 01 04	Approve president's agreement	1	78	75
		1980 09 11	Approve regime	1	69	93
		1988 10 05	Extend president's term	1	44	97
		1989 06 30	Constitution	1	91	85
Costa Rica	0					
Czech Republic	0					
Denmark	6	1978 09 19	Lower voting age	1	54	63

Country	Number	Date	Subject	Number of Items	Yes (%)	Turnout (%)
Denmark (continued)		1986 02 27	Single European Act	1	56	75
		1992 06 02	Maastricht Treaty	1	49	83
		1993 05 18	Edinburgh Agreement	1	57	86
		1998 05 28	Amsterdam Treaty	1	55	75
		2000 09 28	European currency	1	47	89
Dominican Republic	0					
Ecuador	5	1978 01 15	New constitution	1	57	90
		1986 07 01	Electoral procedures	1	30	
		1994 08 28	Constitutional issues	7	*	60
		1995 11 26	Political and economic reforms	11	*	59
		1997 05 25	Political reforms	14	*	59
El Salvador	0					
Finland	1	1994 10 16	EU membership	1	57	71
France	2	1988 11 06	New Caledonia	1	80	37
		1992 09 20	Maastricht Treaty	1	51	70
Germany	0					
Greece	0					
Honduras	0					
Hungary	3	1989 11 26	Elections +	4	*	55
		1990 07 29	Presidency	1	86	14
		1997 11 16	NATO membership	1	85	49
India	0					
Ireland	12	1979 07 05	Adoptions/electoral system	2	*	28
		1983 09 07	Prohibition of abortion	1	67	53
		1984 06 14	Voting rights	1	75	46

Country		Date	Description			
		1986 06 26	Legalization of divorce	1	37	61
		1987 05 26	Single European Act	1	70	44
		1992 06 18	Maastricht Treaty	1	69	57
		1992 11 25	Abortion laws	3	*	65
		1995 11 24	Legalization of divorce	1	50	62
		1996 11 28	Bail reform	1	75	29
		1997 10 30	Confidential meetings	1	53	47
		1998 05 22	N. Ireland / Amsterdam treaty	2	*	56
		1999 06 11	Local government	1	78	51
Israel	0					
Italy	11	1978 06 11	Party subsidies/police powers	2	*	81
		1981 05 17	Abortion laws +	5	*	79
		1985 06 09	Repeal of wage indexation	1	46	78
		1987 11 08	Nuclear power +	5	*	65
		1989 06 18	MEP's mandate	1	88	81
		1990 06 03	Hunting laws/food regulations	3	*	43
		1991 06 09	Electoral law	1	96	63
		1993 04 18	Drug laws/party subsidies +	8	*	77
		1995 06 11	Union rights/broadcasting +	12	*	57
		1997 06 15	Judiciary/civil service +	7	*	30
		1999 04 18	Representation	1	91	50
Japan	0					
Lithuania	7	1991 02 04	Independence	1	93	85
		1992 05 23	Presidential regime	1	73	59
		1992 06 14	Withdrawal of USSR troops	1	92	76
		1992 10 25	Constitution	1	78	75
		1994 08 27	Privatizations +	8	*	37

Country	Number	Date	Subject	Number of Items	Yes (%)	Turnout (%)
Lithuania (continued)		1996 10 20	Parliament/budget	4	*	52
		1996 11 10	Land purchases	1	52	40
Madagascar	4	1975 12 21	Constitution	1	95	92
		1992 08 19	Constitution	1	73	75
		1995 09 17	President	1	72	41
		1998 03 15	Constitutional reforms	1	51	70
Malawi	1	1993 06 14	Multiparty system	1	65	67
Mali	1	1992 12 01	Constitution	1	99	44
Mexico	0					
Mozambique	0					
Nepal	1	1980 05 02	One-party system	1	55	67
Netherlands	0					
New Zealand	11	1975 11 29	Liquor laws	1	a	83
		1978 11 25	Liquor laws	1	a	84
		1981 11 28	Liquor laws	1	a	89
		1984 07 14	Liquor laws	1	a	92
		1987 08 15	Liquor laws	1	a	87
		1990 10 17	Legislative term	1	30	79
		1992 09 19	Electoral system reform	2	*	55
		1993 11 06	New electoral law	1	54	83
		1995 12 02	Fire brigades	1	13	28
		1997 09 05-26	Retirement insurance	1	8	80
		1999 11 28	Size of parliament/victims' rights	2	*	83
Nicaragua	0					
Norway	1	1994 11 28	EU membership	1	48	89

Country		Date	Subject		
Philippines	6	1975 02 27	Martial law / local government	*	91
		1976 10 16	Martial law +	*	97
		1977 12 18	Approve president	90	98
		1981 04 07	Presidential term	75	66
		1984 01 27	Constitutional reform	*	NA
		1987 02 02	Constitution	77	85
Poland	3	1987 11 29	Political and economic reforms	*	67
		1996 02 18	Privatization/economic reforms	*	33
		1997 05 25	Constitution	53	43
Portugal	2	1998 06 29	Legalize abortion	49	32
		1998 11 08	Regionalization	36	48
Romania	2	1986 11 23	Reduce army	100	100
		1991 12 08	Constitution	79	67
Russia	3	1991 03 17	USSR/presidency	*	75
		1993 04 25	Economic reforms +	*	65
		1993 12 12	New constitution	55	58
Slovakia	2	1997 05 24	Presidency/NATO	*	10
		1998 09 26	Stop to privatization	84	44
South Africa	2	1983 11 02	Presidential government	66	76
		1992 03 17	End to Apartheid	69	85
South Korea	3	1975 02 12	Constitution/president	74	80
		1980 10 22	New constitution	92	96
		1987 10 27	Constitutional change	93	78
Spain	3	1976 12 15	Political reforms	94	78
		1978 12 07	New constitution	92	67
		1986 03 12	NATO membership	53	59
Sweden	2	1980 03 23	Nuclear power	a	76

Country	Number	Date	Subject	Number of Items	Yes (%)	Turnout (%)
Sweden (continued)		1994 11 13	EU membership	1	52	83
Switzerland	72		See Chapter 6D	222		
Taiwan	1	1994 11 27	Stop to nuclear reactor	1	90	21
Thailand	0					
Turkey	3	1982 11 07	New constitution	1	92	90
		1987 09 06	Amnesty	1	50	92
		1988 09 25	Local elections timetable	1	35	68
Ukraine	3	1991 03 17	USSR/sovereignty	2	*	84
		1991 12 01	Independence	1	90	84
		2000 04 16	Parliament	4	*	81
United Kingdom	1	1975 06 05	EC membership	1	67	65
United States	0					
Uruguay	9	1971 11 28	Presidency	1	28	92
		1980 11 30	Constitution	1	42	79
		1989 04 16	Amnesty law	1	55	77
		1989 11 26	Index pensions	1	82	88
		1992 12 13	Privatization	1	72	77
		1994 08 28	Electoral laws	1	31	85
		1994 11 27	Education/social security	2	*	90
		1996 12 08	Constitutional reforms	1	51	86
		1999 10 31	Courts/parliament	2	*	92
Venezuela	2	1999 04 25	Constitutional convention	2	*	38
		1999 12 15	New constitution	1	72	44

* Denotes multiple items on ballot.   a Denotes more than two ballot options.   + Denotes other items.

United States, more than two hundred separate issues were on the ballot in forty-one states.[7] There is, however, a great deal of variation among the US states, in both the form and the frequency of referendums and initiatives. Nevertheless, the gains that these institutions have made below the national level in the United States provide a laboratory, rivalled only by Switzerland, in which political scientists can gain a better understanding of the form and functioning of direct democracy in the world today.

Further evidence of the extent to which the referendum has found a place in the political life of modern democracies may be seen in Table 1.1. which displays information on referendums held in all countries in the world with a national population of at least three million people that met certain basic tests of functioning electoral democracy.[8] Of the fifty-eight nations meeting these criteria in 2000, thirty-nine had conducted at least one nationwide referendum between 1975 and 2000. A few countries, such as Italy, Switzerland, and Uruguay used referendums with greater frequency, while in others, such as Canada, Norway, and Brazil, the sole national referendum held during that time was a rare but singularly important political event. Among the minority of major democratic nations that conducted no national referendum over this twenty-five-year period are such established democracies as the United States, Germany, India, and Japan. This suggests that the referendum, although growing substantially in importance over the latter part of the twentieth century, was not ubiquitous. It would, moreover, be difficult to conclude from these observations that there is any clear pattern regarding referendum usage and democratic practice. Few would argue that democracy is healthier in Ireland and Italy than in the United States and Japan merely because Ireland and Italy use referendums more frequently to resolve certain types of political issues. Nor do California and Oregon necessarily enjoy a better quality of democracy than might be found in, say, Pennsylvania or Vermont. Some countries or states whose political cultures are thoroughly democratic manage to live happily without such devices, a few use them extensively, and many others have integrated one or more of them by varying degrees into their political life. In spite of the simplicity of some of the arguments advanced for or against direct democracy, it seems clear that the patterns suggested by real political experience with the instruments of direct democracy are not at all simple.

My objective thus far has been to provide an overview of referendums and citizen initiatives in modern democratic societies. The evidence shows

Table 1.2

Public Attitudes towards Direct Democracy in Four Nations (Percentages)

	Canada	Sweden	Finland	New Zealand
Better to have a referendum	43	75	84	62
Better to let government (parliament) decide	49	22	14	20
Don't know, no opinion	8	3	2	18

Sources: For Canada, 1992 Carleton Referendum Study, cited in Clarke et al. (1996); for New Zealand, 1987 National Election Study, cited in Simpson (1992); Sweden and Finland, 1994 Comparative EU Referendum Study, cited in Jenssen et al. (1998).
Note: The survey question in Canada referred to the 1992 constitutional agreement, in New Zealand to the issue of electoral reform, and in Sweden and Finland to the question of European Union membership.

widespread use in both new and established democracies and a substantial increase over the past two decades, even in countries that had never before used such procedures or that had long ago discarded them. The referendum has been used not only to manage questions of major constitutional change but also to allow citizens to influence the decisions of government directly on a wide range of policy matters, at least partly in response to a widespread sense of dissatisfaction with democratic performance in many countries. We might assume that citizens who have become disillusioned with the performance of more traditional representative institutions would embrace these new developments enthusiastically. But such has not always been the case. Voters in Canada, New Zealand, and Sweden were somewhat divided, for example, on the question of whether important political decisions, even momentous ones such as constitutional revision or European Union membership, were better decided in a referendum or by more traditional political processes (Table 1.2). Their reservations are at least partly explained by the fact that referendums have been rare in these countries and have often not been fully integrated into the existing political culture. In California and Switzerland, where direct votes on a wide range of public issues are considered routine, citizens generally support the process.[9]

While there is often widespread public support for the general principles of direct democracy, referendums, like elections, do not always fulfil their potential. Referendums can appear on one level to be the ultimate

Figure 1.3
Representative and Direct Democracy

Unmediated direct democracy		Pure representative democracy

		Ireland		Germany
	Switzerland	Italy		Canada
	California		Uruguay	Britain

Source: Adapted from Budge (1996).

expression of democratic values, but students of the referendum process in modern democratic societies often cite reservations arising from problems such as low voter turnout, complex wording of questions, manipulation by elites, inadequate information for voters, or the role of special interest groups. Democratic theorists also have long worried that referendums might jeopardize the rights of minorities or exacerbate social and ethnic tensions. There may be good reasons, for example, why referendums have not been used in countries such as Belgium, India, and Israel, where the risks of inflaming social and ethnic tensions are high. In Canada, the historic experience with referendums on divisive issues such as conscription and prohibition produced serious reservations about using them to resolve difficult political issues at the national level.[10] In the United States in recent years, the experience with citizen initiatives in some states has ignited new controversies regarding the disproportionate influence of well-organized and well-funded interest groups in initiative campaigns. Such concerns have led to a critical view of the American experience with these devices as "democracy derailed," rather than fulfilled (Broder 2000).

In theoretical terms, representative democracy and direct democracy are sometimes thought of as representing opposite versions of the democratic vision (shown at opposite ends of the *continuum* in Figure 1.3). Citizens in a democracy either delegate power to elected representatives or retain it for themselves. In reality, however, the choices available to citizens in a modern democracy may not be so stark. Many nations have traditionally combined elements of both direct and representative democracy in their political institutions and have merely shifted the balance more towards one direction or the other at some time in their history. They can therefore be located at some point between the two ends of the continuum. Nations such as Switzerland, for example—which perhaps comes closest today to practising direct democracy on a continuing and entrenched basis—have not discarded the institutions of representative democracy in the process of institutionalizing the referendum. Nor has the Swiss experience led to more serious social tensions, even though Switzerland has many of the same ethnic and linguistic divisions that are found in countries such as Canada or Belgium. It has not done so, in part, because of the constitutional structuring of referendums in Switzerland with provisions requiring, for example, double majorities in certain types of votes. But the controversy surrounding the initiative of November 2002 on asylum seekers in Switzerland suggests that the Swiss, like other frequent users of initiatives and referendums, are not immune to the traditional concerns regarding the rights of minorities.

At the other end of the spectrum, countries such as Britain, which historically have vested political power exclusively in representative parliamentary institutions, are increasingly turning to the referendum in an attempt to resolve long standing political problems or to address new ones. In Europe more generally, the new challenges of the European Union have prompted increased use of the referendum in many of the member countries. The ten countries that are set to enter the EU in 2004 will likely all use referendums to approve their accession, whether they have used them in the past or not.[11] But this does not mean that the representative institutions of nations that are introducing the referendum into their politics in this way are under threat. Rather, many nations have increasingly sought ways to combine some of the elements of direct democracy with their existing political institutions. Thus, while the use of referendums has increased considerably, even in countries that have traditionally preferred representative democracy, it is clear that most of the functioning democracies in the world today would still be located closer to the representative end of the continuum in Figure 1.3. Only Switzerland and perhaps some American states, such as California and Oregon, would be located closer to the "direct democracy" end of the continuum. But even in those cases, most political decisions, including many important ones, are not made in referendums. In Switzerland, voters are called upon approximately four times a year to decide perhaps three or four issues that are put to them on each occasion. The rest of the time, Swiss processes of government function much as they do in other representative democracies.

Given this diversity, it is not surprising to find that the subject matter of referendums also varies widely. In many countries the referendum is

Table 1.3

A Typology of the Subject Matter of Referendums

CONSTITUTIONAL ISSUES. Amendments to the constitution and changes in political institutions, forms of governance, basic laws, etc.

Examples
Australian constitutional referendums
1992 Canadian constitutional referendum
1993 Russian constitutional referendum
1992 and 1993 New Zealand referendums on electoral reform
1993 Brazilian referendum on a presidential system of government
1991 Swiss referendum to lower the voting age

TREATIES AND INTERNATIONAL AGREEMENTS. All agreements between nations, supranational organizations, etc., whether such referendums are constitutionally mandated or not

Examples
1986 Danish referendum on the Single European Act
1986 Spanish referendum on NATO membership
1992 French referendum on the Maastricht Treaty
1994 Austrian referendum on European Union membership
1994 Swiss referendum on participation in UN peacekeeping forces
1998 referendum on the Northern Ireland peace agreement

SOVEREIGNTY. Referendums on territorial questions, issues of "national" self-determination, devolution of authority, federation, secession

Examples
1944 referendum that separated Iceland from Denmark
1948 vote in Newfoundland to join Canada
1991 Ukrainian referendum on independence
1980 and 1995 Quebec referendums on sovereignty
Referendums on statehood for Puerto Rico (1967, 1993, 1998)
1997 referendums in Scotland and Wales to establish national assemblies

PUBLIC POLICY. Referendums on policy questions, including consultative votes on government proposals, abrogative votes on public laws, citizen initiatives, etc.

Examples
Various referendums on prohibition (e.g., Norway, 1926; Iceland, 1933)
New Zealand referendums on conscription (1949) and liquor laws (1967)
1978 Austrian or 1980 Swedish referendums on nuclear power
1992 Uruguayan referendum on privatization of state industries
1993 Italian referendum on decriminalization of drugs
Swiss referendums on social insurance, tobacco and alcohol advertising, casino
　　gambling, sales and gasoline taxes, federal holiday (1993)

reserved for major constitutional changes or exceptionally important issues on which public consultation is a political necessity or is required by law. Yet, as already noted, Switzerland does not limit their use in that way. And in jurisdictions where consultations of the people may be initiated by citizens rather than organized by government, it would be difficult or impossible to limit the range of possible subjects that might be introduced into the public debate. Nevertheless, certain distinct patterns are readily observable among the range of cases displayed earlier in Table 1.1. Referendums most commonly take place on constitutional issues, international agreements and treaties, questions of "national" sovereignty or self-determination, and other more general matters of public policy. I will employ these categories, which make up the typology, or system of classification, in Table 1.3, to analyse specific cases in subsequent chapters of this book.

The typology used here is slightly different from the one used by David Butler and Austin Ranney (1994) in their survey of referendums around the world.[12] It is also easily seen that these categories, however formulated, are not mutually exclusive. A vote on an important public policy question, such as the Irish divorce and abortion referendums, may also involve constitutional matters. Likewise, a treaty may or may not be incorporated into constitutional law. A few cases, such as the 1992 and 1993 New Zealand referendums on the electoral system, may not fit easily into any of the categories unless terms such as "constitutional" are defined fairly broadly. An unusual case, such as the 1998 referendum on the Northern Ireland peace agreement, might conceivably be listed under any of the four categories shown in Table 1.3, although I have included it in category 2 (treaties and international agreements) in this formulation. The categories are nevertheless useful for a general understanding of the kinds of issues on which citizens of democratic nations are most often called upon to vote.

In the subsequent chapters of this book, I will explore some of the theoretical and practical concerns that arise when institutions of direct democracy are used to address these varying types of issues. I will also examine in greater detail several of the specific referendums that have been cited as examples in this chapter within each of the categories in Table 1.3. A more detailed analysis of these cases will provide a good comparative test of some of the arguments that are commonly advanced by commentators who see the referendum as one solution to the malaise afflicting many modern democratic societies. It is important not to idealize the initiative or referendum as a democratic device without knowing a great deal more about its ability to address real political problems. These cases can provide such a test. Taken together, they may be able to give us a more empirically based understanding of both the possibilities and the limitations of the institutions and processes of direct democracy.

NOTES

1. Note especially the declines in turnout that have occurred in recent elections in Canada, Britain, France, and Japan. Turnout statistics for elections in most countries are available from the Institute for Democracy and Electoral Assistance (IDEA) at http://www.idea.int/vt.

2. See Dalton (2002) and Norris (1999) for comparisons of data on political trust, efficacy, and support from surveys in several different countries.

3. See especially the arguments advanced by proponents of the referendum such as Barber (1984) or Boyer (1992a). For an up-to-date survey of thought on this issue, see Mendelsohn and Parkin (2001).

4. New Zealand, for example, adopted new provisions for citizen-initiated referendums in 1993. See Parkinson (2001) for a discussion of the New Zealand legislation.

5. More extensive information on the use of the referendum throughout the world may be found in the archive maintained by the University of Geneva Center for the Study of Direct Democracy at http://c2d.unige.ch/.

6. The states that provide for citizen initiatives are Alaska, Arizona, Arkansas, California, Colorado, Florida, Idaho, Illinois, Maine, Massachusetts, Michigan, Mississippi, Missouri, Montana, Nebraska, Nevada, North Dakota, Ohio, Oklahoma, Oregon, South Dakota, Utah, Washington, and Wyoming. Initiative and Referendum Institute at http://www.iandrinstitute.org. See also Magleby (1994).

7. Initiative and Referendum Institute. See also table 6C1, p. 139.

8. (LeDuc, Niemi and Norris 2002). Tests applied included measures such as the Gastil Political Rights Index (http://www.freedomhouse.org), as well as criteria such as the existence of functioning democratic electoral institutions. The table reflects the status of these fifty-eight countries at the end of 2000, when these classifications were made.

9. In a 1990 survey of California voters, for example, 68 per cent of the respondents said that ballot propositions were "a good thing," 8 per cent felt that they were "a bad thing," and 24 per cent felt that they were "neither good nor bad," or had no opinion. Field Institute poll, cited in Bowler and Donovan (1998).

10. Both the prohibition vote in 1898 and the conscription plebiscite of 1942 led to different results in English and French Canada, thereby creating new political difficulties for the prime ministers (Laurier in 1898; King in 1942) who had initiated the votes in the hope that they would resolve the issue. See Boyer (1992b).

11. Poland, Hungary, the Czech Republic, Slovakia, Slovenia, Lithuania, Latvia, Estonia, Cyprus, and Malta are scheduled to enter the EU under the current enlargement agreement on May 1, 2004.

12. Their categories were constitutional issues, territorial issues, moral issues, and other issues (Butler and Ranney 1994).

2

Theoretical, Conceptual, and Procedural Problems

To this point, I have lumped together the various forms of direct democracy found in different countries using the generic label referendums. It should be recognized, however, that this usage takes in various different forms and does not differentiate among the several types of legal framework within which a direct vote on a public issue might take place. Strictly speaking, the term "referendum" applies when a vote is initiated by a governing body such as a legislature and the result is legally binding on the body that initiated it. In many of the cases documented in Table 1.1, however, the results of such votes were not necessarily binding on the legislative body. In an older form of usage they might therefore have been called plebiscites, but today they are generally referred to as consultative referendums. The 1994 votes in Finland, Norway, and Sweden on membership in the European Union were not legally binding on the governments that initiated them, but the earlier (1972) votes in Ireland and Denmark on European Community membership were. Whether or not a referendum result is legally binding is generally determined by a country's constitution or basic law. However, this distinction is perhaps less meaningful than it once was. Governments in a modern democracy will generally hesitate to ignore a formal vote of their citizens on an important public issue, whether that vote is considered binding on them in a legal sense or not.[1] In Sweden following the 1994 referendum on European Union membership, no member of the Riksdag voted against the enabling legislation, even though only 52 per cent of the public had supported it and many individual members of the Riksdag remained personally opposed.

37

The result may not have been legally binding, but it was clearly treated as politically binding by the legislators, regardless of their personal view.

Votes that result from a petition of citizens rather than from the action of a government are more properly called initiatives or citizen-initiated referendums. In a number of countries citizens may themselves bring about a vote on a public issue by meeting statutory or constitutional provisions for the collection of a minimum number of signatures on a petition. They thus force a vote on a proposal, whether the government wishes it or not. Most Swiss referendums are initiated in this manner, and the results are always legally binding. Many of the US state propositions, particularly in states such as California and Oregon, also reach the ballot by this method. The debate about direct democracy in many jurisdictions today is more often about citizen initiatives than about government-sponsored referendums. New Zealand, which adopted new referendum provisions in 1993, now provides for both types. Italy uses what is generally called the abrogative referendum, or popular veto, in which citizens may, by petition, force a public vote on a law that has already been adopted by the legislature. A petition of five hundred thousand citizens or a vote of five regional councils may force such a vote. A turnout of at least 50 per cent of registered voters is required for such a referendum to be valid in Italy.[2]

Thus, referendums may be used in some instances by governments to consult the people on a particular matter and in others by the people themselves to challenge or bypass the government. Markku Suksi (1993) documents in some detail the variations in legal form of referendums in different jurisdictions, a summary of which is found in Table 2.1. As noted, the categories in the table are general types and several variations are found in the laws of different countries. In many cases more than one of these routes to a referendum is possible. Switzerland, for example, does not use consultative referendums initiated by the government, but all other types are found there. Under the newly adopted New Zealand provisions, a non-binding vote of the people on any issue may be triggered either by citizen initiative or by action of the government. However, throughout this book the generic term "referendum" will be used to denote all these variations.

In the view of many modern political theorists, referendums, regardless of their legal form, enhance the quality of democracy through citizen participation in the political process in a way that elections alone cannot. A "referendum democracy" (Sartori 1987; Mendelsohn and Parkin 2001)

Table 2.1

Forms and Variations of the Referendum

MANDATORY CONSTITUTIONAL REFERENDUM
- Also called compulsory referendum, binding referendum.
- A vote that is required in order to effect a change in the constitution or basic law, the result of which is binding. Rules and procedures for such a referendum are generally entrenched in the constitution or defined by law.
- Used in Australia, Denmark, Ireland, Switzerland.
- Variations: such procedures might be included in a specific piece of legislation rather than a constitution or basic law. In the 1993 New Zealand referendum on electoral reform, the result was made binding by the legislation authorizing the referendum.

ABROGATIVE REFERENDUM
- Also called: rejective referendum, facultative referendum, popular veto.
- A procedure to force a vote of the people on a law that has been passed by the legislature.
- Once initiated, the result is generally binding.
- Used in Austria, Denmark, Italy, Sweden, Switzerland.
- Variations: in Switzerland, the procedure may be initiated by a petition of citizens (50,000). In Sweden and Austria, it is triggered by a minority (1/3) of the members of the parliament. In Italy, the procedure is initiated by legislators, by citizens (500,000), or by regional councils (5). In Italy, the procedure may be used to repeal any existing law, whereas in other cases it is generally applied only to new legislation.

CITIZEN INITIATED REFERENDUM
- Also called initiative, direct legislation.
- A referendum on any subject that is brought about by petition of citizens.
- Used in Switzerland, New Zealand, US states.
- Variations: The number of signatures required varies widely and is generally specified in the constitution or in the law authorizing such votes. Results are normally binding, but are sometimes subject to review by the courts or legislature. CIRs in New Zealand are nonbinding.

CONSULTATIVE REFERENDUM
- Also called: advisory referendum, plebiscite, ad hoc referendum.
- A vote on any subject, usually initiated by the government or legislature.
- The result is generally non-binding.
- Used in France, Britain, Canada, Finland.
- Variations: the rules and procedures for such a vote might be entrenched in a constitution (France), specified in a referendum law (Canada), or provided for in a bill authorizing a referendum on a particular issue (Britain).

Source: Adapted from Suksi (1993).

might be the type of "strong democracy" advocated by Benjamin Barber (1984), or it might at least be capable of curing some of the ills of modern representative democracy. Patrick Boyer, a former Canadian Member of Parliament and long-time advocate of the referendum, puts the case for referendums as follows:

> On many levels and in many ways, people can participate more in the decisions whose consequences affect their lives. Canadians can become less the passive spectators and more the active participants.... Canada's democratic process, under increasing criticism for not providing sufficient voice to the public at large, can be broadened and strengthened through greater use of referendums as an effective means of helping Canadians achieve an energizing degree of self-government. (Boyer 1992a, 21)

A similar line of argument was put forward in the debate leading up to the adoption of new referendum legislation in New Zealand (Simpson 1992) and in a book by Vernon Bogdanor advocating increased use of the referendum in Britain as part of a more comprehensive program of electoral reform:

> Wider use of the referendum could offer real benefits in the operation of British politics. It would prove a powerful weapon against the condition described by Lord Hailsham as "elective dictatorship"—the attempt by governments to implement major changes without ensuring popular support for them.... The referendum could improve the quality of the relationship between government and the people, and that constitutes the central argument in favour of its use. For, in the last resort, the arguments against the referendum are arguments against democracy, while acceptance of the referendum is but a logical consequence of accepting a democratic form of government. (1981, 93)

Thus, the arguments commonly advanced in favour of more participatory forms of democracy are clear and straightforward. The very essence of democracy lies in recognizing that sovereignty rests with all citizens rather than exclusively with a small group of representatives, however carefully chosen. In Bogdanor's words, arguments against the referendum often appear to be arguments against democracy itself. These ideas, of course, are not new, although in countries such as Canada, Britain, and New Zealand, whose political institutions derive from the British parliamentary tradition, they have long been resisted. Why, then, have these and other nations—nations that have long considered themselves democratic—not embraced the referendum sooner or more enthusiastically?

A wide range of objections are often raised, at least some of which are rooted in the classic debates about the ideals and limits of democracy. Perhaps the most serious is the concern about minority rights. James Madison raised the spectre of what he called the "tyranny of the majority," and the idea of regular referendums on major public issues would not have been an appealing concept to the framers of the American constitution in 1787. In large part, this explains why there is no referendum provision in the federal constitution of the United States today. Popular majorities might well use the processes of initiative or referendum to deprive unpopular minorities of their rights. Indeed, questions of minority rights have arisen in referendums held at the state level in the United States (Gamble 1997). In 1992 Colorado voters approved a ballot initiative that would have curtailed the civil rights of homosexuals—a measure which was subsequently overturned by the courts. Californians in 1994 voted to withhold state funding for education and health and social services from noncitizens found to be residing illegally in the state. The increasing occurrence of similar types of ballot initiatives in several US states in recent years suggests that there is good reason to fear that the rights of unpopular minorities could easily be placed at risk in direct votes. In 2002, Swiss voters narrowly rejected a proposal that would have sharply constrained the circumstances under which political refugees could claim asylum in Switzerland and that would also have reduced social benefits for refugees already in the country whose applications for asylum were under review.[3]

Madison believed, as do many critics of direct democratic institutions today, that it was necessary to provide safeguards against the unmitigated power of electoral majorities. Deliberative legislative bodies constitute one such safeguard. The courts, particularly in the United States, provide an additional constraint on the raw power of electoral majorities. But minorities may also be protected, not by forgoing direct democracy or having the courts review its outcomes, but by adjusting the rules for conducting referendums. For instance, concurrent majorities or super majorities (greater than 50 per cent) are sometimes required. In Switzerland, the country with the longest and most extensive experience with referendums in the world today, constitutional amendments must obtain a majority of votes in the federation and majorities in more than half the twenty-six cantons in order to be adopted.[4] Double-majority provisions such as these may help to protect the rights of linguistic, ethnic, and religious minorities in Switzerland against the unmitigated power of the majority groups. But from the perspective of democratic theory, they do not resolve the age-old problems. Such safeguards may protect the rights of some minorities, but in doing so they may also act to thwart the will of the majority, thereby undermining one of the central objectives of the democratic enterprise.

In Canada, an active debate has taken place about whether a majority of 50 per cent plus one would be sufficient to affirm Quebec sovereignty in a referendum and whether a majority of Quebec voters alone should be able to decide an issue of such importance to the entire country. If 50 per cent plus one is not satisfactory, then it becomes all but impossible to specify another threshold that would be both realistic and generally acceptable. To date, the question has not been resolved and may well not be until after a vote has taken place. The issue, however, is crucial to the Anglophone minority in the province, as well as to Aboriginal and other minority groups in Quebec and to the Canadian nation state as a whole. Some commentators have suggested, for example, that the Anglophone or Aboriginal minorities should have the option of remaining within Canada if a narrow majority of the overall Quebec electorate in fact votes to secede.

Other objections that are commonly raised about direct democracy have to do with the interest, engagement, and capacity of ordinary citizens. Indeed, one of the persistent problems in several modern democracies is low citizen interest and involvement and low voter turnout—and this problem is sometimes especially evident in referendums. In recent years, the average turnout in many Swiss referendums has tended to be well below 50 per cent, and in California and other US states it is often far lower.[5] If only a minority of the entire electorate is actually deciding an issue in a referendum, then the question of what constitutes a democratic majority again arises in a different form. For example, the decision by California voters in 1996 to permit the use of marijuana for medical purposes, although it passed with 55 per cent of the votes cast, might be said to have been imposed by only 35 per cent of the voters registered at the time of the election (since many registered voters failed to turn out), or even by only 19 per cent of all California residents of voting age who would have been eligible to vote at the time.[6]

Another potential problem has to do with levels of information and competence. Citizens called upon to vote in referendums routinely complain about insufficient information, confusing question wording, or contradictory lines of argument regarding the possible consequences of a referendum vote. A California Field poll found that the most common complaints of voters about ballot propositions related to confusing wording or to the sheer number of items appearing on the ballot (Bowler and Donovan 1998). Even after a highly intensive eight-week campaign on the constitutional agreement of 1992 (the Charlottetown Accord), 81 per cent of Canadian voters in a national sample felt that "most people didn't understand what the referendum was all about" (Clarke et al. 1996).

Many of the other concerns raised by critics of referendums are technical rather than philosophical, but they are nevertheless not easily dismissed. The large number of items sometimes appearing on US state ballots raises practical questions about how many decisions an individual voter can be expected to compress into a single act of voting. Oregon voters in the 2000 US presidential election faced no fewer than twenty-six ballot propositions dealing with subjects as diverse as education funding, gun control, tobacco settlements, and election campaign finance.

The campaign strategies pursued by groups active in initiative campaigns can also be confusing to voters. Proposals put forward—even occasionally on the same ballot—are sometimes in contradiction with one another. California's Big Green proposal, for example, authored by a coalition of environmental groups in 1990, attracted several competing "lookalike" proposals submitted by industry groups in an effort to draw away votes.[7] It is also often pointed out that budgetary matters are typically not addressed in referendums, even though particular proposals might have significant financial implications. Sometimes ballot propositions include provisions for a bond issue or tax support, but frequently they do not. Should citizens who vote in favour of a new highway or park also be asked to make trade-offs between these and other public projects or to approve tax measures that might support such activities?

A host of other concerns arise in debating the practicality of initiative and referendum legislation, including the following types of questions: Who decides whether or not a particular issue gets to the ballot? What sort of public decisions require a referendum? How many signatures should be required to put a proposal on the ballot? Who writes the questions? Should they be vetted by legal authorities? Who runs the campaigns? What sort of advertising is permitted? How much money can be spent? Can the losing side demand another referendum if a measure passes? Should the courts or the legislature have the right to review decisions made by the voters in a referendum? Questions such as these often arise in nations or localities where referendums are used with some frequency, and they pose difficulties that are not easily resolved.

Although some jurisdictions have attempted to address some of them, the results have not always been successful. Recent court decisions in Ireland, for example, have curtailed the expenditure of public funds and the use of the state television network in referendum campaigns.[8] But these cases have also left considerable uncertainty as to how a governing party that had placed an issue on the ballot could legally put forward its position during the campaign. Similarly, attempts by Quebec authorities to force interested campaign groups to affiliate with umbrella committees were found in a 1997 Canadian Supreme Court decision to be in conflict with free speech provisions protected by the Charter of Rights.[9]

A somewhat different class of objections is sometimes raised by critics who worry that the institutions of direct democracy could undermine those of representative democracy, i.e., that they might weaken the authority of legislatures or lessen the accountability of elected representatives. Countries within the British parliamentary tradition have long recognized that referendums might subvert the sovereignty of parliament, which has always been a central principle of parliamentary government. Further, they might encourage legislatures to avoid grappling with difficult decisions, passing them instead to the voters in a referendum. This problem is less severe when a referendum is used by the government itself for consultative purposes only. But the concept of a citizen-initiated referendum (which might be used to challenge the authority of parliament) or of a mandatory constitutional referendum in a country such as Britain, which does not have a written constitution, does not seem to mesh well with existing political institutions.

These reservations have not prevented countries within this tradition, including Britain itself, from using referendums with increasing frequency. However, in the absence of established constitutional rules regarding the conduct of referendums, it is sometimes difficult to ensure that a referendum will accomplish its intended purposes. In federal systems such as Canada and Australia conflicts can also arise between the different levels of government, and a federal referendum is sometimes regarded with suspicion by the individual states or provinces. Australia, like Switzerland, has a concurrent-majority provision, in which federal constitutional amendments must be approved by a majority of voters both in the federation and in at least four of the six states. In Canada, however, the results of a provincial referendum might not be recognized by the federal parliament, or a federal majority might be attained in a referendum without the concurrence of some provinces. In the absence of any established constitutional rules on such subjects, the possibility that a future Quebec referendum on sovereignty may lead only to new constitutional conflicts, rather than toward any resolution of the national unity question, is very real.

In spite of this rather long list of new and old criticisms, direct democracy in its various forms appears to be flourishing in many countries, including some with Westminster-style parliamentary institutions, such as Britain and New Zealand, and some with federal systems, such as Switzerland or Australia. It seems clear that different types of representative and consultative institutions can coexist within the same polity, because so many countries appear to have successfully adapted various kinds of referendum provisions to their existing forms of government. New Zealand's recently adopted provisions for citizen initiated referendums may over time provide a further test of the ability of Westminster-style parliamentary governments to successfully incorporate new mechanisms of participatory democracy into existing political regimes, just as Switzerland's experience demonstrates that such institutions can operate within the framework of a federal system. New technologies, electronic and otherwise, may over time make regular direct votes of the citizenry on major political questions more feasible, although it is clear that technology alone cannot address many of the classic theoretical criticisms of direct democracy. Ian Budge (1996) argues that, in spite of the many criticisms levelled against it, direct democracy can no longer be dismissed on the grounds of impracticality alone. The evidence shows that many countries have found ways of overcoming some of the impediments and of adapting their existing political institutions to these new challenges. While it remains to be seen whether technology can be successful in overcoming some of the remaining barriers, it is nevertheless clear that further experiments with these types of processes are certain to take place in a wide variety of political environments. Much will be learned from those efforts, whether or not they are able to truly improve the quality of democracy for their citizens.

The observation that many of the classic objections to direct democracy can be and have been overcome in a variety of political systems does not, however, address the question of whether these instruments have necessarily delivered the higher quality of democracy that they seem to promise. Can holding occasional referendums on important issues cure the ills of modern democracy? As noted in Chapter 1, only a few countries use such processes extensively. A closer look at many of the examples that have been cited thus far shows that the referendum sometimes serves objectives in politics other than those associated with creating and sustaining a more participatory or deliberative form of democracy. As we will see in subsequent chapters, governments sometimes call referendums not merely to find out what the people want but rather to advance their own political agendas. In countries that use citizen-initiated referendums, powerful and well-funded interest groups, rather than ordinary citizens, often stand behind particular initiatives. In some instances, political parties may also use initiative processes to advance their views, further indicating that such devices are not restricted only to "citizens."[10] And while its association with the fundamental concepts of democracy has been our main focus here, it might be noted that the referendum has, over the course of history, also been a favoured tool of tyrants and dictators seeking to legitimize and sustain their rule. Several referendums were held in postrevolutionary France, including one in 1802 that made Napoleon consul for life and another in 1804 that endorsed him as emperor. The YES vote in these referendums was in excess of 99 per cent, creating the impression of a broad popular endorsement of what was really an authoritarian regime.

Napoleon has not been the only authoritarian ruler over the years to sense the potential of the referendum, either as a legitimating device or as a means of circumventing more conventional political processes. Contemporary political figures such as Ferdinand Marcos in the Philippines, Hosni Mubarak in Egypt, and Augusto Pinochet in Chile have likewise used the referendum, either to provide a veneer of democratic legitimacy for their regimes or to solicit public approval for particular policies that they supported. Such strategies, however, have not always been successful. Pinochet stepped down in 1989 following a referendum in which a majority of the Chilean electorate declined to extend his

Table 2.2
Political Functions of the Referendum

THE REFERENDUM AS THE "RECOURSE OF THE PRINCE." Implemented by a
state president, head of government, or ruling figure to obtain public endorsement of
a person, regime, or program.

Examples
De Gaulle's referendums on Algeria, the presidency, and political reform
    (France: 1961, 1962, 1969)
Pinochet's referendums on policy, the regime, and the presidency (Chile: 1978,
    1980, 1988)
Yeltsin's referendum on the presidency and economic reforms (Russia: 1993)

THE REFERENDUM AS THE "RECOURSE OF THE CITIZENS." Initiated by citizens
or groups either against the governing authorities or without their approval.

Examples
Swiss initiatives
Italian abrogative referendums
American state ballot propositions

THE REFERENDUM AS "THE RECOURSE OF THE PARTIES." A vote organized
by the governing party as part of its political agenda or to resolve internal political
conflicts.

Examples
1975 British referendum on EC membership
1986 Spanish referendum on NATO
The Irish referendums on divorce and abortion
Australian constitutional referendums

Source: Adapted from Hamon (1995).

presidency. In more democratic regimes also, presidents such as Boris
Yeltsin in post-Soviet Russia or Charles de Gaulle in Fifth Republic
France have sought to use the referendum, not out of a genuine concern
to increase citizen participation in decision making, but to frustrate their
political adversaries or to push through particular policies over determined
legislative opposition. De Gaulle used the referendum first to establish
the constitution of the new Fifth Republic and subsequently to settle the
Algerian conflict. Later, he used it to change the procedures for electing
the president, thereby strengthening his own position within the political
system. But when a further political reform package was turned down by

the French electorate in 1969, de Gaulle, having made the matter an issue of confidence in his presidency, promptly resigned. French presidents after de Gaulle have been much more cautious in the use of the referendum. As President Mitterrand discovered in 1992 at the time of the vote on the Maastricht Treaty on European Union (see Chapter 4 section B), the referendum can often be a two-edged instrument that does not always produce the kind of political results anticipated by its proponents.

Drawing on some of these examples, Francis Hamon (1995) observes that historically referendums have commonly been used in one of three ways (Table 2.2). The first, which he calls the *recourse of the prince*, clearly conforms to some of the instances cited above, in which a state president or head of government has used the referendum to obtain the direct endorsement of the people for a person, policy, or program. The other functions Hamon calls the *recourse of the citizens*, referring to the Swiss, Italian, and American state models of citizen initiative or abrogation, and the *recourse of the parties*, in which governing political parties use the referendum to resolve certain types of policy controversies that cannot be settled by other means. Party government, which is the form existing in most of the democratic world today, works satisfactorily only when political parties are united behind a particular program or policy agenda. Recently, particularly in Europe, issues of major political importance, such as further European economic and political integration, a common European currency, and particular international commitments, have threatened to divide parties internally. Resolving such conflicts through a referendum has been one way of addressing such issues while allowing party government to sustain itself.

Britain's recourse to a referendum in 1975 to resolve the issue of European Community membership, the 1986 Spanish referendum on NATO membership, the Danish votes on the Maastricht and Amsterdam Treaties, and the Irish referendums on divorce and abortion are all examples of the referendum as the recourse of the parties—notwithstanding the different legal frameworks within which these votes took place. In the democratic world of today, where there are perhaps fewer "princes," this may have become one of the most significant functions of the instruments of direct democracy, when they have been deployed in the milieu of party government. As we shall see in subsequent chapters, many of the referendums that take place in democratic nations today come about because of a calculated political decision taken by a governing political party that the referendum is an appropriate instrument for carrying out its political agenda. Except in those few countries where the referendum is exclusively the recourse of the citizens, it might be more appropriate to think of it as simply one of the tools of modern democratic government, which in the majority of countries is also party government.

Because it is a tool rather than an end in itself, it can be used by various political actors to pursue their political goals, as we shall see in some of the examples to be explored further here. Prime ministers, presidents, interest groups, and political parties—as well as ordinary citizens—have all found elements in the processes of direct democracy that they can put to their own uses.

NOTES

1. However, in a few cases governments have ignored a formal vote. In 1955, Swedish voters overwhelmingly rejected a government proposal to switch from left-hand to right-hand driving. The government eventually proceeded with the change anyway, although it took effect twelve years later, in 1967, without any further referendum on the issue. In Ontario the provincial government proceeded with its plan to amalgamate Toronto municipalities in 1997 in spite of the opposition of citizens to the proposal in referendums sponsored by the six municipalities. The provincial government, anticipating a negative outcome, had indicated in advance that it would not be influenced by the city-sponsored referendums.

2. In several recent cases in Italy, this threshold has not been achieved in some instances because of an organized boycott of the referendum by political parties opposing the measure on the ballot. See Uleri (1996, 2002).

3. The overall result was 50.1 per cent NO. Turnout was 44 per cent. Center for the Study of Direct Democracy, University of Geneva http://c2d.unige.ch/.

4. Six of the smaller cantons are half-weighted in making this calculation. See Kobach (1993).

5. Turnout in these jurisdictions also tends to be quite low in elections. In Switzerland, turnout in the 1999 federal assembly election was 44 per cent. In California in the 2000 US presidential election, turnout was 45 per cent compared with the national turnout figure in the same election of 51 per cent.

6. Turnout in US referendums is difficult to calculate because of American voter-registration processes and the complexity of many American state ballots. The number of persons going to the polls might be calculated as the percentage of registered voters or as the percentage of those of voting age. Finally, someone who votes in the election but does not mark a particular ballot question would be counted as a nonvoter for that item but as a participant for other purposes. Using the most stringent criteria, it might be said that as little as 19 per cent of the eligible California electorate voted for the proposition to permit medical use of marijuana in the 1996 election.

7. There were four "environmental-protection" measures on the November 1990 ballot in California. Only one of these passed—a proposal to establish a three-mile "marine protection zone" along the coast.

8. These were, respectively, the McKenna decision (1995) and the Coughlan judgment (1998). For a discussion of the implications of some of these restrictions on government campaigning in referendums, see O'Mahony (1998).

9. The court ruled that third-party campaign activities could in principle be regulated but that the provisions in Quebec's referendum law were too broad. *Libman v. Quebec*, 1997.

10. The 2002 initiative on asylum seekers referred to earlier was put forward by the Swiss Peoples' Party.

3

Referendums on
Constitutional Issues

In the next four chapters of this book, I will examine in some detail several specific referendums that will be classified using the categories set out in Table 1.3 of Chapter 1. The cases considered in this chapter indicate the variety of legal frameworks and political circumstances under which a referendum dealing with a *constitutional* question might occur. In a few countries, notably Ireland, Denmark, Switzerland, and Australia, amendments to the constitution must be approved by a vote of the people in a referendum. In these countries, referendums occur routinely whenever a constitutional amendment is proposed or a matter arises that is considered to be the legal equivalent of a constitutional change.[1] Australia (see section D of this chapter), which has held nineteen referendums on forty-four constitutional proposals since 1901, provides a good example of the use of the referendum as a mandatory part of the formal process of constitutional change. France, in contrast, has within its constitution two alternative methods of constitutional revision, only one of which involves a referendum.[2] In many other countries, however, constitutional referendums are rare; they are used principally to resolve a unique political question that cannot be satisfactorily resolved through more conventional political processes or to effect a major structural change in the institutions of government. Thus, the attempt to implement a program of major constitutional reform in Canada in the late 1980s and early 1990s led eventually to the constitutional referendum of 1992 (see section A, following). Similarly, many new democracies have held a referendum on a new constitution as an integral part of the process of political transition. Russia, for example, conducted such a referendum in 1993 and is examined more closely in section B of this chapter.

As noted in Chapter 1, any attempt to identify referendums by type and subject matter is bound to lead to overlapping categories. Hence, a "constitutional" referendum may involve an important policy question, as did the Irish referendums on abortion (see Chapter 6, section B), or an international treaty, as did the referendums on the Maastricht Treaty in Denmark and Ireland in 1992. We need not be overly concerned with these overlapping categories if we can clearly recognize the variations in the political and legal context under which a referendum might take place. New Zealand (see section C of this chapter) provides a distinct contrast to the examples cited above. The reform of New Zealand's electoral institutions, which was brought about by the referendums of 1992 and 1993, was not part of any systematic process of constitutional change, yet the effect of the referendum was clearly constitutional in nature. I therefore include it for discussion here under this category, since to treat such a referendum as a mere policy matter would greatly understate its significance in effecting a major change in New Zealand's political institutions.

The four cases discussed in the following sections of this chapter all involved major constitutional questions that would clearly have been recognized as such by the citizens who voted in them. Taken together, they provide a broad overview of the varied circumstances under which a referendum process might be used to effect constitutional change.

A. Canada's 1992 Constitutional Referendum

The tangled history of constitutional politics in Canada is not easily summarized.[3] However, the origins of the 1992 referendum, the first such nationwide vote since 1942, lay in Canada's long struggle to patriate its constitution from its British origins and in the events that took place in Quebec following the sovereignty referendum of 1980. Constitutional reform took on a new sense of urgency in 1976 with the election of a separatist government in Quebec. Prime Minister Trudeau, having failed to secure an agreement on a new constitution with all ten provinces, finally acted to patriate the constitution unilaterally in 1982 with the agreement of nine provinces but without the concurrence of Quebec.[4] The election of a new Conservative federal government under Brian Mulroney in 1984 and the defeat of the Parti Québécois (PQ) government in Quebec in the provincial election of 1985 opened the door to the possibility of a new constitutional initiative designed to "bring Quebec in." The new Quebec Liberal government of Robert Bourassa was cautious but open to the idea of a new constitutional proposal. The product of these renewed negotiations—the Meech Lake Accord—was a package of constitutional proposals designed to respond to Quebec's demands for greater autonomy and a more decentralized style of federalism, including recognition of Quebec as a "distinct society." The Meech Lake Accord had been reached in 1987 through secret negotiations between the prime minister and the ten provincial premiers, and the ratification procedure consisted simply of approval by Parliament and each of the ten provincial legislatures within three years. The accord expired in 1990, however, when two provinces, Manitoba and Newfoundland, had failed to ratify it within the established time limit.

A second attempt at an agreement found success in the Charlottetown Accord, reached between the federal government and the provinces in August 1992. This agreement, like the Meech Lake document, might also have simply been put to Parliament and the provincial legislatures for debate and ratification. However, the federal government had by this time effectively lost control of much of its constitutional agenda. Quebec had already committed itself by law to hold its own referendum, either on "sovereignty" or on a federal constitutional proposal, no later than October 26, 1992. The provinces of Alberta and British Columbia had likewise made commitments to hold referendums on any new constitutional proposals. The prime minister and premiers who had negotiated the agreement saw obvious disadvantages in the prospect of separate referendums in Quebec and in other provinces, held at different times and following different electoral rules. A quick federal vote, held on the same day as the already scheduled Quebec referendum (which was then only two months away) became the only plausible strategy. Given this context, it is perhaps not surprising that the public was somewhat ambivalent towards this new political development (Clarke et al. 1996). The referendum seemed to many Canadians like another move in the continuing constitutional chess game rather than the logical conclusion of a truly democratic process.

The Charlottetown Accord was much more comprehensive than previous constitutional proposals. It proposed to create a new Senate in which all provinces would be equally represented—a variation of the type of reform of the Senate that had been sought by the Western provinces during the constitutional negotiations. It carried over from the failed Meech Lake

Accord the provision for recognition of Quebec as a "distinct society," and it further guaranteed to Quebec in perpetuity a minimum of 25 per cent of the representatives in an enlarged House of Commons. The Charlottetown Accord also proposed new arrangements for Aboriginal self-government, recognizing it as an "inherent right," and it set out new divisions of federal and provincial powers in areas such as culture, labour, and resource policy by granting additional powers to provincial governments. Finally, it proposed to give all provinces a veto over fundamental constitutional changes such as those concerning representation or federal institutions.

The referendum ballot provided only for a simple YES or NO on "the agreement of August 28." Because the decision to hold a referendum was taken so quickly, little thought had been given to matters of organization and strategy or even to the wording of the question. As a result, the campaign got off to a very slow start, even though it effectively began as soon as the agreement was announced. For a short time it seemed that a real contest might take place only in Quebec, where an organized opposition was already in place. The Parti Québécois almost immediately announced its intention to campaign for a NO vote, but there was little initial opposition elsewhere in the country. All ten provincial premiers representing three different political parties supported the agreement. The three leaders of the main federal parties each announced that they would campaign actively for a YES vote. Leaders of Aboriginal groups, which had been involved in various phases of the constitutional negotiations, indicated that they would support it. Prime Minister Mulroney, confident of victory, claimed that only "enemies of Canada" would oppose the agreement.

But soon opposition outside Quebec began to surface. The Reform Party, at that time a much smaller and largely Western-based movement, announced that it would oppose the agreement and campaign against it nationally. About the same time, several prominent Quebec Liberals came out against the proposals, revealing a serious split in Premier Bourassa's own party and indicating that the agreement was in serious trouble in Quebec.[5] Within a few weeks other opposition surfaced—from women's groups, from some constitutional lawyers, and finally from a former prime minister—Pierre Trudeau. While it was perhaps not surprising that Trudeau, also a critic of the Meech Lake proposals, would oppose the Charlottetown Accord, his views commanded wide attention, and his intervention in the campaign was timed for maximum effect. Momentum suddenly seemed to shift away from the poorly organized and overconfident architects of the agreement. The YES side in the campaign was often its own worst enemy, airing campaign advertisements that many saw as "scare tactics" and reinforcing some of the feelings of manipulation by elites that had hung over the agreement from the beginning. The various groups and individuals supporting the NO had little in common with each other, ranging widely across the political spectrum and often holding contradictory views on other issues. But arrayed against them were the pillars of the Canadian establishment—business, government, academia, and much of the press and media.

Because there was really no long-term basis of public opinion on many of the specific issues arising from the agreement, the referendum campaign held the potential for even greater volatility and uncertainty about the outcome than would typically be found in an election or in some of the other types of referendums considered in this book. Such is often the case with constitutional questions in which the public has not been highly engaged. Some voters, of course, would have been able to make up their minds quickly on the basis of partisan cues or familiarity with one or more of the long-standing issues in the constitutional debates. A few issues, such as the "distinct society" provision or the proposal for equal representation of the provinces in a reformed Senate were already well known and might by themselves have shaped some voters' views of the entire agreement. In addition, there were the cues provided by the parties and by political leaders such as Trudeau, Mulroney, Bourassa, or Manning—personalities about whom many voters had strong opinions.

Levels of voter interest were high and turnout, at 75 per cent, was 5 per cent higher than turnout in the federal election only a year later. The pattern of voter decision-making was similar to the pattern in Canadian election campaigns (Clarke et al. 1996). Thirty-eight per cent of the respondents in the Carleton Referendum Study indicated that they had made up their minds early—at the time that the agreement was announced or even before. About a third decided on their vote during the early or middle part of the campaign, and a nearly equal number (29 per cent) reserved their decision until the final week. The NO side pulled ahead in the polls during the first week of October and stayed there throughout the remainder of the campaign. With nearly three weeks to go, the contest was effectively over, even though public opinion polls continued to show large numbers of undecided voters until the very end of the campaign.

Table 3A1

Results of the Canadian Constitutional Referendum,
October 26, 1992 (Percentages)

	Yes	*No*	*Turnout*
Newfoundland	63.5	36.5	53
Prince Edward Island	74.1	25.9	71
Nova Scotia	48.9	51.1	68
New Brunswick	62.0	38.0	72
Quebec	44.6	55.4	83
Ontario	50.4	49.6	72
Manitoba	38.4	61.6	71
Saskatchewan	44.5	55.5	69
Alberta	39.9	60.1	73
British Columbia	32.0	68.0	77
Yukon Territory	43.9	56.1	70
Northwest Territories	61.3	38.7	70
Canada	45.6	54.4	75

In the country as a whole, approximately 55 per cent voted NO, compared with 45 per cent who voted YES. Six of the ten provinces voted NO, with strong majorities against the agreement in all of the Western provinces and the Yukon (Table 3A1). The Atlantic provinces, with the exception of Nova Scotia, supported the YES side by fairly substantial majorities. In Ontario, the result was a virtual tie, and the NO majority in Quebec was only slightly higher than in the country as a whole. In Quebec, francophones were more likely to oppose the agreement, while francophones in other provinces were more likely to support it (LeDuc and Pammett 1995). There was a noticeable urban/rural divide, as a disproportionate amount of the YES support came from the larger cities. Older voters and those with higher incomes were slightly more likely to vote YES. Otherwise, there were only modest demographic correlates to the vote, since the national trend against the agreement cut across potential divisions along the lines of social class, gender, age, or education. Public feelings about the substance of the agreement contributed substantially to its defeat. This was true in all parts of the country, although resentment of the distinct-society provision was most pronounced among voters in the West and in Ontario.

While there were partisan divisions in the vote, it is clear that the contest was not fundamentally a partisan one. Since the leaders of all three of the main federal parties had actively campaigned for a YES vote, many of the normal partisan cues that voters might have been expected to respond to were completely absent from the referendum campaign. Bloc Québécois and Reform identifiers, however, voted overwhelmingly NO. For these voters, there was no ambiguity in the messages emanating from the campaign, the parties, or their leaders. For other voters, leaders mattered more. Had those whose task it was to sell this agreement to the Canadian people themselves been more popular, the outcome conceivably might have been different. At the time of the referendum, Brian Mulroney's popularity with the public was close to its nadir, and he would subsequently indicate his intention to resign from office only four months after the referendum. Feelings about some of the provincial leaders, particularly Premier Bourassa and Premier Rae of Ontario, also mattered. But in the final analysis, the agreement failed both because of the message and the messengers. A multivariate analysis (one using a number of statistical variables) suggests that some of the key provisions of the agreement, particularly the distinct-society provision and the guarantee of 25 per cent of the representatives for Quebec, together with feelings about the political leaders, especially the prime minister, sealed the fate of the agreement (LeDuc and Pammett 1995).

Following the referendum, the leaders of all of the main political parties sought to put it behind them as quickly as possible. There was a feeling that the Canadian people had passed judgment not merely on the Charlottetown constitutional proposals but on the political class of the country as a whole. The Reform Party and the Bloc Québécois, however, were able to use the referendum outcome as a springboard for their campaigns in the federal election that followed only a year later.[6] In retrospect it is evident that the referendum defeat set the stage for the Progressive Conservatives' subsequent electoral disaster in 1993. At a minimum it diverted the party's diminishing resources from the critical task of fighting the election, and it ceded crucial electoral ground to the party's most dangerous opponents in Quebec and the West.

The 1992 constitutional referendum was an unusual event in Canadian politics. Although they were not legally required to hold a referendum, it is clear that the architects of the Charlottetown agreement ultimately had little choice but to seek some kind of popular mandate for their project. But as we shall see in some of the other cases examined in this book, a referendum campaign often takes on a life of its own and can be managed only in limited ways by those who initiate it. The 1992 referendum unexpectedly provided Canadian voters with a rare opportunity to pass judgment on the nation's entire political establishment, together with one of that establishment's most cherished projects. The extent to which the NO campaign managed to tap an "anti-politics" or "anti-establishment" streak of opinion became increasingly clear in the final weeks of the campaign. For some, the referendum seemed to represent a battle of the people against the establishment. Seen in this light, it is perhaps more surprising that 45 per cent of Canadians ultimately voted for the Charlottetown agreement than that it went down to defeat.

B. The 1993 Russian Constitutional Referendum

The referendum to approve a new constitution for Russia, which took place in December 1993, originated not in a democratic constitutional process but rather in the struggles between Boris Yeltsin and the Russian parliament, which played out over a period of more than a year. The 1993 constitutional referendum was the third direct vote to take place in Russia, counting as the first Mikhail Gorbachev's all-USSR referendum of March 17, 1991. In that referendum, a second question had been added to the ballot in Russia to create an elected Russian presidency. Following approval of that proposal, a presidential election took place three months later in Russia in which Yeltsin won a landslide victory against five other candidates.[7] The significance of this turn of events was to become clear later, when the Soviet Union itself was dissolved and Gorbachev resigned as its president. Power now rested with the new Russian president—Boris Yeltsin.

That power, largely untested, was shared between the president and the Congress of People's Deputies, which had carried over from the Soviet period.[8] During the year following the collapse of the Soviet Union, relations between Yeltsin and the parliament steadily worsened. Although there were many points of conflict, Yeltsin's determination to impose his choice of prime minister exacerbated the tensions. In December 1992 the replacement of Yeltsin's choice, Yegor Gaidar, by Viktor Chernomyrdin, a candidate acceptable to the Congress, brought the conflict to a head. Claiming a mandate of the people, owing to his position as the elected president, Yeltsin announced that a referendum to endorse his presidency and program would take place on April 25, 1993. Four questions were put to the voters in that referendum: questions about (1) confidence in President Yeltsin; (2) support for his economic and social policies; (3) authorization of early presidential elections; and (4) authorization of early parliamentary elections. The turnout of 64 per cent of the electorate in the April 1993 referendum was respectable, but the results were mixed. In reality, the referendum had no legal standing, and the outcome could be interpreted in various ways. Yeltsin had succeeded in obtaining at least a moderate endorsement of his presidency and program (58 per cent and 54 per cent respectively). The proposals for early elections also carried, but because of the low turnout, they failed to meet a legal threshold of 50 per cent of the entire electorate that had been established by the Constitutional Court.[9]

Yeltsin interpreted the results of the April 1993 referendum both as an endorsement of his presidency and as a mandate to press ahead with a new constitution that would strengthen the powers of the president. Constitutional politics in Russia at the time differed significantly from the politics of Western democracies in that the existing constitution had been carried over from the Soviet era. In the absence of any established process for constitutional renewal, the constitution became essentially a pawn of presidential-legislative politics. The congress itself had in fact debated constitutional matters over several years, and a draft of a new constitutional document had been put forward for discussion before the April 1993 referendum. Emboldened by his "victory" in the April referendum, however, Yeltsin produced his own alternative draft constitution, which provided for wider presidential powers than were contained in the parliamentary proposals. A constitutional conference was established in June 1993 for the purpose of reconciling the two drafts. The conference produced a unified document in July, but the compromises that had been made failed to satisfy Yeltsin's parliamentary opponents. The continuing conflict between the president and congress over the constitution and a wide range of other matters led directly into the crisis of October 1993.[10]

The October crisis was precipitated by Yeltsin's television address of September 21, which effectively suspended the parliament and called for new elections to be held in December. They were to be for a new parliamentary body, to be called the Duma, and would also include a referendum to approve a new constitution. Gaidar was reinstalled as minister of economics, and the president indicated that he would rule directly until the December elections. The deployment of troops and the bombardment of government buildings, together with the street fighting that erupted subsequently, propelled the crisis to a new height of severity. Yeltsin justified his actions by arguing that the Congress of Deputies had repeatedly undermined his program of reform and had failed to agree on a new constitution. To his opponents, however, Yeltsin's actions represented a step toward dictatorship, provoking calls for his removal from office.

In the end, Yeltsin used the crisis to consolidate his position. He produced a new draft constitution that was similar to the compromise document but contained additional presidential powers, and he announced that this version of the new constitution would be put to a direct vote of the people at the elections in December. The time available for deliberation on the new constitutional document was therefore very short. Gradually, however, supporters and opponents began to position themselves along more or less predictable lines. Supporters of Yeltsin promoted the new constitution; opponents were critical. Yeltin's supporters argued that the constitutional impasse could be broken only by this type of direct democratic process.

The rules of procedure for the referendum specified that the constitution would be approved by a simple majority of voters, with a minimum turnout of 50 per cent of the electorate. This provision raised some questions about its validity, since the previous referendum rules had called for approval by an absolute majority of the eligible electorate—a much higher threshold. The outcome of the referendum produced a weak YES majority for the new constitution, with 58.4 per cent of those participating voting in its favour (Table 3B1). There were NO majorities in eight of the twenty-one republics, but the procedures under which the referendum took place did not contain any provisions requiring concurrent majorities. The turnout of 55 per cent was the lowest of any of the three referendums that had been held up to that time in Russia, suggesting that the result might have been ruled invalid under the old referendum law. In fact, given the low turnout, there was some uncertainty as to whether the vote had even cleared the 50 per cent threshold specified in the new procedures. There were numerous other legal challenges to the referendum result, but Yeltsin

Table 3B1
Results of the Russian Constitutional Referendum, December 12, 1993

	Number of Votes	Percentage of Electorate	Percentage of Valid Votes
Yes	32,937,630	31.0	58.4
No	23,431,333	22.1	41.6
Invalid	1,818,792	1.7	
Total	58,187,755	54.8	100.0

Note: Total electorate = 106,182,030

declared that the document had been approved and thus claimed a democratic mandate for his new constitutional order.

White et al. (1997) argue that voting in the referendum tended to be retrospective—voters were more concerned with apportioning blame for the country's political and economic woes than with the details of the new constitution. Those who blamed Yeltsin for the country's problems were more likely to vote NO; those who blamed the communists tended to vote YES. Russians who had suffered the most under the new economic order were more likely to be found among the NO voters. But among both supporters and opponents, there was widespread skepticism about what the new constitution might be able to achieve, and considerable pessimism about its ability to deliver a better quality of democracy.

Almost overlooked in the referendum battle over the new constitution was the fact that elections to the new parliament had taken place at the same time.[11] The elections consisted of votes for members of two houses of a new Federal Assembly: the upper house (the Federation Council), giving two seats to each of the eighty-nine republics and regions, and the lower house (the Duma) consisting of 450 deputies. Half the deputies were elected in single-member districts and half from a list of party candidates using proportional representation. Local elections in some parts of the country also took place at the same time. The voter was thus confronted with various other choices in addition to the referendum vote on the constitution. This arrangement more or less assured that the various political alignments that had arisen out of the struggles between the president and his adversaries would be reflected in the referendum vote. But it also made it more likely that the winners of the constitutional battle would be able to prevail within the new political structures that were being established.

The 1993 constitutional referendum was in some respects unique because of the particular circumstances involved in Russia's process of transition to a democratic regime. In spite of the many difficulties, however, it is clear that the referendum legitimized the new constitution in a way that approval by the old congress or by a constitutional conference could not. Just as Yeltsin's position in the new political order was enhanced and strengthened by his ability to claim a popular electoral mandate, so too the new constitution, for all its potential shortcomings, received its legitimacy through a vote of the people. The referendum is not yet an established part of the process of governance in the new Russia, and it may not become so. However, on constitutional matters, the precedent established by the 1993 vote is likely to ensure that any future constitutional changes will be submitted to the people in a similar fashion.

C. Electoral Reform in New Zealand

The path to electoral reform in New Zealand was long and torturous, involving several governments led by two different political parties, a royal commission, extensive public and parliamentary debates, and two referendums. This is perhaps not surprising when we consider how difficult it is to bring about any change in the electoral laws in most countries. Electoral systems reflect, among other things, vested partisan political interests. Governing parties elected under one set of electoral rules rarely support changes in such institutions unless they are coerced into them. A referendum, precisely because it places decision-making authority in the hands of the people rather than elected officials, is one tool that may be used to effect such fundamental institutional change.

Like Canada and other former British dominions, New Zealand inherited the British system of representation, under which members of parliament are elected from single member districts by simple plurality vote. Defenders of this system value its simplicity, its emphasis on local representation, and its ability to produce stable majority governments. But its critics routinely note its tendencies to inflate parliamentary majorities, to underrepresent the views of political and other minorities, and to disadvantage smaller political parties. Even in Britain itself, the advantages and disadvantages of more-proportional forms of representation have been actively debated.[12] In New Zealand, such a debate began in earnest in the early 1980s following two successive elections in which the party winning the largest number of votes failed to obtain a majority of parliamentary seats. The National party, which had finished second to Labour in total votes in the 1978 and 1981 elections, formed the government in both those instances.[13]

Labour included a commitment to appoint a royal commission on electoral reform in its 1984 campaign platform. Elected with a solid parliamentary majority in 1984, the new Labour government appointed such a commission during its first year in office. Following extensive research and public hearings, the commission recommended in its 1986 report, *Towards a Better Democracy*, that New Zealand adopt a variant of proportional representation similar to that used in Germany, under which a certain number of members of parliament are elected from constituencies but others are elected from party lists to correct a party's parliamentary representation so that it is proportional to its vote. Recognizing that a parliament dominated by the major parties might hesitate to implement such a sweeping change, the commission also recommended that a referendum be held on the issue.[14]

There was widespread cynicism about whether such a referendum would in fact take place, since there was no constitutional mechanism in New Zealand that could force a governing party to call one.[15] Not surprisingly, there were divisions within the Labour caucus regarding the wisdom of a switch to any form of proportional representation, notwithstanding the party's more general commitment to electoral reform. In the end, the recommendations of the royal commission and the issue of a referendum became caught up in party politics and in the 1987 and 1990 election campaigns. Aimer (1999) refers to the events that followed as the "politics of miscalculation." As both major parties attempted to manipulate the issue to their own advantage, they gradually lost control of the reform agenda. Throughout this period, an influential lobby group, the Electoral Reform Coalition, continued to press for implementation of the royal commission's proposals.

Ultimately, however, it was public dissatisfaction with both major parties in New Zealand that fuelled public support for electoral reform and gradually took the issue out of the hands of the political elites. A bipartisan parliamentary committee appointed to review the work of the royal commission and report on its recommendations favoured a weaker alternative to the proposals of the royal commission—an increase in the size of parliament from 99 to 120 seats to correct some of the disproportionality. The committee also proposed a nonbinding referendum on the method of election of the additional members.

Labour reiterated its promise of a referendum on electoral reform during its 1987 election campaign. But although returned to power, the Labour government was unable to proceed further on the matter due to the divisions in its own caucus. Sensing the party's vulnerability on the issue, the National opposition criticized Labour's inaction and promised its own referendum on electoral reform during the course of the 1990 election campaign. Although there was even less support for proportional representation or for a referendum among National parliamentarians than among Labour members, the new National government elected in 1990 was, like its predecessor, stuck with a rashly made campaign promise.

The National government led by Jim Bolger, a staunch opponent of proportional representation, did in fact go forward with a non-binding referendum, which was held in September of 1992. Perhaps hoping to take the steam out of the electoral reform movement, the government proposed four alternatives—the supplementary member system (SM) advocated by the parliamentary committee, the single-transferable-vote system (STV; used in Ireland and in the Australian upper house), the mixed member-proportional (MMP) system favoured by the royal commission, and the preferential vote (used in the Australian lower house). Given four complicated options from which to choose, it appeared unlikely that any one of them could win broad public support. On the ballot, voters were also asked in a separate question whether they favoured change or preferred to retain the current first-past-the-post (FPTP) system, i.e., selection of members of parliament from single-member districts by simple plurality, as in Britain and Canada. They could indicate a preference between the various proposals (part B of the ballot), whether or not they supported change on the first question (part A) (see Table 3C1).

To oversee the campaign, the government appointed an Electoral Referendum Panel chaired by the ombudsman. In addition to ensuring fairness, this panel was charged with the task of educating the public regarding the alternatives presented on the ballot. It issued a six-page brochure entitled *We're Taking It to the People*, which described in some detail each of the five voting systems appearing on the ballot. The pamphlet was published in English, Maori, and Samoan versions and was

Table 3C1

The New Zealand Referendums, 1992 and 1993 (Percentages)

SEPTEMBER 19, 1992

Part A

[ ] Vote to retain the present first-past-the-post system	15.3
[ ] Vote for a change to the voting system	84.7
Total	100.0

Part B

[ ] Vote for the supplementary member system (SM)	5.5
[ ] Vote for the single transferable vote system (STV)	17.4
[ ] Vote for the mixed member proportional system (MMP)	70.5
[ ] Vote for the preferential voting system (PV)	6.6
Total	100.0

Turnout = 55%

NOVEMBER 6, 1993

[ ] For the first-past-the-post system	46.1
[ ] For the mixed member proportional system	53.9
Total	100.0

Turnout = 85%

delivered to every household in New Zealand. In addition to the pamphlet, the Electoral Referendum Panel sponsored various other publications, television programs, and seminars designed to provide information. Concurrently with these activities, the Electoral Reform Coalition waged an active campaign on behalf of the MMP alternative, stressing the fact that this system had originally been recommended by the royal commission. Several interventions by the prime minister and by other cabinet members that were intended to steer voters away from the MMP alternative, or to fan suspicions about electoral reform more generally, created controversies during the campaign and very likely backfired by calling attention to the government's duplicity on the issue.

Although the turnout of 55 per cent was modest, New Zealanders were stunned by the results of the referendum (Table 3C1).[16] They had voted overwhelmingly (84.7 per cent) for change and had also indicated a clear preference (70.5 per cent) for the MMP system proposed by the royal commission and backed by the Electoral Reform Coalition. The strategy of the governing party, which seemed designed to obfuscate the issues and to divide supporters of reform into fragmentary groups favouring different systems had clearly failed. The leader of the opposition and former prime minister, Mike Moore, stated that "the people didn't speak on Saturday; they screamed."[7] As Levine and Roberts (1993) show in their analysis of the referendum vote, there was a strong relationship between dissatisfaction with the government and the vote for change in the referendum.

The unexpected effect of the 1992 referendum outcome was to generate powerful momentum for electoral reform and specifically for the MMP proposal. The result could not be ignored. The government quickly brought in legislation to hold a second binding referendum on reform that would coincide with the next general election, due in a year's time. That referendum would be a straight run-off between the MMP system and the existing FPTP system. While the Electoral Reform Coalition urged immediate implementation of MMP without a second referendum, it seemed that the government intended to stage one more battle against it. However, in the aftermath of the stunning results of the 1992 vote, it also became clear that it had effectively lost control of the issue. The momentum was now with the reformers.

This is not to suggest that the outcome of the second referendum, held in November of 1993, was a foregone conclusion. During the remaining year of its term of office, the governing National Party hovered under a cloud of suspicion regarding its intentions and motives. There was little doubt that most of its members, together with many individual opposition members of parliament, opposed the prospective reforms. But it was difficult to actively campaign against them, given the apparently strong support of the electorate. Opposition therefore mainly took the form of criticizing the MMP proposal and attempting to instil doubts in the minds of voters about how it would actually work in practice.

Also contributing to the momentum behind the reform movement in New Zealand was the growth of the minor parties. For some years, the total share of the vote obtained in elections by the two major parties in New Zealand had been gradually declining, even though third parties found it difficult under FPTP to win seats in parliament. By 1993, two new parties—the Alliance and New Zealand First—had been formed from breakaway factions of the two major parties.[18] Along with the Electoral Reform Coalition, supporters of the minor parties were among the most

Table 3C2
Results of the New Zealand Elections, 1993 and 1996

	1993		1996	
	Vote (%)	*Seats*	*Vote (%)*	*Seats*
National	35.0	50	33.8	44
Labour	34.7	45	28.2	37
New Zealand First	8.4	2	13.3	17
Alliance	18.2	2	10.1	13
ACT	—	—	6.1	8
Christian Coalition*	2.0	0	4.3	0
Others†	1.7	0	4.2	1
	100.0	99	100.0	120
Turnout	85%		86%	

* Christian Heritage in 1993.
† A candidate of the United Party won a constituency seat in 1996. No other party met the five percent threshold required for list representation.

enthusiastic proponents of electoral reform, and particularly of MMP. As the results of the 1996 election, the first held under MMP, would show, their allegiance to this cause was well-placed (see Table 3C2).

Given the results of the 1992 referendum and the political atmosphere that followed in its wake, the outcome of the second (1993) referendum seemed anticlimactic. Yet the campaign itself was hard-fought, and the result could in no way have been taken for granted. The various groups that had opposed the reform proposals at earlier stages, including prominent figures in both major parties, came together under the organization Campaign for Better Government (CBG) to fight the campaign against MMP. This organization enjoyed considerable support from the business community, which feared the prospect of coalition government under an MMP system, and its possible effects on economic policy. The campaign against MMP, which was waged under the banner of the CBG, was better organized and more sophisticated than previous efforts. And because the 1993 referendum was held to coincide with the general election, a higher turnout could be expected and partisan voters more easily mobilized. Many would be voting on the issue for the first time.

The outcome of the referendum demonstrates that the campaign was in every respect a real campaign. The split of the electorate—54 per cent for MMP and 46 for FPTP—shows that in spite of the momentum behind the reform movement, there was in fact a real division of opinion among New Zealand voters on the issue (Table 3C1). There was, of course, a strong correlation between the vote in the 1992 referendum and that of 1993. Voters who had supported change in the first referendum voted overwhelmingly in favour of MMP. But among first-time voters in the 1993 referendum, the division favoured FPTP.[19] There was also a strong partisan component to the 1993 referendum vote. National voters opposed MMP by a ratio of about four to one, while Labour voters were about two to one in favour. As expected, supporters of the minor parties voted heavily in favour of MMP.

The referendum law had been written so that MMP would automatically come into effect upon its approval by the electorate. No further parliamentary review was possible, although the law provided for a review of MMP after two elections and the possibility of another referendum on the issue.[20] The 1996 election, the first held under MMP, represented a sea change in New Zealand politics, but the coalition government that was formed following protracted negotiations between the National Party and New Zealand First after the election also produced a considerable backlash in public opinion (Nagel 1999). Should there be a future referendum on the continuation of the MMP system, the outcome would not be a foregone conclusion, although the reforms now appear to have won greater public acceptance following two further elections held under MMP in 1999 and 2002.

D. A Bill of Rights and a Republic?
The Australian Constitutional Referendums of 1988 and 1999

Referendums have been used in Australia principally to amend the federal constitution, although they have also been employed for other purposes at various times in all the Australian states. Of the forty-seven direct federal votes that have taken place over Australia's history, forty-four have dealt with constitutional proposals.[21] However, the Australian method of amending the constitution through referendums seems to have led to a kind of constitutional gridlock, rather than to a creative process of

Table 3D1

The Australian Constitutional Proposals, September 3, 1988

PARLIAMENTARY TERMS. Would fix the term of office for members both of the House of Representatives and of the Senate at four years instead of the current three years for the House and six years for the Senate.

Percentage voting Yes: 33. Number of states approving: 0.

FAIR ELECTIONS. Would mandate that all parliamentary constituencies would contain approximately the same numbers of voters, thereby equalizing the voting strength of rural and urban constituencies.

Percentage voting Yes: 37. Number of states approving: 0

LOCAL GOVERNMENT. Would grant formal recognition in the constitution to local government.

Percentage voting Yes: 34. Number of states approving: 0.

RIGHTS AND FREEDOMS. Would entrench in the constitution the right to trial by jury, freedom of religion, and fair compensation for any citizen whose property was expropriated by government.

Percentage voting Yes: 31. Number of states approving: 0

Turnout = 92%.

constitutional renewal. Of the forty-four amendments put forward since 1906, only eight have been adopted.[22] One reason for this resistance to constitutional change may be found in the electoral rules, which require a national majority and corresponding majorities in at least four of the six states. But only a few constitutional proposals have failed solely because of this double-majority requirement. Other reasons commonly advanced are public apathy, the effects of partisanship or party loyalties, and the conflicts between levels of government inherent in a federal system (Hughes 1994; Galligan 2001).

Constitutional change in Australia has been primarily a project of federal governments (particularly those headed by Labor), and several federal governments have initiated ambitious programs of constitutional reform in recent years (1974, 1977, 1984, 1988). In this section, I will use as examples the set of constitutional proposals that were put to a referendum by the Labor government of Robert Hawke in September 1988 and the 1999 vote on the issues of replacing the monarchy with a republican form of government and adopting a constitutional preamble affirming Australian social values and principles of government. The 1988 constitutional referendum was fairly typical of the process as it has evolved in Australia, both in the origins of the proposed amendments and in the outcome of the referendum. The 1999 proposals differed somewhat, in that they were first debated by a "people's convention" before being submitted to a vote in the referendum. The 1999 referendum also attracted widespread international attention because of its possible implications for the future of the British monarchy. But in the end all six of the proposals that were put to popular vote in the 1988 and 1999 referendums were rejected. Thus, while the Australian experience is instructive with regard to the role of the referendum in processes of constitutional change, it also highlights some of the difficulties involved in engaging the public at large in sometimes esoteric constitutional debates (Galligan 2001). The 1999 referendum, in particular, also illustrates the importance of the campaign period and provides considerable insight into the decision-making processes of voters in referendums (Luskin et al. 2000; McAllister 2001).

Both the 1988 and the 1999 Australian constitutional referendums involved political stories that played out over several years. The 1988 constitutional proposals were put forward by a constitutional commission that had been appointed by the Labor government in 1985 (Galligan and Nethercote 1989). From the commission's report, completed in 1988, four proposals were selected by the government to be put to referendum (see Table 3D1). The government clearly intended it as the first of a series of such referendums that would, over time, implement many of the commission's recommendations. One of these, a proposal to fix the terms of office of the members of the House of Representatives and of the Senate at four years, had been sought by previous governments (1974, 1977) but had always failed to win the necessary public support. Another proposal would have created an embryonic bill of rights guaranteeing fundamental freedoms such as trial by jury, freedom of religion, and property rights. The other two proposals dealt with entrenching the constitutional authority of local government and with ensuring approximate equality in the size of parliamentary constituencies ("fair elections").

Because many citizens might have been expected to be unfamiliar with issues such as these, the campaign itself was a critical source of information. Voters depended on the political parties, the media, and other participants in the campaign to provide both information and voting cues. The Electoral Commission also played a role, since it was responsible under Australian law for circulating a pamphlet to each voter summarizing the arguments put forward by both supporters and opponents of each proposal.

Although some proposals, such as those relating to entrenching local government and assuring "fair elections," seemed innocuous, all four proposals were soundly defeated in the referendum, in part because, as had often happened in the past, both the state governments and many citizens were suspicious of the federal government's motives in bringing forward such proposals. Partisanship was also a factor. The constitutional commission was widely seen by the opposition parties as a partisan Labor instrument, an attitude that carried over into the referendum campaign. Had the proposals received bipartisan endorsement, their chances of passing might have been greater. But the decision by the opposition Liberal party to campaign actively against them turned the referendum campaign into a partisan fight. As it became more overtly partisan, the campaign began to be assessed in terms of its possible implications for the next federal election, thereby raising the political stakes for all participants.[23]

The strategy followed by opponents of the proposals was not so much to attack them directly as it was to raise doubts about them and to question the motives that lay behind the government's constitutional strategy. The campaign certainly affected the outcome. Public opinion polls only a month before the day of the referendum showed a majority of respondents in favour of all four proposals (Hughes 1994). It might seem strange that a large majority could be persuaded to vote against the "rights and freedoms" proposal, for example, which entrenched constitutional guarantees of trial by jury, freedom of religion, and compensation for expropriated property. But by sowing doubts about the motives of its proposers and the possible unforeseen consequences of constitutional entrenchment of these rights, the opposition succeeded in mobilizing a substantial majority against it. As many analysts of referendums both in Australia and elsewhere have observed, when voters become suspicious or uncertain they tend to vote NO.

Nevertheless, the size of the defeat surprised most observers. Turnout was high (92 per cent), almost comparable to turnout in Australian federal elections, in which voting is compulsory (voting is also compulsory in referendums). Nearly two-thirds of all voters turned down all four items, and none of the proposals carried a majority in any state (Table 3D1). As was the case in the aftermath of Canada's referendum on the Charlottetown proposals (see section A of this chapter), one of the consequences of the 1988 referendum was to suspend any discussion of ambitious new programs of constitutional change in Australia. While many Australians continued to see a need for constitutional renewal, the historical record served only to instil caution regarding the ability of the referendum to bring it about. The comparison with New Zealand here is instructive. In that country the public ultimately succeeded in imposing its will on reluctant elites through the referendums (see section C of this chapter). In Australia and Canada, however, the constitutional proposals put forward by elites failed to win the endorsement of their electorates.

The "moratorium" on new constitutional initiatives in Australia that arose after the 1988 referendum lasted only for a short time. The question of ending the role of the British monarchy in Australia was not new, although it had never before been the subject of a referendum vote. The proposal that was eventually put forward in the 1999 referendum first arose through the initiative of Paul Keating, who had succeeded Robert Hawke as prime minister in 1991. Keating had long favoured severing the connection to the British monarchy in Australia, and he vowed to accomplish this goal in time for Australia's constitutional centennial in 2001. Thus, an intensive national debate developed in the mid-1990s between "monarchists" and "republicans" about both the desirability of replacing the monarchy and the related issue of exactly what should replace it.

Labor's defeat in the 1996 election slowed the momentum of what had come to be called the "republican movement," but it did not end the debate. The new prime minister, John Howard, who personally favoured retaining the monarchy, instead shifted both the terms and the milieu of the debate. Recognizing that the movement to create a republic enjoyed considerable support among Australians and that some members of his own party also favoured ending the monarchy, Howard allowed the debate to be taken up by a specially constituted constitutional convention — the "people's convention" mentioned earlier.[24] This innovation depoliticized the process somewhat, allowing the debate to be carried on outside parliament and in a less partisan atmosphere. Increasingly, the debate focused not on the monarchy itself but on various proposed alternatives, and the convention became deeply divided between models calling for an elected

Table 3D2

The Australian Republic Referendum, November 6, 1999

REPUBLIC. "To alter the constitution to establish the Commonwealth of Australia as a republic, with the Queen and Governor General being replaced by a President appointed by a two-thirds majority of the members of the Commonwealth Parliament."

Percentage voting Yes: 45. Number of states approving: 0.

PREAMBLE. "To alter the constitution to insert a preamble."*

Percentage voting Yes: 39. Number of states approving: 0

Turnout = 95%.

* For the text of the preamble, see note 25.

state president and one appointed by parliament. The convention finally voted to support the concept of a president chosen by a two-thirds vote of parliament. It also endorsed a constitutional preamble that had been initially proposed by Howard.[25]

The raucous campaign that followed saw both proposals soundly defeated (Table 3D2). Neither proposal won a majority in any state, and nearly two-thirds of the country voted against the preamble.[26] While the concept of a republic itself continued to enjoy considerable public support, according to public opinion polls conducted near the time of the referendum, the divisions among republicans regarding the proposed presidency prevented the formation of any real consensus on the issue as it appeared on the ballot paper. Many Australians who favoured a president elected in a direct nationwide vote found themselves opposed to the proposal for election by members of Parliament, which came to be derided during the campaign as a proposal for "a politician's republic." Others were willing, even if reluctantly, to accept a nonelected president in order to secure the primary objective of bringing an end to the role of the British monarchy in Australia. A "deliberative poll" conducted during the referendum campaign shows that the process of opinion formation among voters was complicated (Luskin et al 2000). As republican-leaning voters learned more about the proposals, they were more inclined to vote YES. But the population at large assimilated new information more slowly. Even though the evidence indicates that Australians continued to favour replacing the monarchy both before and after the referendum campaign, the proposals went down to defeat (McAllister 2001). The NO forces succeeded in effectively changing the subject of the campaign discourse and in dividing their opponents over the issue of an elected presidency. Republicans who preferred an elected presidency joined with monarchists to defeat the proposal.

Following the referendum, republican groups vowed to fight on. Howard quickly ruled out a second referendum, but the leader of the opposition committed his party to holding separate referendums on the issue of a republic and on the question of an elected presidency if Labor formed the government after the next general election. Thus, rather than being resolved by the referendum, the issue is likely to arise again in a more partisan electoral context sometime in the future.

Both the Australian and Canadian experiences suggest that securing any large-scale constitutional change through the referendum process is often very difficult. Even constitutional initiatives with seemingly strong popular support fail more often than they succeed. Voters generally come to such a process with relatively little information about the debates that have preceded the referendum campaign, and they therefore depend on the various campaign actors for information and cues. A campaign provides opportunities for distortion and misinformation and allows opponents to plant doubts in the minds of voters that are not easily resolved over a short period. Yet the New Zealand experience indicates that such obstacles can be overcome. Constitutional politics are normally the exclusive preserve of the political elites. When the mass public becomes engaged, the stakes are raised, and the outcome becomes dependent on developing and implementing an effective communications strategy. Under such conditions poorly prepared or poorly organized campaigns seem doomed to fail. Often they fail because the elites who organize and conduct them overestimate their abilities to control the political forces that such campaigns may unleash.

NOTES

1. In Denmark, for example, transfers of sovereignty such as those that would have occurred under the Maastricht Treaty or through joining the single currency would normally have to be submitted to the people under article 20 of the Danish constitution. While a referendum on such issues might be avoided under some cir-

cumstances, it has now become a convention in Denmark that they will be submitted to referendum.

2. The alternative procedure allows the president to submit a proposal to a joint session of the National Assembly and Senate, and requires a three-fifths majority for approval.

3. See especially Cairns and Williams (1991) and Russell (1993) for a more comprehensive discussion of the issues and events leading up to the 1992 referendum.

4. The constitution, which included a new amending formula and a charter of rights came into effect on April 17, 1982, following its approval by the British Parliament and proclamation in Ottawa by Queen Elizabeth.

5. Legally speaking, the referendum in Quebec was separate from the one conducted under federal jurisdiction in the rest of the country. This had various implications for the conduct of the campaign, particularly with respect to advertising, campaign organization, and finance. See Côté et al. (1992).

6. The Bloc Québécois went on to win 14 per cent of the total vote (49 per cent in Quebec) and fifty-four seats in the 1993 federal election, becoming the official opposition. The Reform Party won 19 per cent of the vote and fifty-two seats. The Conservatives and NDP were devastated in the 1993 election, winning only two and nine seats respectively. For an analysis of the possible linkages between the referendum and the federal election, see Clarke et al. (1996) and Saint-Germain and Grenier (1994).

7. The proposal to create an elected Russian presidency was approved by 70 per cent of voters in the March 17 referendum in Russia. Seventy-one per cent of Russian voters approved the Gorbachev proposal to maintain the union. Turnout in Russia in the March 17th referendum was 75 per cent of the eligible electorate.

8. The parliament had been elected in 1990. Two hundred and fifty-two members of the 1,068-member Congress of People's Deputies formed the working parliament, which was known as the Supreme Soviet. On the dissolution of the Soviet Union in 1991, this body became the sole legislative authority in a sovereign Russia.

9. The proposal for early presidential elections obtained 49.5 per cent of the votes cast (31.7 per cent of the entire electorate), and the proposal for early parliamentary elections won 67.2 per cent (43.1 per cent of all eligible voters). White et al. 1997.

10. On the dramatic events of the October crisis, see Brown (1993) or Ahdieh (1997).

11. Ironically, the election of the Duma was being held under provisions of a constitution that was itself subject to approval in the referendum taking place concurrently.

12. For an overview of the electoral reform debate in Canada, New Zealand, and other countries, see Milner (1999).

13. In the 1978 election, Labour won 40.4 per cent of the vote and forty-two of the ninety-two seats, while the National Party formed the government with 39.8 per cent of the vote and fifty-four seats. In 1981, Labour won 39.0 per cent of the total vote and forty-five seats, compared with 38.8 per cent and forty-nine seats for National, which again formed the government.

14. Report of the Royal Commission on Electoral Reform, *Towards a Better Democracy* (Wellington 1986).

15. New Zealand did, however, adopt new provisions for nonbinding citizen-initiated referendums in 1993. See Parkinson (2001).

16. There was a more typical turnout of 85 per cent in the 1990 and 1993 general elections.

17. Moore was quoted in Levine and Roberts (1993).

18. The Alliance was a coalition of five smaller parties, including initially the Greens, which formed in 1991. New Zealand First was formed in 1993 by Winston Peters, a former National Party cabinet minister who had broken with the National Party and had been expelled from its caucus. Peters was overwhelmingly re-elected to parliament as an independent candidate in a by-election in March 1993 and proceeded to form New Zealand First three months later.

19. First-time voters favoured the FPTP system by a margin of about 57 to 43 per cent (Levine and Roberts 1994; Vowles et al. 1994).

20. The review did in fact take place in 2000, and the parliamentary committee which conducted the review declined to recommend another referendum on the issue.

21. The other three referendums dealt with military conscription (1916, 1917) and the national song (1977).

22. For a list of constitutional proposals put forward in Australia since 1906, see Hughes (1994), Miles (1998), or Galligan (2001).

23. The election took place in March 1990. The Labor government was returned in that election by an extremely narrow margin, winning seventy-eight seats in the House of Representatives on a mere 39 per cent of the first preference vote. The combined Liberal-National opposition won sixty-nine seats.

24. Polls continued to show that as many as two-thirds of Australians favoured ending the monarchy (*Sydney Morning Herald*, August 26, 1999). There was considerably less consensus, however, on the question of what sort of institution should replace it.

25. The text of the proposed preamble was as follows:

> With hope in God, the Commonwealth of Australia is constituted as a democracy with a federal system of government to serve the common good.
>
> We the Australian people commit ourselves to this Constitution:
>
> proud that our national unity has been forged by Australians from many ancestries;
>
> never forgetting the sacrifices of all who defended our country and our liberty in time of war;
>
> upholding freedom, tolerance, individual dignity and the rule of law;
>
> honouring Aborigines and Torres Strait Islanders, the nation's first people, for their deep kinship with their lands and for their ancient and continuing cultures which enrich the life of our country;
>
> recognising the nation-building contribution of generations of immigrants;
>
> mindful of our responsibility to protect our unique natural environment;
>
> supportive of achievement as well as equality of opportunity for all;
>
> and valuing independence as dearly as the national spirit which binds us together in both adversity and success.

26. The republic proposal did carry in the Australian Capital Territory, however, with 63 per cent of voters in that jurisdiction voting YES.

4

Referendums on Treaties and International Agreements

In this chapter, I consider several cases in which a referendum was held to ratify a treaty or international agreement that had been entered into or contemplated by a government.

As noted in Chapter 1, this usage of the referendum has become well established in a number of countries, and in several important instances in recent years a major international treaty or agreement has been put to a referendum, either because a particular country's constitution required such a ratification process or because its government deemed that such a vote was politically expedient. In the case of the 1986 referendum on NATO in Spain (discussed in section A of this chapter), the agreement in question was already in force at the time of the referendum, a circumstance similar to that of the referendum held in Britain on European Community membership in 1975. Referendums on the 1992 Maastricht Treaty in Denmark, France, and Ireland provide additional examples, even though the specific legal circumstances varied considerably among the European countries that acceded to Maastricht. By the time of the 2000 referendum on joining the European currency (section D of this chapter), the convention had become well established in Denmark that all European agreements that involve a transfer of sovereignty are submitted to referendum, even though an alternative process exists under article 20 of the Danish constitution when an agreement enjoys broad parliamentary support.[1] In Ireland a referendum on international treaties is mandatory when a constitutional amendment is involved. If there is a dispute regarding the ability of the state to enter into a treaty without a referendum, it may be up to the courts to resolve the issue.[2]

In Switzerland article 89 of the constitution has a provision specifically covering international treaties that do not require a constitutional amendment.[3] However, referendums involving international associations may arise under any one of several provisions governing referendums in Switzerland (see Chapter 6, section D). As a result, there have been several votes in Switzerland on participation in international bodies, including votes involving UN membership (1986, 2002), the International Monetary Fund (IMF) and the World Bank (1992), participation in UN peacekeeping operations (1994), the initiation of negotiations to join the European Union (1997), and closer economic ties with the European Union (EU) (2000). While participation in international treaties and organizations accounts for only a small part of the diverse subject matter of Swiss referendums, they have tended to enjoy a greater profile in national politics and have sometimes attracted a higher turnout.[4]

While referendums on international treaties or agreements can arise under various legal or constitutional provisions, the decision to put an agreement to a referendum may also be a simple political one. In the case of the 1994 referendums on European Union membership in Austria, Norway, Sweden, and Finland, the referendum was a politically necessary step in the process of joining the European Union but not a formal legal requirement. A similar argument might be made in Britain today. No British government would risk joining the monetary union without obtaining public approval in a referendum, even though such a course is not legally mandated. François Mitterrand made what was clearly a strategic decision to submit the Maastricht Treaty to a referendum in 1992, no doubt believing that it would be easily approved by French voters. But the close outcome in that case demonstrates that the volatility and uncertainty of a campaign can quickly escalate the risks of such a strategy (see section B of this chapter). While there is nothing specific about referendums on these subjects that make them inherently different from those on other high-profile issues, the fact that they are often central to a government's foreign or economic policy frequently ensures that they will involve real political conflicts. As will be seen in several of the examples treated in this chapter, the campaigns have often been intense, the turnout high, and the outcomes difficult to predict.

A. Spain's 1986 Referendum on NATO

Spain's decision to join NATO was linked indirectly to its transition to democracy and the process of its integration into Europe. From the death of General Franco in 1975 to the attempted coup of 1981, Spain's political future remained in some doubt. For many of those seeking to ensure that the process of integrating Spain more completely into a democratic Europe would continue, NATO membership was seen as a logical first step. Membership in the European Community, while not tied directly in any way to joining NATO, would follow in due course, according to this view.[5] The Union of the Democratic Centre (UCD) government of Adolfo Suarez first announced its intention to take Spain into NATO in 1980, but the policy faced widespread public opposition.[6] Many Spaniards were suspicious that US influence over Spanish foreign policy would increase as a result of membership in NATO, and membership had also become linked in the public mind to the emotionally charged issue of American military bases in Spain. Sensing that public opinion was strongly against Spanish entry into NATO, the opposition parties demanded a referendum.

The government, however, had little interest in risking a referendum on the issue. The proposal for Spanish membership in NATO was formally presented to the Cortes (Spanish parliament) in August 1981. The Socialist and Communist deputies were firmly opposed. Using its parliamentary majority, the government prevailed by a vote of 186 to 146. On May 30, 1982, Spain formally became a member of NATO.[7] But the question was not fully resolved by these events, in part because Spain was on the eve of a general election. Inevitably, the debate over NATO carried forward into the election campaign. The Socialist opposition, let by Felipe Gonzàlez, promised that it would hold a referendum on the issue if elected. In the election, which took place in October 1982, the Socialists won a majority of seats in the Cortes, with 48 per cent of the popular vote, and Gonzàlez became prime minister. The UCD and its successor party, the Popular Democratic Party (PDP), were decimated, and the opposition was formed by the Popular Alliance (AP), led by the former Francist Manuel Fraga. The election thus produced not only the first change of government in Spain's fledgling democracy but also a new polarization of the party system between left and right.

Gonzàlez's position with regard to NATO began to shift soon after he assumed power. While the Socialists had taken advantage of anti-NATO sentiment among the public during the election campaign, their platform had not explicitly called for withdrawal from the organization. In promising a referendum on the issue, the party had been able to avoid such a commitment, while at the same time implicitly positioning itself on the anti-NATO side of the debate. In power, however, Gonzàlez soon began to hint at a change in his position, increasingly linking the NATO commitment to Spain's desire to join the European Community, which he supported. In October 1984 the prime minister formally announced a change of position. Spain, he maintained, had to honour its international commitments. The prospective referendum provided the necessary political cover. If the Spanish people decided otherwise, Gonzàlez indicated, he would of course take Spain out.

There was, however, no rush to a referendum. For a time some observers felt that Gonzàlez would instead wait until the next general election to consolidate his change of policy. The political circumstances were complicated by the fact that anti-NATO sentiment in the country had grown as the various anti-NATO groups became more closely aligned with the European peace movement. A peace demonstration in early 1985 drew more than one hundred thousand people. The organizers of the demonstration called on the government to dismantle the US military bases in Spain and to sever all NATO ties. There was no assurance that Gonzàlez could win a referendum on NATO or that he could avoid a damaging split in his own party over the issue. Many prominent Socialists, including the foreign minister, Fernando Moran, continued to be opposed.

At the 1984 party congress, largely on the basis of his own extraordinary personal popularity within the party, Gonzàlez pushed through a resolution in support of his NATO policy over the strong objections of the youth and trade-union wings of the party. With the party thus formally behind him, Gonzàlez began to position himself for the referendum. Public opinion polls continued to suggest that he would lose a referendum on the issue, but the prime minister pressed ahead. A cabinet shuffle in mid-1985 removed Moran from his key position in the cabinet and demoted other opponents of the new policy. The Cortes passed the referendum legislation in December, and the date was set for March 12, 1986.

Gonzàlez had gambled that his own popularity and careful repositioning of the party on the issue could carry the day. But the support of voters, many of whom remained suspicious of NATO, would have to be won in a difficult campaign. Gonzàlez's position was strengthened somewhat by the strategic difficulty that his non-Socialist opponents faced as a result of his U-turn. It was, after all, the centre-right government that had taken Spain into NATO, and the opposition Popular Alliance and its leader were strong supporters of NATO, as was the military. By adopting what had previously been their position, the prime minister had left them with the difficult choice of either rallying to the support of the government or revising their own views.

Fraga, the Popular Alliance leader, resolved this dilemma by calling for a boycott of the referendum. Such a vote was unnecessary, in his view, because Spain was already in NATO. Further, Fraga indicated that his party disagreed with the terms of continued membership that the government had set, because they stressed the gradual process of political and military integration rather than the simple fact of NATO membership.[8] The call for abstention would also maximize the electoral strength of Socialist opponents of NATO, thus providing greater embarrassment to Gonzàlez should he lose. While this seemed a clever strategy—enabling the AP to avoid being drawn into overt support of the government in the referendum—it ultimately backfired. By calling for a boycott, Fraga himself had to persuade his pro-NATO supporters to stay away from the polls. He thus made the referendum into more of a vote of confidence in the government and the prime minister than it might otherwise have been. Gonzàlez took full advantage of this strategic opening in the campaign, stressing that the referendum was not just about NATO but that it was in reality a vote of confidence in him and the young Socialist government. He hinted broadly that he might be forced to resign as a consequence of defeat in the referendum and that Spain faced the prospect of a return to a government led by former supporters of Franco.[9] Spain's young democracy itself was at stake according to some of the more extravagant rhetoric of the campaign.

The wording of the referendum question (Table 4A1) had also been carefully crafted to stress the support of the government's position rather than just the issue of NATO membership, and it referred to the terms of membership, which included a ban on nuclear weapons and reductions in the number of American troops stationed on Spanish soil. As the campaign progressed, it became increasingly a partisan fight. But towards the end, Gonzàlez also began to stress the possible unforeseen consequences of leaving NATO, a tactic that was designed to appeal more to pro-NATO supporters of the opposition parties but that would not alienate Socialist voters. The partisan atmosphere helped Gonzàlez to rally his supporters,

Table 4A1

Results of the Spanish Referendum on NATO, March 12, 1986

Do you think it advisable for Spain to remain in the Atlantic Alliance under the terms set down by the government?

Result	Percentage of Electorate	Percentage of Votes Cast	Percentage of Valid Votes
Yes	32	53	57
No	24	40	43
Invalid	4	7	
Abstentions	40		
Total	100	100	100

even those who remained skeptical about NATO.[10] And it also made it more difficult for Fraga to persuade his partisans to stay away from the polls. The prime minister's strategy of appealing to opposition voters was inadvertently aided by the announcement that the king and queen intended to vote in the referendum, implicitly defying Fraga's call for abstention.

Gonzàlez's own political charisma should also not be underestimated in explaining the dramatic turnaround which his victory in the referendum represented. Anthony Gooch (1986) colourfully describes the atmosphere of his referendum-eve appeal to the nation in a televised debate:

> His entry into the television studios for his last appearance before the vote was described "like Jesus Christ entering Jerusalem on Palm Sunday." As he answered the questions put to him, Spain's great communicator was completely at ease. The incomparable attraction that the man exerts just by being there, with that voice of his that is sheer magic, sheer charisma, almost as if he had some gift from the Almighty himself. (312)

The support for the YES side (53 per cent of the votes cast; see Table 4.1) might not at first glance seem like a ringing endorsement of the government's position. But given the widespread expectation that it would be all but impossible to persuade the Spanish people to endorse NATO—an expectation that had prevailed almost until voting day—it represented a stunning personal victory for the prime minister. A turnout of 60 per cent represented an even greater achievement, because it indicated that Fraga's call for a boycott had clearly failed. Ironically, Gonzàlez's position was salvaged as much by the pro-NATO votes of the opposition forces as by his own supporters. By gaining votes from two completely different sources—from Socialist party supporters who suppressed their own views on NATO and rallied to his cause and from the pro-NATO Popular Alliance voters who defied their leader's call for abstention and voted for NATO—Gonzàlez managed to change the electoral arithmetic, which would have otherwise led to almost certain defeat.

Like the Canadian constitutional referendum (Chapter 3, section A) or the Swedish nuclear power referendum (Chapter 6, section A), Spain's referendum on NATO was a unique political event. As the only referendum held on an important political question in modern Spain, it may or may not be typical of what instruments of direct democracy might produce in that country if used on other issues. However, it does demonstrate the importance of several factors that appear in other referendum cases—the significance of turnout, the relevance of the question wording, the potential role of partisanship, and the power of political leadership. The campaign itself was crucial to the outcome, an observation that might also be made about many other referendums examined in this book. Even on an issue on which many Spanish voters held strong opinions and on which competing partisan forces seemed to be clearly aligned, the three-month referendum campaign was capable of changing the result from almost certain defeat to a dramatic and unexpected victory.

B. The 1992 French Referendum on the Maastricht Treaty

The Treaty on European Union was signed at the Dutch town of Maastricht by the foreign ministers of the twelve European Community members on February 7, 1992. From that time until the treaty finally came into force on November 1, 1993, it was the subject of a wide-ranging political debate throughout Europe. Building upon the foundations laid by the Single European Act of 1986, the Maastricht Treaty represented another significant step forward in the ongoing process of European political and economic integration. Even the change in the formal name of the organization—from the original European Economic Community (EEC) to European Community (EC) in 1986 to European Union (EU), with the implementation of Maastricht—was meant to signal that the new Europe had become a real political entity rather than a mere trading bloc. Given the controversy that such a move was bound to engender, it is not surprising that the debate over the treaty and its provisions was intense. But only three of the twelve member nations at the time—Denmark, Ireland, and France—put the treaty to a vote of the people in a referendum. In Denmark and Ireland, constitutional provisions mandated that a referendum take place. In France the decision was taken by the president alone.[11] François Mitterrand's decision to opt for a referendum was thoroughly political, driven as much by considerations of French domestic politics as by any of the provisions of the treaty itself (Appleton 1992).

Perhaps the single most important event on the road towards ratification of the Maastricht Treaty occurred not in France but in Denmark. When Danish voters rejected the treaty by a vote of 51 per cent to 49 per cent in their referendum on June 2, 1992, the short-term future of the entire European project was cast into doubt. Before the Danish vote, it had generally been expected that ratification by the member states would proceed slowly but smoothly. The Danish rejection sent shock waves through European capitals, and elsewhere in Europe greater attention began to be focused on some of the more controversial aspects of the treaty.[12] As one observer noted at the time, like most of its predecessor documents, it had never been intended for public debate in an intense campaign (Hartley 1992). Rather, it was a "web," designed to conceal divergent interests and shade ambiguities. But the Danish electoral laws had required that the main provisions of the document be translated into simple language and summarized in a campaign pamphlet distributed to each household. This thrust the details of the treaty into the open and subjected it to intense public scrutiny at the hands of a well-organized and well-funded coalition of Danish Euroskeptics (see section D of this chapter).

President Mitterrand announced his intention to hold a referendum immediately following the Danish vote. While there had been considerable previous discussion of the desirability of a French referendum on Maastricht, the outcome of the Danish vote may have made one inevitable. It also signalled clearly to all concerned the dangers inherent in the process and strengthened the position of Euroskeptics within the various parties. Although Mitterrand had earlier suggested to an interviewer that the treaty would be handily endorsed by the French electorate, the outcome of a referendum on the issue could no longer be taken for granted. In his Bastille Day (July 14) address, the president announced that the referendum would take place on September 20. It was to be a long and difficult campaign.

The principal opposition to Maastricht in France came initially from the political extremes, in particular the Communists (PCF) and the National Front (FN). But there were opponents in all of the other parties, including a small number in Mitterrand's own Parti Socialiste.[13] The Gaullist opposition (RPR) was deeply divided. Its leader, Jacques Chirac, positioning himself for the next presidential campaign, supported the YES side but attempted to maintain as low a profile as possible on the issue. Two prominent Gaullist Euroskeptics—Charles Pasqua and Philippe Séguin—assumed leadership roles in the NO campaign, as did Philippe de Villiers and Michel Poniatowski, both members of former president Valéry Giscard d'Estaing's Union for French Democracy (UDF). These figures provided the anti-Maastricht forces with respectable and articulate leadership figures, ensuring that the NO campaign would consist of more than "a clutch of xenophobes and Marxists" (Criddle 1993). It also produced greater risks for Chirac, as several of the UDF and RPR figures on the NO side were potential presidential rivals. Broadcast time in the campaign was allocated by party on the basis of proportion of seats in the National Assembly, rather than divided evenly between the YES and NO camps. This arrangement appeared initially to give some advantage to the Socialists, who had maintained a greater degree of party unity on the issue. But the deeply divided Gaullists split their share of the allocation between their YES and NO factions, thereby providing Pasqua and Séguin with an important platform.

Like the Canadian constitutional referendum (Chapter 3, section A) or the Danish referendum of a few months earlier, the YES side in the campaign seemed to be composed of a broad cross-section of the political establishment. In addition to Mitterrand and prominent members of the government, the YES side had the support of a former president (Giscard), Mitterrand's 1988 presidential opponent (Chirac), the leaders of the mainstream parties, most of the business establishment, many trade unions, and a wide variety of prominent religious, entertainment, sports, and literary figures. The NO side, consisting of the political fringes and party dissidents such as Pasqua and Jean Pierre Chevènement, had little in common except for their opposition to Maastricht. But the opponents' ability to portray themselves as political "outsiders" captured the mood of

Table 4B1

Results of the French Referendum on the Maastricht Treaty,
September 20, 1992

Do you approve the draft law put to the French people by the President of the
Republic authorizing the ratification of the treaty on European Union?

	Percentage of Electorate	*Percentage of Valid Votes*
YES	34.4	51.0
NO	33.0	49.0
Invalid	2.3	
Abstentions	30.3	
Total	100.0	100.0

disenchantment with the political class that was widespread in France at
the time. Mitterrand's own declining popularity and the deficiencies of his
government provided weaknesses that could be readily exploited (Franklin
et al. 1995).[14]

Philippe Séguin articulated this mood effectively, and emerged as
the principal spokesman for the NO campaign. Attacking the European
"technocracy," Séguin defended the NO case in a televised debate with
Mitterrand on September 3. The positions put forward by both sides had
less to do with the specifics of the treaty than with the spirit and philoso-
phy of the new Europe. According to its critics, Maastricht was but one
more step in the relentless march towards an undemocratic, remote, and
uncontrollable European superstate that threatened national sovereignty.
Supporters of the YES side argued that rejection of the treaty would put
at risk all the progress towards a new Europe that had been achieved in
the previous thirty years. The final weeks of the campaign saw the YES
side in a desperate fight to save the treaty. The prospect of a NO result
pulled both Giscard and Chirac more actively into the campaign. German
chancellor Helmut Kohl made an unprecedented television appearance on
behalf of the YES side. At the margins, the scare tactics of the YES side,
which emphasized the dire consequences for Europe of a rejection of the
treaty, seemed to turn the tide. Polls shifted from forecasting a narrow NO
victory to a narrow YES in the final few days.[15] The extremely close result
(Table 4B1) discloses the essential unpredictability of the outcome.

Of France's twenty-two regions, only nine returned a majority for the YES. But Paris was strongly in the YES camp, as were several other large cities. A number of distinct sociodemographic patterns emerged in the vote, with the more affluent parts of the country being more likely to vote YES (Dubois and Keraudren 1994). Beyond Paris, there was a sharp rural/urban divide, with rural (and particularly farming) areas being more likely to vote NO. Nearly four of five Socialist voters supported the YES. But these alone were not enough to produce a victory for the president. Mitterrand's victory was achieved as much with support from the UDF and Green voters, both of which groups split approximately 60-40 to the YES side (Habert 1992). RPR voters also helped, although these split 60-40 to the NO. As well as reflecting the weaknesses of the Socialist government and doubts about the treaty, the referendum exposed the divisions over Europe within all of the political parties.

The narrow French YES, along with the approval by Danish voters of a revised document eight months later, "saved" Maastricht.[16] However, the extent to which the European project was ever really at great risk is doubtful. What the Danish and French governments and their European partners were actually seeking in the referendums was not so much the active endorsement of the voters as a continuation of the "permissive consensus" that has characterized the European project during much of its modern history. Had French voters said NO only three months after the Danes administered their reprimand to the architects of the new Europe, the result would more likely have been an intense new round of negotiations, rather than the actual death of Maastricht. The French and Danish referendums had indeed demonstrated the size of the gap that had opened up between the public and the elites over the form and structure of the new Europe (Wallace and Smith 1995). But the voters in reality were capable only of slowing down or modifying the project, rather than vetoing it outright.

While there have been other referendums on issues of European integration in some EU countries since 1992, there has not been another in France. The narrow outcome of the 1992 referendum, along with the Danish experience, awakened European leaders to the potential strength of Euroskepticism in their electorates. Combined with other feelings of political discontent, such attitudes represented a potentially powerful political force. Where referendums on European issues could be avoided, other means might be found to ratify future agreements. But where a vote of the people on such issues was constitutionally or politically mandated, the political groundwork would henceforth be laid more carefully.

C. The Nordic Referendums on European Union Membership

The expansion of the European Community began in the early 1970s with the addition of Denmark, Ireland, and the United Kingdom to the original six members. The policy that had effectively prevented the addition of new members ended formally with a referendum in France held in April 1972 in which 68 per cent of the French electorate approved the policy of enlargement of the community. All three of the new members held referendums on EC membership—Denmark and Ireland in order to meet their own constitutional requirements, and the United Kingdom because of the decision of Harold Wilson's Labour government to submit the issue of British membership to a national vote. Although it was not constitutionally required to do so, Norway also held a referendum on membership, largely because of internal party disagreements on the issue. The Irish referendum, in which 83 per cent of the voters said YES to EC membership was held only two weeks after the French referendum on enlargement. Norway and Denmark followed in September and October of 1972, respectively, with Norwegian voters turning down the proposal for EC membership by a vote of 47 per cent to 53 per cent, and Danish voters approving it by a margin of 63 per cent to 37 per cent.

The Norwegian NO and the debate that took place over EC membership in Denmark signalled the political difficulties that the issue would face in the Scandinavian countries. This was later to be confirmed by the relatively narrow margin of Danish approval of the Single European Act in a referendum held in 1986 (56 per cent to 44 per cent) and in the rejection of the Maastricht Treaty in the 1992 Danish referendum. The result in Norway put an end to the debate on membership in the Community (for the time being), but Norway, along with Sweden, remained a member of the European Free Trade Area (EFTA). The Delors Initiative to create a European Economic Area between the EU and the EFTA revived the debate on full membership in both countries. But public opinion polls consistently indicated that the issue would face difficulty with Nordic electorates. Polls in December 1993 placed support for EU membership in Norway at 24 per cent and in Sweden at 33 per cent (Jenssen et al. 1998).

The governing parties in both countries would proceed cautiously, and they were themselves internally divided on the issue.

The road to the 1994 referendum in Finland took a somewhat different course. The issue of Finnish membership in the EU could not have arisen before the break-up of the Soviet Union and the end of the Cold War. Those events opened the door to a change in Finland's traditional position of neutrality and made more compelling the arguments of those who, for both economic and political reasons, sought to tie Finland more closely to the democracies of the West. For many Finns, membership in the EU was as much a question of establishing their identity in the new Europe as one of political or economic integration (Arter 1995). But support for Finnish membership was also enhanced by the economic circumstances in which Finland found itself in the early 1990s. Because the country was hit hard by the economic recession of those years and faced unemployment rates of nearly 20 per cent, there were fewer domestic impediments to membership in Finland than in its Nordic neighbours. Parties of both the left and the right, excluding the Communists and the small populist Finnish Rural Party (SMP), supported EU membership.

While there was no constitutional requirement for a referendum to secure Finnish membership, it was clear from the beginning that a popular vote would take place. In fact, the issue of Finnish membership became closely tied to the debates in the neighbouring countries. The idea that the referendums to be held in all four countries that were conducting membership negotiations with the EU (Austria, Finland, Norway, and Sweden) might be synchronized emerged out of the talks. The resulting "domino strategy"—in which referendums in the countries which were most likely to vote YES would take place first, thus bringing pressure on the more reluctant electorates—was nowhere formally recognized as a policy, but it nonetheless clearly served the agenda of officials in Brussels who were supporting the cause of enlargement as much as it did the domestic political agendas of proponents of EU membership. Thus, a series of referendums was held, with the Austrians voting in June, the Finns in October, and the Swedes and Norwegians two weeks apart in November. Favourable votes in Austria and Finland might be enough to tip the balance in Sweden. And a YES vote next door in Sweden would bring enormous pressure to bear on the reluctant Norwegians voting only two weeks later (Jahn and Storsved 1995).

Table 4C1

Results of the Nordic Referendums, 1994 (Percentages)

	Finland* (1994 10 16)	*Sweden†* (1994 11 13)	*Norway‡* (1994 11 28)
Yes	57	52	48
No	43	47	52
Blank	—	1	—
Turnout	74	83	89

* The question wording in Finland was, "Should Finland become a member of the European Union in accordance with the negotiation that has been achieved?"
† The text of the question in Sweden was, "Do you think that Sweden should become a member of the EU in accordance with the agreement between Sweden and the member states?"
‡ In Norway, the wording used on the referendum ballot was, "Should Norway become a member of the EU (European Union)?"

This domino strategy was, as Jahn and Storsved argue, "nearly successful." Austria, as expected, voted in favour of membership in the June referendum by a margin of two to one (67 per cent YES). The stage was thus set as favourably as possible for the three Nordic referendums that would take place in the fall. In October, Finland voted YES by a narrower, but relatively safe, margin of 57 per cent to 43 per cent. Sweden followed a month later, approving membership in a very close vote of 52 per cent to 48 per cent. But two weeks later Norwegian voters nevertheless turned down membership in the EU by a margin of 48 per cent to 52 per cent (Table 4C1). The domino strategy may have had some effect on the Swedish result, but in Norway it failed to achieve the outcome desired by the supporters of EU membership.

Those supporters had included the governing parties in all three countries, which in Finland was a centre-conservative coalition and in Norway and in Sweden social democratic. In Sweden membership had first been proposed by the SAP (Social Democratic) government of Ingvar Carlsson in 1990, but following the SAP's loss to a four-party conservative coalition in the 1991 election, the SAP reverted to its traditional policy of opposition to EU membership. However, the coalition, which was led by Carl Bildt, was strongly supportive of Swedish membership, which had not been a major issue in the election campaign. Bildt moved the process steadily forward, committing his government to hold a referendum when it submitted the accession bill to the Riksdag in August 1994. But the SAP's return to power as a minority government in the election of September 1994 once again placed Swedish membership in doubt.[17] Carlsson, having previously committed himself to support the policy but, leading a divided party, opted for a low-key strategy for the referendum following his return to power. Members of his party who disagreed with the policy formed an organization—Social Democrats against the EU—that campaigned actively against it. They were joined by the Communist and far-left parties and also by the Greens, who in Sweden were among the strongest opponents of EU membership. But membership enjoyed broad support from the business community, the powerful trade union confederation, major farm organizations, and all other mainstream political parties. Yet in spite of this broad spectrum of support, the YES option managed to attract only 52 per cent of Swedish voters.

In Norway it was the NO side that enjoyed broader support. Parties of both the left and the right were found among the opponents of Norwegian EU membership. While business was generally supportive, the powerful trade union congress voted by a narrow margin to oppose it. Agricultural organizations and fishermen remained unpersuaded that their interests were adequately protected, in spite of the careful attention that had been given to these areas during the negotiation of the accession treaty. On the other hand, the Labour Party (DNA) government of Gro Harlem Brundtland was in a somewhat stronger political position than was its Swedish counterpart. Reelected in 1993, Brundtland was able to maintain a greater degree of party unity on the EU by emphasizing security issues, Nordic unity (given that Sweden and Finland had just voted themselves in), and the need for a full Norwegian presence in European decision-making processes. She had also managed the negotiations well. Known Euroskeptics were placed in several key cabinet positions, and their support was eventually secured once they were satisfied with the terms of the treaty of accession in their respective areas. But this strategy was not enough. Remarkably, in spite of the seemingly favourable conditions under which the vote took place, the results differed little from those of the 1972 referendum.

In all three countries, several clear sociodemographic patterns emerged in the vote. Urban voters, particularly in Helsinki, Stockholm, and Oslo, provided the core of support for EU membership in all three cases, while

Figure 4C1

Regional Voting Patterns in the Nordic EU Referendums

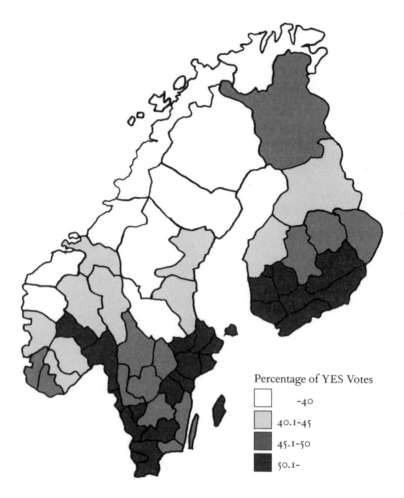

Percentage of YES Votes

☐ -40

▨ 40.1-45

▦ 45.1-50

■ 50.1-

Source: Jahn and Storsved (1995, 24).

opposition tended to be concentrated in the rural areas (Figure 4C1). In part, this pattern reflected the concerns of fishing and farming interests mentioned earlier. But class and economic cleavages were also reflected in the vote in various ways, as were partisanship and ideology. Partisanship mattered more in countries where the parties had managed to maintain a greater degree of internal unity on the issue. Over 70 per cent of Social Democratic/Labour voters in both Finland and Norway voted YES. But in Sweden, where divisions among the governing Social Democrats were more apparent, SAP voters split only about 55 to 45 to the YES side (Jenssen et al 1998).

The three Nordic referendums provide a rare opportunity for a comparative study of a direct vote on the same issue in different countries, a vote that was conducted at approximately the same time. They are also somewhat unique in that the outcome of one was intended to influence the outcome in others. But the different results in the three cases demonstrate that domestic political factors remain the dominant force in referendum voting, paralleling in many ways the patterns found in national elections. However, these referendums also demonstrate that, while well-known political and economic cleavages may have been instrumental in each of the outcomes, referendums nevertheless provide considerable opportunity for shifts in public sentiment, no matter how skillful the management of the campaign. The fact that, over a four-year period, public opinion polls had suggested possible alternative outcomes in all three cases indicates that these referendums were never entirely predictable, whatever strategies might have been followed. In part because of the close result and continued divisions within the governing SAP, Sweden opted to remain outside the monetary union, which came into effect on January 1, 1999. Acceptance of the Euro, the common European currency, thus became a continuing political question in Sweden and the subject of a future referendum.[18] The outcome of that referendum and Swedish handling of the issue of participation in the European Monetary Union (EMU) more generally is certain to influence the approach to this issue in Britain and Denmark as well. Enlargement of the EU to twenty-five members, now slated to take place in 2004, will extend these debates to new political environments.

D. Denmark Says "No" Again:
The 2000 Referendum on the European Currency

Since Denmark first joined the European Community in 1973, the European issue has been at the centre of Danish politics. Denmark, Ireland, and Britain entered the EC at the same time in January 1973, bringing the number of member nations to nine. The path to enlargement

Table 4D1

Results of Six Danish Referendums on European Issues,
1972–2000 (Percentages)

Date	Issue	Yes	No	Turnout
1972 10 01	EC membership	63.3	36.7	90
1986 02 27	Single European Act	56.2	43.8	75
1992 06 02	Maastricht Treaty	49.3	50.7	83
1993 05 18	Edinburgh Agreement	56.7	43.3	87
1998 05 28	Amsterdam Treaty	55.1	44.9	75
2000 09 28	Single currency	46.7	53.3	89

of the community from its original six members had been cleared by a referendum held in France in April 1972 in which French voters endorsed the principle of enlargement.[19] Referendums took place in all three of the new member nations, although the political and legal circumstances were different in each. Britain held its referendum two years after entry, following Labour's victory in the elections of 1974. Of the three countries, only Ireland had a constitutional requirement for a referendum, since joining the EC involved several necessary changes to the Irish constitution regarding parliamentary sovereignty (Gallagher 1996). In Denmark a referendum was necessitated by the fact that the proposal to join the EC lacked the five-sixths level of support in the Folketing (the Danish parliament) that would have been necessary to avoid one (Svensson 1996, 2002).[20] In Britain the decision by the Wilson government to hold a referendum was purely political, having no direct legal consequences for the continuation of British membership.

In all three cases, the vote in favour of membership in the European Community was strongly tilted to the YES side. Even in Denmark, "Europe" was not then as politically contentious as it would later become. But the signs of the developing European cleavage in national politics were present even at that time. Of the three countries that voted to join the community in the early 1970s, the NO vote was highest in Denmark. Thirty-seven per cent of the Danes voted NO to Europe in the October 1972 referendum, compared to 33 per cent in Britain and 17 per cent in Ireland. Turnout in the Danish referendum was 90 per cent, compared with 70 per cent in Ireland and 65 per cent in Britain. This relatively high

NO vote, combined with the split in the governing party over the issue, was a precursor of things to come in Danish politics.

Over the next two decades, Denmark would hold five more referendums on various European issues. The progression of these referendums (see Table 4D1) reflects the evolution of the European project, covering the Single European Act (1986), the Maastricht Treaty and Edinburgh Agreement (1992-1993), and the Amsterdam Treaty (1998) and culminating in Denmark's vote against participation in the Euro in September 2000. Although the vote against the Single European Act in 1986 was substantial (44 per cent), the watershed of this period was Denmark's narrow rejection of the Maastricht Treaty in the June 1992 referendum. This event sent shock waves throughout Europe, since it represented a major political setback for the architects of the new Europe. Although a NO vote in tiny Denmark might not by itself have been sufficient to derail the European project, it reverberated in other countries. Certainly, the Danish vote, along with the issues that it raised, was a factor in the referendum on Maastricht held in France three months later (see section B of this chapter). The Danish vote against Maastricht exposed the political vulnerability of the European project in Denmark and elsewhere. Although a compromise that allowed several specific Danish exceptions to Maastricht was cobbled together in Edinburgh and although the resulting Edinburgh Agreement was ratified in another referendum barely a year later, the vote against Maastricht in Denmark had lasting effects in European politics generally and in the national politics of several other member countries. Out of the NO campaign in the 1992 referendum was born one of the first well-organized political groups (the June Movement) that articulated the reservations that many observers outside the political elites felt about the speed and direction of European integration. From 1992 onwards, Euroskepticism, as it came to be known in Britain, was a powerful political force in several EU countries. But it was in Denmark that it first found its political voice.

Given this background, it is not surprising that the prospective entry of Denmark into the European Monetary Union (EMU) proved to be politically contentious. It was clear from the beginning that there would have to be a referendum on the issue and that the chances of passage were doubtful. Nevertheless, the outcome of the vote conceivably might have gone either way. Prime Minister Poul Nyrup Rasmussen (a Social Democrat) himself led the YES campaign (Best for Denmark) and used the considerable resources of the government on its behalf. The timetable, under which the Euro had already been launched on January 1, 1999, allowed the government to plan its campaign well in advance and to anticipate many of the sources of opposition to the common European currency. All of the mainstream political parties, holding 140 of the 179 seats in the Folketing, supported Danish participation in the EMU.[21] Also lined up behind Danish participation in the Euro were the leaders of the major trade unions, nearly all elements of the business community, and most of the nation's newspapers. On the surface it appeared that the chances of success in such a setting were fairly good. Some public opinion polls taken in the spring of 2000 suggested a YES lead of as much as 15 per cent (Downs 2001). But by midsummer, this lead had evaporated. Polls in June showed the race at a dead heat and the number of undecided voters in the 15 per cent to 20 per cent range (Marcussen and Zølner 2001).

Much depended on the government's ability to convince skeptical Danish voters that entry into the Euro-zone was necessary to protect the Danish economy. A considerable part of the YES campaign therefore stressed the potential economic dangers of Danish nonparticipation in EMU—slower economic growth, a weaker currency, higher interest rates, unemployment. Members of the governing coalition also sought to separate the Euro question from larger European issues, stressing that the EMU was an economic issue that did not necessarily entail closer political union. This strategy however was undermined by a report published by the Danish Economic Council (members of which were dubbed the "three wise men") in May. This report stated quite clearly that participation in the EMU would make little difference to the Danish economy, since the Danish currency, the krone, was already pegged to the Euro. In the view of the economists, the issue was purely political. Although the report said little that was really new, its timing and conclusions exposed the thin veneer of the YES campaign. The Euro could not be detached from wider political questions and defended on purely economic grounds.

The NO campaign, in contrast, was more diverse and wide-ranging. It did not so much have to make a coherent case against the Euro as to raise doubts and suspicions about the arguments being put forward by the YES side. Ranging from far-left to far-right, campaigners for the NO had various reasons for opposing the Euro. One of their leaders was Pia Kjaersgaard, who was also leader of the small Danish Peoples' Party. Relying heavily on patriotism and Danish nationalism, Kjaersgaard employed slogans such as "Defend the krone" and "Danes will decide."

Other NO campaigners raised the spectre of a dominant European central bank (located in Frankfurt!) or portrayed EU institutions and practices as a threat to Danish democracy. The left parties that opposed the EMU tended to stress potential threats to the safeguards of the Danish welfare state. The NO campaign was also aided inadvertently by the Euro itself, which had declined steadily against other currencies, particularly the US dollar, since its official launch. In the end, however, one of the strongest weapons that the NO side possessed was the psychology of the underdog. For many, left or right, the campaign was an epic battle of the Danish people against the political elites—or little Denmark against the European superstate.

By voting day, the outcome appeared certain, although the YES side seemed genuinely shocked by its loss. The prime minister portrayed the outcome as a "defeat for Denmark," but other European leaders sought to downplay the importance of the vote on the larger European stage. All sides had seemingly learned something from the 1992 Maastricht referendum and its aftermath, of which the 2000 referendum on the Euro was something of a reprise. But what Danish voters most appeared to have learned was that the real costs of voting NO in a referendum were much less than the overheated rhetoric of an intense campaign implied. The government's own economists had told them so!

NOTES

1. Support by five-sixths of all members of the Folketing is required. Qvortrup (2001) notes that joining the European single currency did enjoy this level of parliamentary support but that the government submitted the issue to referendum anyway.

2. The Supreme Court decided in 1987, for instance, that the constitution did not permit ratification of the Single European Act without a referendum. The precedent established in that decision has been interpreted as applying to later treaties involving issues of European integration such as Maastricht (1992), Amsterdam (1998), and Nice (2002). See Gallagher (1996) for a more detailed discussion of Irish referendum practices.

3. Fifty thousand voters or eight cantons can request a referendum on such a treaty. Only a simple majority of the national electorate (not a double majority, as is normally the case in Swiss referendums) is required to confirm the treaty. If the treaty involves a constitutional amendment, however, a referendum is mandatory, and the normal double-majority provision (a majority of voters and a majority of the cantons) applies. See Chapter 6, section D for a more detailed discussion of the referendum process in Switzerland.

4. Turnout in Swiss referendums is generally low. However, the 1992 referendum on membership in the European Economic Area drew a turnout of 78 per cent, the

highest for the 1990s during which the average turnout in referendums was only 44 per cent (see Chapter 6, section D).

5. Spain first applied for membership in the European Community in 1977 but did not become a member until 1986.

6. The Union of the Democratic Centre was a broad coalition of centre and centre-right groups that had won the 1977 and 1979 elections. It began to break apart in 1981 and was succeeded by several other groups, including the Democratic and Social Centre (CDS) and the Popular Democrats (PDP). These groups continued to form the governing coalition until the Socialist victory in 1982.

7. The provision was that integration into NATO would take place in stages. The first stage would be Spanish participation in all NATO political bodies, to be followed by gradual increases in Spanish participation in NATO military operations.

8. The Socialists had also added provisions for reductions in the number of American troops that could be stationed in Spain and a complete ban on nuclear weapons on Spanish soil.

9. Fraga had served as a cabinet minister under Franco.

10. Boix and Alt (1986) estimate that about seven out of ten 1982 Socialist voters in the referendum supported the YES side.

11. Two articles of the French constitution might have applied. Article 11 places in the hands of the president the authority to call a referendum on any matter that "would affect the functioning of institutions." Article 89 outlines the process of constitutional amendment under which a proposal may be submitted either to a referendum (following passage by both houses of parliament) or to a joint session of parliament convened as a Constitutional Congress (in which a three-fifths vote is required). Mitterrand in effect chose both these options in the case of the Maastricht Treaty, submitting three specific items that required constitutional change to the Congress and the treaty as a whole to a referendum under the provisions of Article 11.

12. A detailed analysis of the 250 articles of the Maastricht Treaty is beyond the scope of this discussion. For a summary of the main provisions, see Best (1994).

13. The most prominent of whom was Jean Pierre Chevènement, a left-wing member of the PS.

14. Edith Cresson, who had been Mitterrand's prime minister since May 1991, was replaced by Pierre Bérégovoy in April, partly as a consequence of the steep losses that the Parti Socialiste had suffered in the local elections in March.

15. French electoral law provides for a ban on publication of public opinion polls for a period of seven days before voting day.

16. The Edinburgh Agreement, designed to address the Danish reservations about Maastricht, was signed on December 11, 1992.

17. The results of the general election of September 18, 1994 in Sweden were as follows (1991 figures shown in parentheses):

	Votes		Seats	
Social Democrats (SAP)	45%	(38)	161	(138)
Moderate Party (Conservative)	22	(22)	80	(80)
Centre Party	8	(9)	27	(31)
People's Party (Liberal)	7	(9)	26	(33)
Left Party (Communist)	6	(5)	22	(16)
Greens	5	(3)	18	(0)
Christian Democrats	4	(7)	15	(26)
New Democracy	1	(7)	0	(25)

18. The government of Goran Persson has indicated its intention to hold a referendum on the Euro in September 2003.

19. Until then, enlargement of the community had been blocked by the threat of a French veto. The resignation of President de Gaulle in 1969, followed by the 1972 referendum initiated by President Pompidou, effectively removed this obstacle. Sixty-eight per cent of those participating in the 1972 French referendum voted in favour of enlargement.

20. The decision to join the EU enjoyed broad cross-party support but was opposed by the far left parties. There was also some opposition within the governing Social Democrats and the Radical Liberals. The vote in the Folketing was 141 in favour and 34 against, with the NO votes including twelve Social Democrats and four Radical Liberals. Since 150 YES votes would have been required to meet the five-sixths rule, a referendum was therefore obligatory under article 20 of the constitution.

21. Opposed were two right-wing parties (the Danish Peoples' Party, with thirteen seats, and the Progress Party, with five seats), one centre-right party (the Christian Peoples' Party, with four seats), and two left-wing parties (the Socialist Peoples' Party, with thirteen seats, and the Red-Green Alliance, with four seats).

5

Referendums on Sovereignty, National Self-Determination, and Devolution

Referendums on subjects such as sovereignty, national self-determination, and devolution are relatively rare, in part because jurisdictions that might desire a change in their political status often lack the legal competence to undertake a binding referendum on self-determination. In the case of Quebec the two referendums held on "sovereignty" by the provincial government (1980 and 1995) might well have met legal challenges from the federal government had they been successful. In Puerto Rico, while the commonwealth government in each of the three instances (1967, 1993, 1998) was seeking stronger ties with the United States rather than independence, it nevertheless would have been impossible to accomplish this objective without the cooperation of the US federal government in Washington (see section D of this chapter). In the case of the devolution referendums in Scotland and Wales, however, local autonomy was a project of the central government itself—in Wales it was foisted upon a skeptical and somewhat reluctant Welsh electorate. But while the circumstances of these referendums varied considerably, they had in common the principle that in a democratic political culture, changes in the basic form of the nation-state cannot be made without some form of popular consent.[1]

However, in some instances such changes have been accomplished without resorting to a referendum. The "velvet divorce" of Slovakia and the Czech Republic in 1992 was accomplished without a referendum, even though there was considerable evidence that the citizens of both parts of the former Czechoslovakia would have preferred this approach.[2] Similarly, the secession of Singapore from Malaysia in 1965 was accomplished quickly through negotiations between political leaders and without any formal process of public consultation.[3] More typically, however, such cases of peaceful secession would involve both types of processes, i.e., extensive negotiations among the elites followed by ratification of the new political arrangements by citizens in a referendum.[4] This is what occurred in the protracted disengagement of Norway from its union with Sweden, which was first negotiated by specially constituted parliamentary committees and finally endorsed by Norwegian voters in a plebiscite in 1905.[5] The secession of East Timor from Indonesia might also serve as a more recent example of such a process culminating in a referendum, although it would be more difficult to describe that case as one of peaceful secession.[6]

The breakup of the Soviet Union in the early 1990s provides several additional examples in which referendums were used in the creation of newly independent states. In a final attempt to hold the union together, Mikhail Gorbachev initiated an "all-union" referendum that took place on March 17, 1991. Although it applied to all fifteen constituent republics, only three (Belarus, Turkmenistan, and Tajikistan) held the referendum exactly as instructed by the central government, with no changes of wording or additional questions. In the three Baltic republics, the movement towards independence was already well advanced at the time of Gorbachev's referendum, and all three (together with Georgia, Armenia, and Moldova) boycotted the vote. In Ukraine, a second question was added to the ballot asserting the "sovereignty" of Ukraine (see section B of this chapter). In Russia, a second question was added on the creation of a Russian presidency.[7] Rather than achieving his goal of preserving the union, Gorbachev's referendum had exactly the opposite effect. By the end of 1991, ten of the fifteen former Soviet republics had held successful referendums on independence.[8] While their respective paths to independence were shaped by events taking place within the Soviet Union, referendums played a key role in the process.

Several prominent Canadian examples of state building through referendums should also be noted here. When Newfoundland entered Confederation in 1949, it was as a result of a protracted process that involved a two-stage referendum.[9] More recently, the creation of Nunavut involved three direct popular votes that took place over a ten-year period.[10] Finally, the experience of Quebec (see section A of this chapter) has clearly established the precedent that any future changes in its political status can come about only through the consent of its citizens in a referendum. While matters such as question wording and minimum majorities are likely to continue to be contested in any future vote, the principle that a referendum must be a key part of any process leading to the independence of Quebec now seems well established.[11]

Finally, in the evolving case of Northern Ireland referendums have played and are likely to continue to play a role in any change in its political status. While at one time the future of the six counties that remained part of Britain after the 1921 partition might have been resolved through negotiations between the United Kingdom and Irish governments, it is now clear that such a solution is no longer possible. This does not imply that resolution of this long-standing issue would be any easier to accomplish in a referendum than by other means. In fact, it would likely be rendered more difficult by the complexities of a direct vote. But as in Quebec, the principle that a substantial change in the political status of Northern Ireland cannot be accomplished without the consent of its citizens now seems well established and accepted by all parties.

Thus, while referendums on sovereignty are still rare, they have increasingly become an essential part of the process of national self-determination throughout the democratic world.

A. The Quebec Sovereignty Referendums

Quebec's quest for independence, or "sovereignty," began with the victory of the Parti Québécois in the 1976 provincial election. The PQ's strategy in that election had been to decouple the question of separation from Canada from other election issues by promising a separate referendum on sovereignty, thereby avoiding the sharp polarization of the electorate that had caused the party's defeat in 1973 (Pinard and Hamilton 1977). The 41 per cent of the popular vote obtained by the PQ in the 1976 election was still substantially higher than the public support for any sovereignty option that was estimated at the time, and it was clearly less than would be required to carry a referendum. During its first term in office, much attention was given by the PQ government to matters of question wording, timing, and strategy for the referendum to follow.

Table 5A1

The Quebec Sovereignty Referendums, 1980 and 1995

1980 REFERENDUM QUESTION

> The Government of Quebec has made public its proposal to negotiate a new agreement with the rest of Canada, based on the equality of nations;

> This agreement would enable Quebec to acquire the exclusive power to make its laws, levy its taxes, and establish relations abroad—in other words, sovereignty—and at the same time, to maintain with Canada an economic association including a common currency;

> No change in political status resulting from these negotiations will be effected without approval by the people through another referendum;

> On these terms, do you agree to give the Government of Quebec the mandate to negotiate the proposed agreement between Quebec and Canada?

REFERENDUM RESULT, MAY 20, 1980

> Yes: 40.4%; No: 59.6%; Turnout: 86%

1995 REFERENDUM QUESTION

> Do you agree that Quebec should become sovereign, after having made a formal offer to Canada for a new economic and political partnership, within the scope of the bill respecting the future of Quebec and of the agreement signed on June 12, 1995?

REFERENDUM RESULT, OCTOBER 30, 1995

> Yes: 49.4%; No: 50.6%; Turnout: 94%

When the text of the 1980 referendum question was released to the public, its wording (Table 5A1) was considered by many observers to provide a potentially winning formula, based on extensive public opinion polling. It provided the reassurance of a continued economic association with Canada and a common currency and asked only for a "mandate to negotiate" an agreement with the rest of Canada, not for sovereignty itself. Further, it specified that any agreement that might be achieved would have to be approved in another referendum. Polls commissioned by the government suggested that this strategy could attract the support of well over 50 per cent of the electorate. Yet the proposal ultimately went down to a rather decisive 60 per cent to 40 per cent defeat, in part because the federalist side was able to effectively shift the terms of the debate over the course of the campaign, arguing for "renewed federalism" as an alternative to the sovereignty-association proposed in the referendum question. While renewed federalism as such was not on the ballot, the NO campaign ultimately persuaded voters to view the choice in such terms rather than as a choice between the status quo and sovereignty.

Opinion shifted steadily away from the YES side over the course of the 1980 campaign, reflecting in part the struggle between the two sides to redefine the referendum question in their own competing terms. The relative newness of these issues at that time, the complexity of the ballot question, and the nature of the discourse itself meant that the decision was not clear-cut or easy for many voters. Nevertheless, many voters had in fact made up their minds even before the referendum was actually called or had come to a decision fairly early in the campaign, leaving only 5 per cent still undecided by the final week, according to one survey conducted at the time of the 1980 referendum.[12]

The defeat of the PQ in the 1985 provincial election brought about a pause in the sovereignty debate, but support for sovereignty surged again with the failure of the Meech Lake Accord in 1990. The Parti Québécois returned to power in 1994 and moved quickly towards a second referendum in 1995. The 1995 referendum question was shorter and still proposed a negotiated agreement with the rest of Canada. But it put a one-year limit on any such talks, after which Quebec would become sovereign regardless of their outcome.[13] There was no promise, as in 1980, of a second referendum. In the wake of the failure of previous federal constitutional initiatives, a concept like "renewed federalism" retained little credibility.[14] The NO side in the 1995 campaign did not even seriously attempt to counter the PQ strategy by offering constitutional counterproposals. Instead, the NO side resorted to essentially negative campaign themes that stressed that a YES vote effectively meant separation.

Participants in the 1980 referendum would have immediately recognized many of the themes and arguments put forward in 1995. Even for those who had not voted in 1980 or who may have entered the electorate subsequently, fifteen years of ongoing debate on sovereignty provided considerable familiarity with the basic issues and positions of the leading actors.[15] Further, the parties in Quebec, long polarized around the sovereignty issue, themselves provided ample cues to voters. Thus, in 1995 many voters were able to come to a decision much more quickly on the issue. Seventy per cent of respondents in one survey indicated that they knew how they would vote even before the referendum was called. Yet the percentage of voters reserving judgment until the final week was also significant.[16] The actual call of the referendum seemed an unimportant part of the dynamic in 1995, perhaps because it had been so widely anticipated. But the campaign itself was important, producing a shift towards the YES side in the final weeks and making the outcome extremely close.

The role of the parties and their leaders was crucial in the two Quebec referendums. Because the party system in Quebec is polarized around the sovereignty issue, in both instances the two major political parties themselves formed the core of the umbrella committees that carried on the campaign. While the link between partisanship and the vote in both of the Quebec referendums was thus very strong, one important difference between the 1980 and 1995 contests was the extent to which partisanship itself had weakened within the electorate over this fifteen-year period.[17] By 1995 nearly a quarter of the Quebec electorate did not identify with either of the two main provincial parties, thus introducing a greater element of uncertainty into the referendum outcome.[18] Appeals to partisanship alone, however strongly felt, were even less likely to carry the day in 1995 than in 1980.

At the time of the 1980 referendum, the two main provincial parties stood about equal in overall public support. Premier René Lévesque scored well above the provincial Liberal leader of the time (Claude Ryan) in personal popularity. However, the leadership deficit on the federalist side in 1980 was more than compensated for by the presence of the federal Prime Minister, Pierre Trudeau. Although not at the peak of his national popularity at the beginning of his fourth term as prime minister, Trudeau was nevertheless still well regarded by Quebec voters. The message of "renewed federalism" that ultimately swung the 1980 referendum result to the NO side was thus delivered to a relatively receptive electorate by a highly credible and popular federal prime minister, who more than counterbalanced the provincial popularity enjoyed by Premier Lévesque. While both sides held certain advantages, the political circumstances of the 1980 referendum campaign favoured the federalist side from the beginning.

The position of the political parties and their leaders during the 1995 referendum was very different. Public support for the Liberals relative to that for the PQ had slipped considerably. Substantially fewer Quebec voters identified themselves as Liberals than had done so in 1980.[19] Premier Jacques Parizeau, while not as popular as Lévesque had been, was regarded positively by francophone voters. The Liberal leader (Daniel Johnson) was by far the most unpopular of the Quebec party leaders and represented a serious liability for the NO side in the campaign. His federalist ally, Prime Minister Jean Chrétien, was equally unpopular. The entry of Lucien Bouchard, then the federal leader of the Bloc Québécois, into the campaign tilted the balance even further toward the YES side.[20] In some respects, Bouchard played a role comparable to that of Trudeau in 1980. His personal popularity, particularly among francophone voters, was nearly as high as was that of Trudeau during the 1980 referendum. An electorate frustrated with the record of failed constitutional initiatives of the past fifteen years was prepared to listen to the arguments put forward by Bouchard during the course of the campaign.

The extraordinarily high turnout in the 1995 referendum indicates the extent to which the sovereignty issue was capable of engaging and mobilizing the Quebec electorate. The call of the referendum itself had little effect in motivating voters, because partisan attitudes were already well entrenched. As the campaign progressed, however, small groups of voters with weaker leanings for or against sovereignty were gradually pulled into the respective camps. Although the NO side appeared initially to do better among these uncertain voters, as some became wary of the possible implications of a YES result by the final week, more voters with positive but slightly weaker feelings toward sovereignty decided for the YES. Unlike the pattern in 1980, the YES side in the 1995 referendum was quite successful in gaining and holding the support of "soft nationalist" voters as the campaign drew to a close (Pammett and LeDuc 2001).

It is hard to escape the conclusion that ineffective leadership of the federalist side made a major difference in the outcome, even though part of the explanation also lies in the overall growth of sovereignist sentiment among Quebec francophones (Cloutier et al. 1992) and in demographic changes in the electorate (LeDuc 1997). The two Quebec referendums clearly demonstrate that a result may often depend on factors such as the presentation of the issue (question wording), the framing of the options, the effectiveness of the campaign message, and the trust of the principal messengers, even when opinions on the issue of the referendum itself are strongly held. The outcome of a possible third referendum on sovereignty in Quebec thus remains difficult to predict, although public support for sovereignty appears to have declined somewhat in recent years.[21] Moreover, with the defeat of the PQ in the 2003 provincial election, the timetable for such a third referendum, if it takes place at all, may be moved further into an unknowable future.

B. The 1991 Independence Referendum in Ukraine

Mikhail Gorbachev's accession to power in the Soviet Union in 1985 opened the door to a new process of political and economic reforms. But in the USSR's constituent republics the reform agenda inadvertently strengthened the hand of nationalist reformers, whose ambitions ranged well beyond Gorbachev's twin goals of *glasnost* and *perestroika*. In Ukraine an active reform movement (Rukh) pushed for implementation of Gorbachev's reforms, but, as also occurred in the Baltic republics, the reform movement quickly acquired nationalist overtones. Birch (2000) notes that reformist and nationalist ideologies of the late 1980s coalesced into four distinct political groupings that might be represented as follows:

	Nationalist	*Antinationalist*
Proreform	National democrats	Liberals
Antireform	National communists	Imperial communists

Either of the antinationalist groups could easily have supported Gorbachev's reforms, but for quite different reasons. The nationalist groups, however, increasingly began to frame their support in terms of greater autonomy from Moscow. The more radical among these groups saw the reforms as a step toward full independence.

The parliamentary elections that took place throughout the USSR in 1989 and 1990 strengthened Gorbachev's position in relation to domestic opponents of his reform agenda, but they also brought nationalist reformers into greater prominence in many of the republics. In Ukraine the Democratic Bloc, comprising various opposition groups, gained 125 parliamentary seats in the March 1990 elections. Demands for language rights and greater autonomy merged with the democratic reform movement and unleashed powerful new political forces. As Gorbachev began his struggle with Boris Yeltsin in Russia, he also had to contend with the

Table 5B1
Results of the Referendums in Ukraine, 1991

MARCH 17

1. "Do you consider it necessary to preserve the USSR as a renewed federation of equal sovereign republics in which human rights and the freedoms of all nationalities will be fully guaranteed?"

    Yes: 71.5%; No: 28.5%

2. "Do you agree that Ukraine should be part of a Union of Soviet Sovereign States on the basis of the declaration of sovereignty of Ukraine?"

    Yes: 83.5%; No: 16.5%
    Turnout: 84%

DECEMBER 1: INDEPENDENCE

    Yes: 90.3%; No: 9.7%
    Turnout: 84%

various centrifugal forces that were threatening the existence of the union itself. Lithuania's declaration of independence and Gorbachev's attempt to suppress it brought the union issue to a head. He attempted to head off disintegration of the USSR by holding a referendum on March 17, 1991.

Like the parliamentary elections a year earlier, Gorbachev's "all-union" referendum provided new opportunities for other political actors. In Russia, Boris Yeltsin and his supporters used the opportunity to create a new Russian presidency. Leaders in other republics tinkered with the wording of the question or added questions of their own. Ukrainian nationalists were divided between strategies of boycotting the referendum or attempting to turn it to their own purposes. An alternative question on Ukrainian "sovereignty" was drafted in parliament but was unable to secure majority support. In the end, the national communist leader, Leonid Kravchuk, negotiated a compromise formula, under which both questions would be put to the voters.[22] The two questions that appeared on the March ballot (see Table 5B1) were independent of each other and to some extent contradictory. Strong nationalists were inclined to vote NO on the union question and YES on sovereignty, while hard-line communists favoured the opposite combination. But Kravchuk advocated a YES vote on *both* questions, and successfully campaigned for this course. Thus, Gorbachev won his vote on the union question, securing 78 per cent in favour throughout the USSR and 71 per cent in Ukraine. But as subsequent events were to demonstrate, it was indeed a pyrrhic victory.

The outcome of the all-union referendum throughout the USSR was thus subject to different interpretations, allowing all sides to claim victory. On the basis of the outcome, Gorbachev continued to pursue his agenda of preserving the union by drafting a new Union Treaty for ratification by the republics. Ukraine and other republics repeatedly postponed consideration of the draft treaty, clearly playing for time as new events unfolded in Moscow. In the end Gorbachev's treaty was pre-empted by an attempted coup in August 1991. As the union continued to disintegrate in the aftermath of those events, parliament scheduled a referendum on independence to coincide with presidential elections to be held on December 1, 1991. In that vote Ukrainians voted overwhelmingly in favour of independence and elected Leonid Kravchuk as president.[23] More than any other single event, the Ukrainian referendum signaled the end of the Soviet Union. Within days the leaders of Russia, Ukraine, and Belarus met to devise a new Commonwealth of Independent States and thus seal the fate of the Soviet Union. Gorbachev resigned as president three weeks later.

Referendums played a key role at both ends of this remarkable chain of events. Of the fifteen republics of the former Soviet Union, all but four achieved independence through a referendum.[24] Gorbachev's ill-fated all-union referendum of March 1991 allowed the nationalist agenda to be pushed forward more rapidly and gave national communist figures such as Kravchuk the opportunity to make the transition to an agenda of independence. The overwhelming vote in favour of independence in the December referendum provided legitimacy and effectively merged the reform and antireform agendas under a single nationalist banner.

C. Local Self-Government for Scotland and Wales

Scotland and Wales have twice been called upon to vote on a question of devolving limited government powers to an elected assembly. The referendums differ in one very significant way from the Quebec example, which otherwise provides a useful comparison. In Scotland and Wales, devolution was an initiative of the central government itself, rather than an attempt by a constituent territory to break away from the United Kingdom. But in the Scottish case particularly, the desire by the government at Westminster to find a new framework for self-government was driven in part by the rise of nationalist parties. Although the initiative may have come from the centre, the 1979 referendums were a response to the rise of nationalist forces in Scotland and Wales during the 1970s.[25] Labour, which held the majority of parliamentary seats in both Scotland and Wales, saw a key part of its traditional political base threatened by the growth of nationalist parties. A policy response that could dampen the appeal of nationalism was therefore clearly in its political interest.

A royal commission had issued a report recommending devolution in 1973. The issue was not immediately pursued by the new Labour government that was elected in 1974, however, because it was divided on the question and lacked an overall parliamentary majority. Furthermore, it was more preoccupied with economic issues in the mid-1970s. By 1978, however, the government was ready to bring forward its devolution legislation. The Scotland Act provided for an elected parliament at Edinburgh that would have limited tax-raising powers and would generally have been responsible for policy matters previously handled by the Scottish Office. The Wales Act also provided for an elected assembly, but with more limited powers paralleling those of the Welsh Office. Although, as noted in earlier chapters, referendums have not historically been a part of the British political tradition, the Northern Ireland "border poll" of 1973 (affirming the status of Northern Ireland as part of the United Kingdom) and the European Community membership referendum of 1975 had established important new precedents in Britain regarding public consultation on constitutional matters. Holding a referendum also allowed Labour to finesse its internal party divisions on the devolution issue, just as it had successfully done on the issue of European Community membership. The date of the two votes was set for March 1, 1979, in both Scotland and Wales.

The political context in which the two referendums took place contains a major part of the explanation for their failure. A general election had been widely expected in the fall of 1978, but the likelihood that Labour would lose at that time caused it to delay. By spring, the Labour government's days were numbered, even though Harold Wilson had been succeeded by James Callaghan as prime minister. The "winter of discontent," in which the government faced extensive labour unrest only added to

Table 5C1

The Scottish Devolution Referendums

MARCH 1, 1979

Do you agree that the provisions of the Scotland Act 1978 should be put into effect?

	Percentage of Electorate	Percentage of Votes cast
Yes	32.9	51.6
No	30.8	48.4
Abstentions	36.3	
Total	100.0	100.0

SEPTEMBER 11, 1997

[ ]   I agree that there should be a Scottish parliament.
[ ]   I do not agree that there should be a Scottish parliament.
[ ]   I agree that a Scottish parliament should have tax-varying powers.
[ ]   I do not agree that a Scottish parliament should have tax-varying powers.

		Percentage of Electorate	Percentage of Votes cast
Yes	Parliament	44.7	74.3
	Tax powers	38.2	63.5
No	Parliament	15.5	25.7
	Tax powers	22.0	36.5
Abstentions		39.8	

Callaghan's political difficulties. The referendum was thus conducted by an unpopular governing party during its waning days in office. Internal party divisions on the devolution issue, with some prominent Labourites campaigning on the NO side, created an air of uncertainty for many voters. Many nationalist voters saw the limited powers of the new assembly as inadequate, but traditionalists feared that any form of devolution could become the first step towards the breakup of the country. In a campaign in which the parties themselves were divided, it was easy for opponents of the legislation to create doubts among the electorate as to what was really being proposed.

Table 5C2

The Welsh Devolution Referendums

MARCH 1, 1979

Do you agree that the provisions of the Wales Act, 1978, should be put into effect?

	Percentage of Electorate	Percentage of Votes cast
Yes	11.9	20.1
No	46.9	79.9
Abstentions	41.2	
Total	100.0	100.0

SEPTEMBER 18, 1997

[ ] I agree that there should be a Welsh Assembly.
[ ] I do not agree that there should be a Welsh Assembly.

	Percentage of Electorate	Percentage of Votes Cast
Yes	25.2	50.3
No	24.9	49.7
Abstentions	49.9	
Total	100.0	100.0

In Scotland the government's strategy was complicated by a provision known as the Cunningham amendment. During the parliamentary debate on the Scotland Act, dissident Labour members, with the support of the opposition parties, had forced through this amendment, which provided that the legislation would be recalled if it secured the support of less than 40 per cent of the eligible electorate in the referendum. The Cunningham amendment all but doomed the devolution proposal in Scotland. While a thin majority of the votes cast were in favour of the Scotland Act, these comprised the votes of less than a third of the total electorate (Table 5C1), well short of the 40 per cent threshold.

In Wales, there was never much chance that the referendum question would pass under the political circumstances in Britain in 1979. The nationalist cause in Wales did not have the depth of support that the Scottish National Party enjoyed, and many of the arguments in favour of Welsh devolution rang hollow. An assembly without significant powers would be a mere "talking shop," a useless appendage, according to its opponents. It would create more bureaucracy (paid for by higher taxes), and it was being proposed only because of the pressures in Scotland for greater autonomy. Led largely by Conservatives, the *No Assembly* campaign was able to effectively submerge the issue of home rule in a campaign against "more government." Labour's overall unpopularity made the task easier, and the Wales Act went down to a crushing defeat in the referendum (Table 5C2). Along with the outcome of the referendums, the victory of Margaret Thatcher in the British general election only two months later ended the devolution debate at the national level, but the issue did not disappear from the Scottish political agenda. Various groups continued to agitate for a greater measure of home rule in Scotland, a cause to which Thatcher's Conservatives remained firmly opposed. Eventually, Labour's return to power under Tony Blair in the election of May 1997 opened the way for a new initiative.

Events moved quickly following Blair's accession to power. The new secretary of state for Scotland, Donald Dewar, was a long-time proponent of devolution who had drafted a new plan for a Scottish parliament in 1987. The Referendum Bill was the first piece of legislation introduced in the new parliament. Labour's overwhelming parliamentary majority ensured passage without the sort of compromises that had to be made in 1979. The framework for the new 129-member Scottish parliament, which would be elected by a mixed formula of single-member districts and proportional representation and would have the power to adjust income tax rates in Scotland, was set out in a government white paper. Two separate questions would be put to Scottish voters in the referendum—the principle of a Scottish parliament and the issue of whether the parliament should have the power to adjust income tax rates in Scotland. The referendum date for Scotland was set for September 11, barely three months after the election of the Labour government.

The Welsh proposal proceeded along a similar track, but with an obviously much tougher electoral deficit to overcome. Ron Davies, Labour's new secretary of state for Wales, a previous opponent of devolution, would now have to lead a campaign in its favour. The plan for a Welsh assembly provided for a 60-member assembly; one-third of the members would be elected by party-list proportional representation. Unlike the Scottish proposal, there was no issue of powers to adjust income tax rates, although the economic responsibilities of the new assembly were carefully outlined. The new structure was presented under a theme of "modernization," rather than autonomy, thereby avoiding some of the divisive rhetoric of the earlier devolution debates (McAllister 1998). Wales would vote on September 18, a week later than Scotland, possibly creating a beneficial "domino" effect.

The Scottish and Welsh campaigns were very different, both in style and in how the key issues were characterized. In Scotland the two campaigns were managed by cross-party umbrella groups—*Scotland Forward* and *Think Twice*—which campaigned respectively for what came to be known as the "double YES" and "double NO" on the two ballot proposals (Table 5C1). However, other groups and individuals supported the principle of a Scottish parliament but advocated a NO vote on the proposal for tax powers. Unlike the situation in 1979, Labour maintained considerable unity behind both proposals, losing very few of its prominent members to the NO side. The cross-party nature of the campaign was also important, making it easier for Liberal Democrat and Scottish National Party voters in particular to support the double YES. Scottish newspapers, with remarkably few exceptions, endorsed the YES side, as did many prominent figures from the worlds of sports and entertainment. Given the large cross-section of different groups supporting the double YES, and the relative isolation of the Conservatives, who had recently been devastated in the general election, the overall outcome of the 1997 Scottish referendum was never really in doubt. The Scottish parliament proposal was supported by three out of every four Scottish voters, and even the more uncertain tax powers proposal was endorsed by nearly two-thirds. Turnout, while relatively low at just over 60 per cent, was not a factor as it had been in 1979.

The *Yes for Wales* campaign was led effectively by Ron Davies, who stressed the themes of "partnership" and "cooperation." While *Yes for Wales* attempted to construct the same type of broad, inclusive all-party coalition of support that *Scotland Forward* had achieved, there was more dissent, even within Labour ranks. Several Welsh Labour MPs refused to support the proposal. The Welsh nationalist party, Plaid Cymru, never impressed by the relatively powerless assembly, gave its support unenthusiastically. The *Just Say NO* umbrella group was formed late, just as the campaign got under way, and served mainly as an organizational device for Conservative opponents of the government's proposals. However, because of greater skepticism in Wales about the value of devolution, *Just Say No* quickly found a ready audience for its many criticisms of the plan. In the end, the razor-thin victory that the YES side achieved in Wales may have been due as much to the popularity of the young Labour government as to support for the devolution proposal itself. Appeals to "Back Blair" carried more weight with some voters than did the prospect of a new group of politicians installed in an assembly at Cardiff. Nevertheless, the result hung in doubt until the very end. The unimpressive turnout of 50 per cent of the electorate suggests that Welsh voters lacked enthusiasm for devolution, even in the form of a proposal backed by Tony Blair.

The outcome of the Scottish and Welsh referendums provides only a temporary conclusion to the long-running saga of "home rule" in the various parts of the United Kingdom. For Scots the parliament that now sits in Edinburgh may seem like the fulfilment of a three-hundred-year-old quest for the return of Scottish self-government, but for some nationalists the new institutions are only a first step in the restoration of full Scottish political sovereignty. For Tony Blair, Scottish and Welsh devolution fulfilled an election commitment, but it is only one part of a larger Blairite program of political and constitutional reform that has yet to be completed. From both these points of view, further referendums would likely be required in order to move on to the next phase. The attempt to create new autonomous institutions for Northern Ireland has already led to a subsequent referendum, in May 1998, on the Good Friday peace agreement and may well lead to others in the foreseeable future. The restructuring of the institutions of government in the United Kingdom, of which Welsh and Scottish devolution is a significant part, remains a work in progress.

D. Statehood for Puerto Rico?

The political status of the US Commonwealth of Puerto Rico has been a matter of intense debate ever since the United States acquired the island in the Spanish-American War of 1898. The military administration of the newly acquired territory ended quickly in 1900 when Congress passed the Foraker Act, which provided for an appointed civil government. While the act allowed for a popularly elected legislature, political power was concentrated in the hands of a governor, executive cabinet, and supreme court, all of who were appointed by the US president. The Jones Act of 1917 granted US citizenship to Puerto Ricans and provided for somewhat greater local autonomy. But it was not until 1947 that federal legislation was amended to allow Puerto Ricans to elect their own governor. In 1948 the man who was in many ways the architect of modern Puerto Rico, Luis Muñoz Marin, became its first elected governor.

Muñoz and his Popular Democratic Party (PPD), along with sympathetic officials in Washington, invented the unique commonwealth arrangements under which Puerto Rico enjoyed considerable political autonomy while remaining under American sovereignty. Muñoz saw the self-governing British dominions, such as Canada and New Zealand, as his model, believing that Puerto Rico's political and economic interests were best served by a status that took full advantage of Puerto Rico's unique position in the Caribbean world. In 1950, the US Congress passed the Puerto Rico Federal Relations Act, commonly known as Public Law 600, which formalized the commonwealth arrangement. The Puerto Rican electorate approved Public Law 600 by a margin of 77 to 23 per cent in a referendum held in April 1951. In the following year Puerto Rican voters, again in a referendum, approved a new constitution that had been drafted according to the provisions of Public Law 600.[26] While the US Congress carefully preserved its exclusive right to alter the political status of Puerto Rico, these events enshrined the commonwealth arrangement within a tight legal framework.

In spite of the large margins of approval by Puerto Rican voters of Public Law 600 and the new constitution, the events of 1950-52 did not end the debate over Puerto Rico's political future. Some saw the commonwealth as at best a temporary arrangement or at worst as a relic of the colonial past. When other US territories such as Alaska and Hawaii became states in 1959, support for statehood in Puerto Rico grew. The party system gradually polarized around the two principal alternatives of statehood and continuation of the status quo. The pro-statehood forces in Puerto Rico reorganized themselves in 1965, under the leadership of Luis Ferré, as the New Progressive Party (PNP), providing the first real challenge to the hegemony of the PPD. However, the shifting political currents in Puerto Rico itself provide only part of the explanation for the resumption of the debate about political status. No change in the status of Puerto Rico is legally possible unless authorized by the US Congress. In 1964, President Lyndon Johnson appointed what was to be the first of three presidential

Table 5D1

Results of the Three Puerto Rico Political Status Plebiscites

	1967 07 23	1993 11 14	1998 12 13
Commonwealth*	60.4	48.6	0.1
Free association†			0.3
US statehood	39.0	46.3	46.5
Independence	0.6	4.4	2.5
None of the above†			50.3
Blank/invalid		0.7	0.3
Turnout	60	74	71

* In the 1998 referendum, the commonwealth option was on the ballot as "free associated territorial state." It was interpreted as affirming the status quo, but this interpretation was one of the subjects of debate in the campaign, causing the PDP, which has traditionally supported commonwealth status, to switch its support to "none of the above."

† This option appeared only on the 1998 ballot.

commissions for the purpose of making recommendations to Congress with respect to the political status of Puerto Rico. This resumption of the political status debate led to the first of the three nonbinding plebiscites in 1967, which occurred partly as a response to one of the recommendations of the commission.

Like all subsequent popular votes on the subject, the results of the 1967 plebiscite were inconclusive. The PPD government, attempting to head off growing sentiment in favour of statehood, defined the ballot options largely on its own terms, thereby precipitating a boycott of the referendum by other groups. The boycott was only partially successful, producing a relatively low turnout of about 60 per cent of the registered electorate. Among those voting, 60 per cent voted in favour of continuing the commonwealth, while 39 per cent supported statehood, thus confirming two principal political options. Fewer than 1 per cent of those voting chose the third alternative of independence (Table 5D1). But ironically, in the gubernatorial election of the following year the New Progressive Party won its first election victory, and Luis Ferré became the first overtly pro-statehood governor of Puerto Rico. The PNP, which would continue to alternate in power with the PPD for the next twenty years (Table 5D2), became the principal actor in the continuing drive to bring about statehood.

FIVE · Referendums on Sovereignty

Table 5D2

Votes Cast for Governor in Commonwealth
Elections in Puerto Rico, by Party (Percentages)

	1984	1988	1992	1996	2000
Popular Democratic Party (PPD)	48%	49%	46%	45%	49%
New Progressive Party (PNP)	45	46	50	51	46
Independence Party (PIP)	4	5	4	4	5
Others	3	*	*	*	*

* Less than 1 percent.

In the years following, the attitude of Washington to the question of the political status of Puerto Rico might best be described as inattention. While no change is possible without Washington's consent, it was unlikely that any drive towards a new political status would be initiated in Washington. The second presidential commission, appointed by President Nixon in 1973, recommended several amendments to Public Law 600, but they were not acted upon by Congress. Partly out of frustration with continued congressional inaction, the PNP launched a new referendum initiative following its return to power in the 1992 election, one in which the PNP hoped that a pro-statehood result, although non-binding, would nevertheless bring pressure to bear on Washington. To ensure that the referendum would be "fair" and to increase the probability that its outcome would be recognized as valid by all concerned, each of the political parties was allowed to draft its own option. The option put forward by the PPD was for an "enhanced" commonwealth status or "associated free state" (estado libro asociado). The PPD clearly hoped that such an option would attract the support of both those favouring the status quo and proponents of limited reform. Like "renewed federalism" in the 1980 Quebec referendum (see section A of this chapter), it provided a cloak of ambiguity within which the existing commonwealth arrangements could be promoted, but, as a result, the status quo was not really on the 1993 ballot in any direct form. The votes of those favouring change could thus be divided and interpreted in several different ways.

The outcome of the 1993 plebiscite was numerically very close (Table 5D1), but it did not provide a clear majority for any of the three options. The gain in support for statehood was evident, as the option favoured by the PNP government garnered 46.3 per cent of the vote. But the "enhanced commonwealth" option could still be said to have won, thereby depriving statehood proponents of any claim to victory. Further, the option of full independence, which had been vigorously promoted by the Independence Party (PIP) in its campaign, had obtained a crucial 4.4 per cent. While the 1993 plebiscite, with a solid turnout of 75 per cent of the electorate, had perhaps been the fairest test of public opinion on political status yet held in Puerto Rico, the ambiguities of the result were immediately evident. Not surprisingly, the vote, which had been intended to restart the drive toward statehood, led only to renewed frustration.

The 1993 referendum did, however, attract attention in Washington. If nothing else, it served notice that the federal authorities could not continue to play the role of disinterested bystanders. President Clinton appointed the third presidential commission on Puerto Rico in 1994, and sympathetic members of Congress began to take upon themselves the cause of resolving the Puerto Rican "dilemma." A Republican member of the House of Representatives, Don Young, introduced legislation known as the Young Bill (HR856), which laid out a series of conditions that would have to be met in order for Congress to take any action on the political status of Puerto Rico.[27] One of these provisions was for a third non-binding referendum, which would take place before December 31, 1998. The political status options to be specified were worked out in consultation between congressional leaders and the Puerto Rican political parties. However, the manner in which a continuation of commonwealth status would be defined on the referendum ballot remained a matter of contention, as it had been in 1993. The PPD clearly hoped to once again promote a "reformed" commonwealth arrangement as an alternative to either the status quo or statehood. But the ruling PNP, hoping to limit the appeal of this option, added the word "territorial" to the commonwealth definition, raising echoes of the old colonial status. In protest, the PPD campaigned instead for the "none of the above" option on the ballot, one of the five choices that was presented to the voters under the terms of the legislation in the 1998 referendum (Table 5D1).

The effectiveness of the PPD protest campaign is evident in the outcome. Only a handful of voters supported the traditional commonwealth option in the form that appeared on the 1998 ballot, while statehood received about the same percentage that it had in 1993. But "none of the above" gained a clear majority of all votes cast, as the PPD was able to combine its traditional supporters with other protest groups to defeat the pro-statehood initiative. While the PNP lamely tried to claim the outcome as a victory for statehood, arguing that the "none of the above" votes did not really count, few were willing to accept this interpretation of events. With a turnout of 71 per cent, the result of the referendum could hardly be ignored, but whatever the interpretation, the Puerto Rican electorate had delivered a serious blow to the hopes of supporters of statehood, both at home and in Washington.

While past voting trends and the events of the 1998 campaign both suggest that the vote closely followed existing party lines, there is no available survey analysis to conclusively support this interpretation. Nor is it likely that the result of the 1998 referendum will put an end to the political status debate. Puerto Rican politics remain polarized around the issue of statehood. The pro-statehood PNP, which had held power since 1992, used the institutions of the Commonwealth government during that period to support its cause, just as the provincial government in Quebec has used its position to promote the sovereignty agenda. Unlike the PQ, the PNP also enjoyed support, from time to time, among several key actors in Washington. However, the PDP regained the governorship in the 2000 election, and it also holds a majority of seats in both houses of the commonwealth legislature. A new initiative to promote statehood is therefore unlikely to be undertaken unless the PNP returns to power. Any such initiative, whether undertaken by the PNP or by others, would almost certainly involve some type of referendum. If and when it occurs, question wording, particularly in reference to the commonwealth option, would continue to be of major importance, and the political parties would again be the principal actors in the campaign. Under the existing commonwealth provisions, such a vote, whatever form it might take, would continue to be non-binding. The US Congress, if it chose, could conceivably alter these arrangements and set its own rules for a fourth vote. But with the status quo forces once again in power in Puerto Rico, Washington is more likely to return to a policy of benign neglect.

NOTES

1. For a theoretically oriented discussion of this issue with particular reference to Quebec, see Dion (1996).

2. The evidence also suggests that the separation of Slovakia and the Czech Republic would probably not have been approved by citizens in a referendum. For a

further discussion of this case, see Young (1994) and Leff (1997). On the process of political transition in Eastern Europe and the former Soviet Union more generally, see Linz and Stepan (1996).

3. See Bedlington (1978) and Chan Heng Chee (1971) for a discussion of the creation of the state of Malaysia in 1963 and Singapore's secession from it in 1965.

4. On the dynamics of this process in several of the cases mentioned here, see Young (1994).

5. Dissolution of the union with Sweden was overwhelmingly approved by Norwegian voters in the plebiscite of August 13, 1905. See Lindgren (1959).

6. There was considerable violence in the period preceding the August 30, 1999 referendum, which took place under UN supervision. The ballot question offered a choice between a new status as a "special autonomous region" within Indonesia or independence. Seventy-nine per cent of those voting opted for independence. East Timor, a former Portugese colony, had been annexed by Indonesia in 1976.

7. Boris Yeltsin was elected in the presidential election held three months later (June 12, 1991). For a more detailed chronology of these events, see Marsh (2002). See also Linz and Stepan (1996).

8. Moldova held its referendum on independence in 1994. Russia, Belarus, Kazakhstan, and Tajikistan became independent states without holding a referendum on the issue upon dissolution of the union.

9. In the first round of the 1948 Newfoundland referendum (June 3), voters were presented with three options: (1) responsible self-government, (2) confederation with Canada, and (3) continuation of the Commission government. As the outcome of this first round produced no clear majority, a second vote forcing a choice between the first two options was held on July 22, 1948. In that runoff, 52 per cent voted for confederation with Canada over responsible self-government (48 per cent). See Noel (1971) and Eggleston (1974).

10. Although the federal government made it clear that these were nonbinding "plebiscites," they nevertheless served to legitimize the division of the Northwest Territories. In the first vote, held on April 14, 1982, 56 per cent of NWT residents voted in favour of division of the territory into two parts. In the second vote (May 5, 1992), the issue of the boundary line between the territories was addressed. Finally, in the referendum of November 3-5, 1992, the creation of Nunuvut was approved by residents of the eastern Arctic: 69 per cent of its citizens voted in favour of the proposal. On these and other Canadian examples of referendums, see Boyer (1992).

11. In its Clarity Act of 2000, the federal government mandated that a "clear" majority on a "clear" question would be required before any negotiations leading to secession might be undertaken. But since neither term was precisely defined in the act, the exact standards of a clear question and whether a simple majority of fifty per cent plus one is sufficient are likely to remain hotly contested in any future Quebec referendum. Alternatively, these issues could conceivably be subjects of negotiation before a future referendum. On the evolution of these issues more generally, see Young (1999).

12. In 1980 49 per cent of voters indicated that they had made up their minds how to vote before the referendum was called. Most of the balance decided during the campaign, with only 5 per cent indicating that they had waited until the final week (compare table 7.2) Data reported are from the 1980 Canadian National Election

Study, of which a subsample of Quebec voters were reinterviewed at the time of the referendum (Pammett et al. 1983).

13. The bill referred to in the referendum question (table 5.1) declared that Quebec is a sovereign country, stated that an independent Quebec would continue to use the Canadian dollar and would allow its residents to retain concurrent Canadian citizenship, and authorized the Quebec government to negotiate a new association between Quebec and Canada. The bill was to come into force one year following its approval in the referendum. The June 12 agreement referred to in the question was reached between Premier Parizeau, BQ leader Bouchard, and Mario Dumont, leader and only elected member of the Parti Action Démocratique du Québec. The agreement stated that an offer to negotiate a formal treaty of economic and political partnership would be made to Canada following a YES vote in the referendum.

14. Various unsuccessful attempts to find a settlement of the "unfinished" 1982 constitution in Canada also provided the background to the 1992 federal constitutional referendum. See Chapter 3, section A.

15. At least a third of the electorate would have consisted of different individuals in 1995 than in 1980, due to patterns of aging, population replacement, and migration, etc. (LeDuc 1997).

16. The percentage was about twice as many as in the 1980 referendum. Eleven per cent of a sample of 1995 Quebec voters indicated that they had decided how to vote in the final week, compared with 5 per cent in a comparable 1980 study (see note 12).

17. In 1980, 84 per cent of YES voters identified with the Parti Québécois, while 87 per cent of NO voters were Liberals. The pattern in 1995 was similar, but slightly weaker, because of the overall decline in partisan attachment among the Quebec electorate (Pammett and LeDuc 2001).

18. In the 1993 Canadian National Election Study (CNES), 38 per cent of Quebec respondents identified themselves as Liberals and 36 per cent as PQ; 26 per cent reported no party identification. This compares with 1980 figures of 51 per cent Liberal, 39 per cent PQ, and 9 per cent non-identifiers (Pammett and LeDuc 2001).

19. See note 18.

20. Bouchard subsequently became premier of Quebec, succeeding Jacques Parizeau, who resigned following the loss of the referendum.

21. A poll by Groupe Léger et Léger in early 2000, for example, placed support for sovereignty at about 41 per cent of the Quebec electorate.

22. In the province of Galicia, the opposition controlled local council added a third question, which read as follows: "Do you want Ukraine to become an independent state which independently decides its domestic and foreign policies, and which guarantees equal rights to all of its citizens, regardless of their national or religious allegiance?" This question attracted the support of 88 per cent of those voting in Galicia, while the first two questions received 39 per cent and 64 per cent respectively.

23. Kravchuk received an absolute majority in the first round, winning 62 per cent of the vote in a field of six candidates.

24. The exceptions were Russia, Kazakhstan, Tajikistan, and Belarus.

25. In the February 1974 election, which brought the minority Labour government of Harold Wilson to power, the Scottish National Party (SNP) won 22 per cent of the total vote in Scotland and seven of the seventy-one Scottish seats in the parliament at Westminster. In the October election of the same year, the SNP won 31 per cent

of the vote in Scotland and eleven seats. In Wales, the Welsh nationalist party (Plaid Cymru) won two of the thirty-six Welsh seats in February 1974 and three in the October election with about 11 per cent of the total vote in each instance.

26. The constitution was approved by a margin of 82 per cent to 18 per cent in the 1952 referendum.

27. A more detailed analysis of HR856 is beyond the scope of this discussion. However, among its provisions were requirements regarding official language legislation and a timetable for transition to any new political status. The Young Bill passed the House of Representatives by a vote of 209 to 208 on March 4, 1998. A summary of the provisions of HR856, including a number of amendments offered during the congressional debate, may be found at http://thomas.loc.gov/cgi-bin/bdquery/z?d105: h.r.00856.

6
Referendums on Public Policy Issues

Referendums are more commonly used to resolve large and difficult political or constitutional questions than to deal with routine policy matters. But there are polities, such as Switzerland, in which the institutions of direct democracy are more fully integrated into the ordinary processes of government, allowing various other types of political issues to be decided by referendum. Section D of this chapter provides an overview of Switzerland's referendum processes and gives a sense of the diversity of issues on which Swiss citizens are regularly called upon to vote three or four times a year. During the 1990s, referendums in Switzerland dealt with such diverse issues as taxes, public transport, unemployment insurance, maternity leave, medical research, agriculture, drugs, and casino gambling. In Switzerland, such issues may be placed on the ballot by the initiative of citizens or groups rather than by the government.

Similarly, the wide range of ballot propositions that are regularly presented to voters in many US states are often citizen initiatives rather than government-sponsored proposals. While the exact rules and procedures for placing items on the ballot vary considerably from state to state, the practice is most commonly associated with Western states, notably California, Oregon, Arizona, Colorado, and North Dakota. Although my interest in this chapter is in the practice more generally, rather than in the politics of any single state, I refer to these examples as the "California model" (section C of this chapter), because the evolution of direct democracy in that state typifies many of the practices found elsewhere in the United States.

In some of the other examples to be discussed in this chapter, particular policy questions may be placed on the ballot by a government for its own political reasons, sometimes to avoid being forced to deal with the issue in an election or to reconcile different views on a contentious issue within a governing party or coalition. The referendums in Austria (1978) and Sweden (1980) on nuclear power took place because divisions within a governing party over a difficult policy question created political circumstances in which a popular vote became the preferred means of resolving the issue. For many years New Zealand placed on the ballot at each general election a question regarding liquor laws, largely for the purpose of removing this contentious area of policy from the partisan political arena.[1] In Uruguay, referendums have been held on several important policy issues, including privatization of state industries, pensions, education policy, and social security.

Switzerland, Italy, and Ireland have provisions under which legislation that has been adopted by parliament may be forced to a referendum.[2] In these instances the abrogative, or facultative, referendum (see Chapter 2) provides a means by which the losing side in a parliamentary battle might carry on the fight through direct democratic processes. Ireland, although it does not have provisions for citizen initiatives, has held referendums on a number of contentious policy matters, such as divorce (1986, 1995) and abortion (1983, 1992, 2002). These referendums are difficult to classify according to the typology of subject matter set out earlier (see Table 1.3) because they involve policy questions that can only be dealt with through constitutional amendment. There are also numerous examples of such a combination of factors in many of the US state referendums, where enactment of an amendment to the state constitution by citizen initiative becomes the preferred method of forcing governments to follow a particular direction in a contentious area of public policy (e.g., gun control, tax policy, education). In the Irish case (see section B of this chapter) such referendums, although initiated by the government itself, are sometimes a response to pressures from particular groups. In the case of the abortion issue, three referendums over nearly twenty years have failed to produce any real societal resolution of this deeply divisive moral question. On the other hand, putting the matter to a referendum has also served the interests of the government, courts, and political parties, who can then allow such intense pressures to be directed elsewhere.

A. Sweden's 1980 Referendum on Nuclear Power

Referendums are relatively infrequent in Sweden. Although a provision for consultative referendums authorized by the Riksdag (Swedish parliament) has been enshrined in the Swedish constitution since 1922, only five such consultations have taken place to date: a 1922 vote on prohibition, a 1955 referendum on changing to right-hand driving, a 1957 referendum on pensions, a 1980 referendum on nuclear energy, and the 1994 vote on European Union membership (see Chapter 4 section C). In each of these cases, the referendum came about because of a political decision, taken by the governing party or parties, that it was necessary or desirable to seek public consultation on a contentious matter of public policy. As Ruin (1996) notes, the circumstances generally involved significant intraparty divisions. A referendum thus provided the party leadership with a convenient means of defusing a controversial political question.

The 1980 referendum on nuclear energy fits this model perfectly. Responding to the oil price shocks of the 1970s, the Social Democratic (SAP) government of Olof Palme expanded the country's capacity for nuclear electric power generation. While this policy was formally approved by the Riksdag in 1975, it was not without controversy. Two parties, the Agrarians (subsequently renamed the Centre Party) and the Communists (renamed the Left Party), were firmly opposed. Divisions within the ruling Social Democrats were also apparent, and the "nuclear issue," involving both the production of nuclear power and the proliferation of nuclear weapons, gradually became a major political issue in Sweden, as well as in other European countries. It was significant in the 1976 general election, in which the Social Democrats were narrowly defeated by a three-party coalition of Agrarians, Liberals (the People's Party), and Conservatives (later the Moderate Party).

The three-party coalition, led by Agrarian Thorbjörn Fälldin, found it difficult to agree on a common nuclear policy. The Conservatives favoured nuclear energy as an alternative to oil-fired electric generation, while the Agrarians remained firmly opposed to this strategy. In October 1978, Fälldin's government collapsed, in part because of these continued differences within the coalition, and was replaced by a minority People's Party (Liberal) government under Ola Ullsten. Early in 1979, the profile of the nuclear issue throughout the world was raised by the accident at the Three Mile Island nuclear plant in the United States. The former SAP

Table 6A1

Results of Swedish General Elections, 1976-82

	1976		1979		1982	
	Votes (%)	Seats	Votes (%)	Seats	Votes (%)	Seats
Social Democrats (SAP)	43	152	43	154	46	166
Moderate Party (Conservative)	16	55	20	73	24	86
Centre Party (Agrarian)	24	86	18	64	16	56
Liberal (People's Party)	11	39	11	38	6	21
Left Party (Communist)	5	17	6	20	6	20
Others	1	0	2	0	2	0

prime minister, Palme, now in opposition, proposed a referendum on the issue, in part to prevent it from becoming a major focus of the parliamentary elections expected in 1979. His suggestion was quickly accepted by the other parties, and it was agreed that the referendum would take place six months after the general election, which was scheduled for September 1979. For purposes of the election at least, the issue was thus effectively sidelined.

Palme's referendum strategy was largely successful in suppressing partisan debate on the issue during the election campaign. However, the small gains registered by the left parties in the election were not sufficient to oust the three-party centre-right coalition from power (Table 6A1). A new Centre Party government, again headed by Thorbjörn Fälldin, assumed office in coalition with Moderates and Liberals. The agreed upon referendum took place on March 23, 1980. Although it was constitutionally non-binding, all the parties undertook to respect the results. The exact alternatives to be placed before the voters on the ballot were arrived at through lengthy interparty negotiations. Given the climate of opinion at the time, there was no overtly pro-nuclear option put forward. Rather, the alternatives presented provided for gradations of opposition to nuclear power and differed in the timetable, as well as in the inclusiveness, of the policy alternatives proposed. The ballot provided for three options: (1) the status quo, (2) gradual reduction, and (3) phasing out all nuclear power sources. The ballot options, each of which spelled out a policy direc-

Table 6A2

Sweden's 1980 Nuclear Power Referendum, March 23, 1980 (Percentages)

ALTERNATIVE 1. ENERGY FOR SWEDEN   18.9

Nuclear power generation to be phased out at a pace which would
safeguard employment and welfare. No more than 12 nuclear plants
would be allowed to operate during the transition period.

ALTERNATIVE 2. PHASE OUT, BUT SENSIBLY   39.1

As in #1, nuclear power would be phased out at a measured pace,
and no more than 12 nuclear plants would be allowed to continue
in operation. However, these goals would be pursued through a
rigorous program of energy conservation. State sponsored research
into additional sources of renewable energy would be intensified,
and greater attention would be given to environmental protection
and safety factors.

ALTERNATIVE 3. ATOMIC POWER?—NO THANKS   38.7

All nuclear power sources would be phased out over a ten year
period. No new plants would be allowed to begin operation, and
existing plants would be subject to a safety review. Mining of
uranium would be prohibited in Sweden, as well as reprocessing of
nuclear fuels and export of nuclear technology. Energy conservation
and disarmament would also be prioritized.

Blank votes	3.3
Total	100.0
Turnout	76%

tion in some detail, were given the short form names of (1) *Energy for
Sweden*, (2) *Phase out, but sensibly*, and (3) *Atomic power?—no thanks* (see
Table 6A2). Although there continued to be some differences of opinion
within all of the parties, the first alternative was formally supported by
the Conservatives, and the second alternative by the Liberals and Social
Democrats. The parties supporting the second alternative, both of which
had been recently in government, sought to portray this option as representative of the "sensible" middle ground between inaction and radical
antinuclearism. The Left Party (Communist) and Centre Party backed the
much more strongly anti-nuclear third option.

The results, while not producing a majority for any of the alternatives, confirmed the broadly anti-nuclear leanings of the Swedish electorate (Table 6A2). Granberg and Holmberg (1988) found strong links between voting behaviour in the referendum and the actual policy preferences of voters. This linkage may have been due to the presence of three alternatives on the ballot (rather than the simple YES/NO choice found in many referendums), which allowed voters to register a more nuanced opinion. The fact that differences continued to exist within many of the parties, even those that had formally endorsed one of the alternatives, may also have afforded voters greater freedom to vote their "true" feelings. While the campaign had an effect, there was not the dynamic process of opinion formation and change sometimes found in other referendums. Rather, the campaign provided an opportunity for parties and voters to find accommodation between the strongly held views of many citizens on these issues and the positions of the parties and government. Turnout, at 76 per cent, was significantly lower than is typical of Swedish general elections.[3] The fact that the second alternative (sensible phase-out) only narrowly out-polled the more aggressively anti-nuclear third option set the tone for Sweden's energy policy in the years following the referendum.

The referendum was in many respects inconclusive in policy terms, because the combination of responses to the three alternatives could be interpreted in different ways (Setälä 1999). The "winning" second alternative did not specify any precise timetable for phasing out nuclear power, and it included the relatively high cap of twelve installations that had also been specified in option 1. The Riksdag set 2010 as the deadline for phasing out nuclear power generation, but it also permitted the completion and start-up of nuclear plants already under construction. The result, however, did have significant implications for the evolution of the party system in Sweden. By accepting the referendum outcome as interpreted by the Riksdag, the Centre party lost considerable credibility as an anti-nuclear alternative and steadily lost support in each of the next three parliamentary elections.[4] The Ecologist (Green) party, formed in the following year, eventually gained the support of many non-Communist voters who had supported option 3 (Bennulf and Holmberg 1990). While the referendum result seemingly settled the nuclear issue in Sweden in the very short term, the Chernobyl disaster of April 1986 once again made nuclear policy a central focus of Swedish politics. In the 1988 election, the Greens surged to twenty seats in the Riksdag, breaking the 4 per cent representation threshold for the first time.[5] The 1980 referendum can thus be said to have had several unforeseen consequences for both public policy and the political system.

Other lessons of the 1980 Swedish nuclear power referendum may affect some of our broader conclusions about processes of direct democracy. While the parties were still the principal actors guiding the campaign, this referendum seemed less partisan than many of the other cases considered here, and the campaign less intense. The motives of the main parties in holding the referendum were clear—to keep the difficult nuclear issue out of the general election campaign and to avoid debilitating splits over the question within the main parties and between parties in coalition. The three options on the ballot may have allowed both the parties and the country as a whole to avoid a polarized YES/NO, winner take all debate on the issue of nuclear power. Clearly it was in the parties' interest to avoid such a debate because their internal divisions would likely have become more unmanageable in a more polarized situation. On the other hand, this decision may also have limited the actual impact of the referendum on public policy, because the absence of a clear winning (i.e., majority) alternative allowed the results to be interpreted in different ways. The government may well have taken the result into account in formulating its nuclear policy, but it enjoyed considerable policy freedom in spite of the outcome. The referendum exposed divisions over the issue and set at least a broad general direction for future policy. But in accomplishing these more limited objectives, it may have failed to provide the clear and decisive resolution of a difficult issue that referendums are often thought by their proponents to be capable of achieving.

B. Ireland's Referendums on Divorce and Abortion

The referendum occupies a significant place in Irish politics. The 1937 constitution provides that all constitutional amendments proposed by the Dáil (lower house) must be ratified by a majority of voters in a binding referendum. To date, nineteen referendums on twenty-seven specific issues have been held under the provisions of the 1937 constitution, which was itself approved by the people in a referendum.[6] While the constitution also provides for a rejective referendum on ordinary legislation that can be triggered by a petition to the president endorsed by a majority of the

Seanad (upper house) and one-third on the members of the Dáil, this process has never been used. There are no provisions for citizen initiatives in Ireland. Thus, Irish referendums have invariably been binding constitutional votes brought about through the decision of a governing party to pursue a particular policy change by means of the constitutional process.

Ireland, like many other European countries, has used the referendum to deal with institutional matters such as voting rights or representation and also to ratify European treaties such as the Single European Act (1987), Maastricht (1992), Amsterdam (1998), and Nice (2001, 2002).[7] But Ireland differs somewhat in the extent to which it has also made contentious moral questions the subject of popular votes. This difference is explained in part by the role that religion has traditionally played in Irish society and by the special position given the Catholic Church in the 1937 constitution.[8] The referendums on moral issues, however, have been tightly bound up with Irish party politics. The 1983 referendum, which inserted a "pro-life" clause into the constitution, came about largely as a result of pressure from anti-abortion groups in the run-up to the 1982 general election. Although abortion was already illegal in Ireland, pro-life groups feared that the existing legislation might be amended by more liberal governments or that the legislative ban on abortion might eventually be overturned by the courts. In the pre-election period, promises were obtained from both of the major parties—Fianna Fáil and Fine Gael—to support a pro-life constitutional amendment. Following the election of November 1982, which returned a Fine Gael/Labour coalition to office, the Dáil approved the pro-life amendment in an acrimonious debate. Although the wording of the amendment was essentially what had been proposed by Fianna Fáil before the election, the political parties largely refrained from playing an active role in the referendum campaign that followed.[9] The Fine Gael and Labour deputies were divided, but Catholic priests and bishops took an active part in support of the YES campaign. The new amendment was endorsed by 67 per cent of Irish voters in the referendum of September 7, with a low turnout of 53 per cent of the eligible electorate.[10]

But rather than settling the contentious issue of abortion in Ireland, the 1983 referendum ensured that the issue would remain high on the political agenda for the next twenty years. The successful entrenchment of the pro-life amendment in the constitution meant that it could be removed or changed only by means of a similar process. Although the 1983 amendment ensured that the ban on abortions in Ireland would continue, it did not prevent an estimated five thousand women from travelling to Britain each year to obtain an abortion (Girvin 1993). Legal battles over the provision of information about abortion also continued to generate conflict. The issue arose again in a somewhat indirect manner, in the context of the debate over the Maastricht Treaty. Concern that provisions of the treaty might come into conflict with the pro-life amendment (now article 40 of the constitution) had led to the insertion of a special protocol in the treaty.[11] But this did not satisfy critics who feared that the process of European integration itself might ultimately undermine the Irish stand on abortion. The political atmosphere was intensified by the controversial "X case," in which the Supreme Court overturned a lower-court decision preventing a fourteen-year-old rape victim from travelling to Britain for an abortion. In this highly charged environment, the government feared that the abortion debate would spill over into the referendum on Maastricht. The newly elected Taoiseach (prime minister), Albert Reynolds, sought to prevent this by committing the government to hold a separate referendum on the abortion issue. This referendum would take place after the Maastricht Treaty had been ratified, thus effectively decoupling the two issues.

The 1992 abortion referendum took place, as promised, in November, five months after the Maastricht Treaty had been approved by Irish voters.[12] The government proceeded cautiously, reflecting the many divisions within the governing Fianna Fáil and the strongly held opinions on the issue of both politicians and voters. As Girvin (1993) notes:

> The objective of the government, one shared by the opposition parties, was to retain control of the agenda on abortion and not let it slip into the hands of the extra-parliamentary groups.... Fianna Fáil was attempting to balance the reality that the Supreme Court had overturned the absolute ban on abortion with a recognition that conservative opinion, especially the Church, was concerned to restrict *any* opportunity for abortion in Ireland.

In drafting the amendments, the government hoped to steer cautiously between the boundaries set by the Supreme Court decision in the X case and the hostility of the Church and to resist the pressures of pro-life groups, which sought to fully restore the 1983 ban. Public opinion polls generally indicated support for freedom to travel and greater freedom of informa-

Table 6B1
The Irish Referendums on Abortion (Percentages)

SEPTEMBER 7, 1983

The "pro-life" amendment	Yes	66.9
	No	33.1
	Turnout	53%

NOVEMBER 25, 1992

1. Restrict availability of abortion	Yes	34.6
	No	65.4
2. Affirm freedom to travel	Yes	62.4
	No	37.6
3. Affirm freedom of information	Yes	59.9
	No	40.1
	Turnout	65%

JUNE 3, 2002

To entrench the Protection of	Yes	49.6
Human Life in Pregnancy Act	No	50.4
in article 40 of the constitution	Turnout	43%

tion, but there were wide differences on the more substantive issues. In the end, the government drafted three questions to put to referendum. The substantive question, the most difficult of the three, sought to narrow the scope of the Supreme Court decision by recognizing the threat to a mother's life, but not "health," as possible grounds for abortion.[13]

The complexity of the issue and the confusing language of the substantive item made position-taking difficult. The pro-life campaign, after some deliberation, advocated a NO vote on all three items. So also did some Catholic bishops, but the official position of the Church hierarchy recognized early on that any outcome was unsatisfactory, because it would result in abortions being performed under some circumstances. A YES vote on the substantive item would entrench "threat to life" as grounds for legal abortion. But a NO vote would effectively allow the Supreme Court decision in the X case to stand. Many women's groups that would otherwise have supported a more liberal abortion law opposed the substantive amendment because of the distinction it drew between "health" and "life." The Trades Union Congress also opposed this amendment, as, in the end, did Fine Gael. The fact that the referendum took place at the same time as a general election also complicated the issue for voters, deflecting some attention from the referendum issue and encouraging candidates to take individual positions sometimes at variance with those of their party.

The outcome of the referendum (Table 6B1) was a defeat of sorts for Fianna Fáil, which had campaigned for a YES vote on all three items. Its attempt to steer a narrow compromise course on the substantive item failed to attract support in sufficient numbers from either side of the heated debate. However, the government had accomplished its original goal of decoupling the entire abortion debate from Maastricht. Furthermore, neither pro-life nor pro-choice groups could claim any kind of meaningful victory. The less controversial travel and information items appeared to be resolved, given the substantial majorities in favour of both. But the defeat of the substantive item ensured that abortion would remain on the Irish political agenda for some time.

In the years following, pro-life groups continued to lobby vigorously for a third referendum on abortion, hoping to restore the full weight of the 1983 ban and limit the future role of the courts. Because of the emotional intensity and intra-party divisions, subsequent governments hesitated to reopen the issue. But the combination of group pressures and the ambiguity of further court decisions eventually led the Fianna Fáil/Progressive Democrat coalition government of Bertie Ahern to promise a third referendum. This referendum also hinged on the government's ability to draft language that would close loopholes created by the court decisions but also satisfy the contending groups. The language of the amendment drafted for the June 2002 referendum in the end satisfied some, but not all, of the pro-life groups.[14] Pro-choice groups solidly opposed the new amendment, but pro-life groups were divided. Following a highly emotional campaign, the proposed amendment was narrowly defeated (49.6 per cent YES to 50.4 per cent NO). Turnout (43 per cent) was substantially lower than it had been in the two previous referendums on the issue (Table 6B1).

In contrast to the abortion referendums, the two votes on the divorce issue were relatively straightforward, even though they also involved an attempt to resolve a complex moral/religious question by means of a referendum. Article 41 of the 1937 constitution stated that "no law shall

Table 6B2

The Irish Divorce Referendums (Percentages)

To remove the constitutional ban on divorce (article 41)

JUNE 26, 1986		NOVEMBER 24, 1995	
Yes	36.5	Yes	50.3
No	63.5	No	49.7
Turnout	61%	Turnout	62%

be enacted providing for the grant of a dissolution of marriage." Various groups had lobbied for some time for an end to the constitutional ban on divorce, but the influence of the Catholic Church was clearly felt on the issue. Garret FitzGerald's announcement in 1981 of his government's desire to "secularize" the constitution opened the door to the possibility of change.[15] Public opinion, however, was closely divided on the issue of divorce, making governments cautious. An opportunity arose in 1985-86, when public opinion polls on the issue seemed to indicate a shift in sentiment (Sinnott 1995). In 1986 the governing Fine Gael/Labour coalition put forward a new amendment to lift the ban and to specify in its place a set of restricted circumstances in which a divorce could be granted.[16]

In the referendum campaign that followed, the YES side was led by Fine Gael and Labour, but some backbench Fine Gael deputies were also active on the NO side. Fianna Fáil took an officially neutral position in the campaign, but many Fianna Fáil politicians were active supporters of the NO position. So, too, were many Catholic organizations and individuals, even though the Church as an organization took no official position. As the campaign progressed, opinion in favour of the proposed amendment declined sharply. The extreme rhetoric of the campaign, coming from various sources, seemed to have a strong effect on public sentiment. The irony of the lopsided outcome (Table 6B2), which saw nearly 64 per cent of voters support the NO, was that opinion polls had shown as much as 77 per cent of the public favouring a change in the divorce law only a few months earlier. Within a few months after the referendum, public opinion seemed to once again return to this "normal" reading (Darcy and Laver 1990). Hence, the 1986 campaign on the divorce amendment demonstrates clearly the potential for volatility in referendum campaigns, even ones involving a moral issue on which individual opinions might be thought to be more strongly held.

Like the abortion issue, the divorce question was not settled by the 1986 referendum, despite its decisive outcome. Successive Irish governments proceeded with family law reform legislation, dealing with matters of "separation" rather than legal divorce. Over time, the stage was set for a second referendum on the issue in 1995. By then, the process of secularization of Irish society was much further advanced. The moral authority of the Church had also been significantly eroded by a series of scandals involving clergy. Thus, on the surface, the climate for change in 1995 appeared much more auspicious. The partisan climate was also different in 1995 than it had been in 1986. This time, a more united Fine Gael/Labour/Democratic Left coalition led the YES campaign, and the Fianna Fáil opposition also endorsed the proposal. Yet in spite of this broad phalanx of support, the outcome of the 1995 referendum (Table 6B2) was extremely close (50.3 per cent YES; 49.7 per cent NO). As in 1986, what had seemed to be widespread public support for a change in the divorce law deteriorated rapidly in the face of a vigorous campaign, carried on largely by nonparty groups. Perhaps only the personal popularity of the president of the republic, Mary Robinson, saved the measure from defeat (Adshead 1996).

Again it was difficult for anyone to claim victory in the face of the 1995 referendum outcome. The losing NO side immediately demanded recounts and launched a court challenge to the results. The fact that an all-party grouping in support of the YES had been able to produce only such a marginal result led to many questions regarding the efficacy of the parties and their leaders. However, the Catholic Church was undoubtedly the biggest loser, in spite of the narrow result. Irish voters had, however cautiously, voted in a referendum for a more secular future.

C. The "California Model"

The variations of direct democracy in the United States have almost no parallel elsewhere in the world, except perhaps in Switzerland (see section D of this chapter). Although there has never been a national referendum in the United States, all states except Delaware provide for amendments to their state constitutions to be submitted to a popular vote, and thirty-one of the fifty states permit some other type of referendum device. Twenty-four states have provisions for citizen initiatives. Western states such as California and Oregon have tended to use instruments of direct democ-

Figure 6C1

Frequency of Initiatives in California, 1910-2000

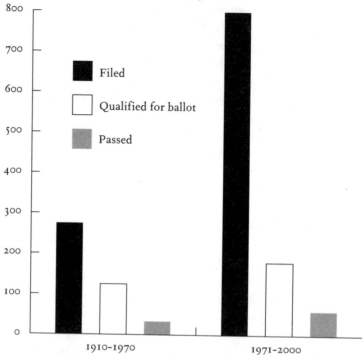

Sources: Bowler and Donovan (2000); Initiative and Referendum Institute (http://www.iandrinstitute.org); California Ballot Propositions Database (http://www.uchastings.edu/library/ballotprops.htm).

racy, particularly the initiative, more extensively, in part because of the populist traditions that are more firmly rooted in the political culture of the American West. These devices have been used with dramatically increased frequency in recent years, prompting an active debate about their effects on American democracy. Some see these developments as a healthy expression of American democratic values, while others believe that the initiative process, in particular, has been captured by well-financed special-interest groups and now represents a threat to the very democracy that such institutions were originally intended to enhance.[17]

Both the form and the frequency of referendums vary considerably among the US states. Some indication of this variation may be seen in Table 6C1, which lists all the propositions that appeared on state ballots

Table 6C1
Propositions on the November 2000 Ballot, by State

N	State	Type	Subject	YES (%)	Turnout (%)		
					VAP	PRES	Drop-off
26	Oregon	L	Payments to Local Government	84	53	61	-8
		L	Special Fund for War Veterans	75	54		-7
		L	Excess General Fund to Taxpayers	62	54		-7
		L	Federal Income Tax Deductions	51	55		-6
		L	Regulation of Adult Establishments	47	55		-6
		L	Formation of Counties	45	52		-9
		L	Use of Tobacco Settlement Money	43	54		-7
		I	Limits on Asset Forfeiture	67	53		-8
		I	Education Funding	66	53		-8
		I	Home Care	63	54		-7
		I	Gun Control	62	56		-5
		I	Private Property Valuation	53	54		-7
		I	Public Funds for Political Purposes	47	54		-7
		I	Teaching of Homosexuality	47	55		-6
		I	Payroll Deduction without Written Authorization	45	55		-6
		I	Tobacco Settlement Proceeds	45	54		-7
		I	Federal Income Tax Deduction	45	55		-6
		I	Administration Rule Reform	44	52		-9

N	State	Type	Subject	YES (%)	Turnout (%)			Drop-off
					VAP	PRES		
	Oregon (continued)	I	Limit on State Appropriations	44	52			-9
		I	Public Financing of Campaigns	41	53			-8
		I	Banning Certain Animal Traps and Poisons	41	55			-6
		I	Vote Requirement for Tax Increase	40	54			-7
		I	Increase Difficulty of Initiative Process	38	52			-9
		I	Teacher Pay Based on Job Performance	35	55			-6
		I	Mandatory Minimum Sentences	26	54			-7
		I	Utility Rate Regulation	13	51			-10
14	Alabama	L	State Trust Fund Allocation	70	37	50		-13
		L	Auburn University Board of Trustees	69	34			-16
		L	Supernumerary Program for Winston County	63	26			-24
		L	Establish State Improvement Trust Fund	63	42			-8
		L	Collection of Ad Valorem Taxes	62	34			-16
		L	Allow Interracial Marriage	60	40			-10
		L	Supernumerary Program for County	60	26			-24
		L	Supernumerary Program for Town of White Hall	57	27			-23
		L	Supernumerary Program for Green County	57	27			-23
		L	Supernumerary Program for Chiltern County	55	28			-22
		L	Supernumerary Program for Lowndes County	54	26			-24
		L	Supernumerary Program for Clay County	54	27			-23

	State	Type	Issue				
		L	Supernumerary Program for Sumter County	54	26		-24
		L	Supernumerary Program for Marion County	53	27		-23
14	Arizona	L	Exempting Tax on Burial Plots	68	34	42	-8
		L	Freezing Residential Property Tax	64	34		-8
		L	Modernizing Constitutional Wording	61	35		-7
		L	Increase Education Funding	53	35		-7
		L	Increase Commissioner Term Limits	52	34		-8
		L	Growth Limitation on Land Use	48	33		-9
		L	Initiatives for Wildlife Laws	38	35		-7
		L	Legislative Pay Increase	36	35		-7
		I	Tobacco Settlement Funds	63	35		-7
		I	Bilingual Education	63	35		-7
		I	Tobacco Settlement Funds	58	35		-7
		I	Redistricting of Electoral Boundaries	56	34		-8
		I	Urban Growth Management Plans	30	35		-7
		I	Telecommunications Deregulation	20	35		-7
12	Colorado	L	Obsolete Language in State Constitution	72	48	57	-9
		L	Redistricting Timetable	60	46		-11
		L	Property Tax Relief for Seniors	55	50		-7
		L	Expanding State Lottery	52	53		-4
		L	Allowing Appointment of County Surveyors	45	47		-10
		L	Education Funding	44	51		-6

N	State	Type	Subject	YES (%)	Turnout (%)		
					VAP	PRES	Drop-off
	Colorado (continued)	I	Gun Control	70	56		-1
		I	Medical Marijuana	54	56		-1
		I	Increase in Education Spending	53	55		-2
		I	Abortion Waiting Period	40	55		-2
		I	Tax Reduction	34	55		-2
		I	Environmental Growth Limitations	30	40		-17
11	Georgia	L	Homeowner Tax Relief	88	38		-6
		L	Appointment of Legislators	82	38	44	-6
		L	Compensation for Law Enforcement Officers	82	38		-6
		L	Military Tax Exemption	79	37		-7
		L	Compensation for Teachers	75	38		-6
		L	Tax Exemption on Farm Equipment	71	37		-7
		L	Compensation of State Employees	70	37		-7
		L	Experience Requirement for State Court Judges	65	37		-7
		L	Tax Exemption on Manual Labor Tools	63	37		-7
		L	Property Classification of Marine Vessels	48	35		-9
		L	Ad Valorem Tax Exemption	22	36		-8
9	Nebraska	L	Filling Legislative Vacancies	78	44	56	-12
		L	Identify Powers of Initiative and Referendum	69	42		-14
		L	Judicial Compensation	56	43		-13

	Type	Issue				
	L	Election of Lieutenant Governor	52	47		-9
	L	Gender Neutrality of Constitution	43	46		-10
	L	Requirements for Initiative Petitions	38	45		-11
	L	Change Process for Constitutional Amendments	37	43		-13
	I	Ban on Same Sex Marriage	70	52		-4
	I	Establishment of Term Limits	56	48		-8
8 California	L	Veterans Bonds	67	36	44	-8
	L	Campaign Finance Reform	60	36		-8
	L	Legislative Pay	39	35		-9
	I	Drug Treatment Program	61	37		-7
	I	Government Contracting Competition	55	36		-8
	I	Local School Bond Approval	53	37		-7
	I	Redefinition of Taxes and Fees	48	35		-9
	I	School Choice - Vouchers	29	38		-6
8 Massachusetts	L	Redistricting	70	51	57	-6
	L	Prisoner Voting	64	53		-4
	I	Tax Credit for Charity Giving	72	52		-5
	I	State Income Tax Cut	59	54		-3
	I	Prohibition of Dog Racing	49	53		-4
	I	Comprehensive Health Care System	48	53		-4
	I	Drug Treatment Tax Fund	47	52		-5
	I	Commuter Tax Credit	43	53		-4

N	State	Type	Subject	YES (%)	Turnout (%)		
					VAP	PRES	Drop-off
7	Washington	L	Invest State Money in Trust Funds	64	40	57	-17
		I	Class Size Reduction	71	42		-15
		I	Teacher Pay Increase	62	43		-14
		I	Vote Requirement for Tax Increase	57	41		-16
		I	Banning Certain Animal Traps and Poisons	54	43		-14
		I	Sponsoring Public Schools	48	42		-15
		I	Funding of Road Construction	42	42		-15
6	Alaska	L	Constitutional Amendments	43	49	64	-15
		L	Wildlife and Hunting Referendums	36	50		-14
		L	Constitutional Amendment re Corporations	27	49		-15
		I	Acceptance of Hunting Law on Wolves	53	50		-14
		I	Legalizing Hemp	39	52		-12
		I	Capping Property Taxes	29	51		-13
6	Maine	L	Property Taxes on Commercial Fishing	49	59	67	-8
		L	Gay Rights	49	65		-2
		L	Voting by Mentally Ill	40	61		-6
		I	Physician-Assisted Suicide	49	67		0
		I	Gaming/Property Tax Relief	40	62		-5
		I	Protection of Forests	28	62		-5
6	Rhode Island	L	Water Quality Bonds	75	44	54	-10

		L	Environmental Bonds	73	44		-10
		L	Transportation Bonds	68	43		-11
		L	Higher Education Bonds	67	44		-10
		L	Call for Constitutional Convention	66	42		-12
		L	Harbor Museum Bonds	49	44		-10
6	South Dakota	L	Investment of State Funds	56	56	58	-2
		L	Property Taxes on Commercial Fishing	55	56		-2
		L	Initiatives and Local Governments	55	55		-3
		I	Prohibition of a State Inheritance Tax	80	58		0
		I	Change Gambling Maximum Bet	52	58		0
		I	Prohibit Video Lottery	46	58		0
5	Arkansas	L	Property Relief Tax	62	42	48	-6
		L	Revision of Judicial Article	57	39		-9
		L	Redevelopment Bonds	55	41		-7
		I	Tobacco Settlement	64	41		-7
		I	Legalize Lottery/Gaming	36	44		-4
5	Missouri	L	Budget Reserve Fund	59	50	57	-7
		L	Commission on Compensation	39	49		-8
		L	Legalize Bingo	32	50		-7
		I	Regulation on Billboards	49	54		-3
		I	Campaign Finance Reform	35	51		-6
5	Montana	L	Tobacco Settlement Proceeds	73	58	62	-4

N	State	Type	Subject	YES (%)	Turnout (%)		Drop-off
					VAP	PRES	
	Montana (continued)	L	Repeal Inheritance Taxes	68	59		-3
		L	Vehicle Taxes	58	59		-3
		L	Investment of State Compensation Fund	52	56		-6
		I	Game-Farm Reform	52	59		-3
5	New Mexico	L	Senior Citizen Facility Improvement Bonds	61	37	47	-10
		L	Public Education Bonds	60	37		-10
		L	Making Bernalilo County an Urban County	54	34		-13
		L	Equipment Bonds	47	36		-11
		L	Eliminating Term Limits on County Officials	26	37		-10
5	Oklahoma	L	Sale of Wine	70	45	49	-4
		L	Tobacco Settlement Proceeds	69	45		-4
		L	State Budget	57	45		-4
		L	Eliminating School Millage Elections	55	44		-5
		L	Funding for County Health Departments	36	45		-4
4	Louisiana	L	Tax Exemptions for Food	53	44	54	-10
		L	Income Taxes	38	44		-10
		L	Industrial Development	36	43		-11
		L	Economic Development	32	44		-10
4	Nevada	L	Transportation Bonds	49	21	44	-23
		L	Investment of State Funds	41	41		-3

		I	Banning Same Sex Marriage	70	43		-1
		I	Medical Marijuana	65	42		-2
4	Utah	L	County Government	69	46	53	-7
		L	Tobacco Settlement Trust Fund	61	47		-6
		I	Uniform Procedure for Asset Forfeiture	69	49		-4
		I	Establishing English as Official Language	67	50		-3
3	Florida	L	Circuit Court Judge Selection and Retention	34	45	51	-6
		L	County Court Judge Selection and Retention	31	45		-6
		I	Developing Statewide High-Speed Monorail	53	47		-4
3	Hawaii	L	Duties of Reapportionment Commission	79	43	41	2
		L	University of Hawaii Autonomy	77	49		8
		L	Tax Review Commission Extension of Terms	37	48		7
3	South Carolina	L	Reduction of Property Taxes	84	43	46	-3
		L	Vehicle Taxes	65	42		-4
		L	Establishing Lottery	54	46		0
2	Idaho	L	Terms of Public School Fund	69	49	54	-5
		L	Establishment of Municipal Bonds	54	46		-8
2	Kansas	L	State-Held Stock in Banking Institutions	62	45	54	-9
		L	Aircraft Taxes	49	44		-10
2	Kentucky	L	Change Legislative Sessions	53	36	52	-16
		L	Abolish the Railroad Commission	51	36		-16
2	Maryland	L	Terms of Office for Cecil County Officers	69	31	52	-21

N	State	Type	Subject	YES (%)	Turnout (%)		
					VAP	PRES	Drop-off
2	Maryland (cont'd)	L	Eminent Domain	38	31		-21
2	Michigan	I	Home Rule — Interference in Municipal Affairs	33	51	58	-7
		I	School Choice — Vouchers	31	54		-4
2	New Jersey	L	Public Disclosure of Sex Offenders	79	34	51	-17
		L	Redistribution of Taxes to Transportation	63	34		-17
2	Ohio	L	Conservation Bond Authorization	57	44	56	-12
		L	School Trust Fund	49	44		-12
2	Virginia	L	Lottery Proceeds Fund	83	45	52	-7
		L	Right to Hunt	60	45		-7
1	Connecticut	L	Abolish County Sheriffs	66	35	58	-23
1	Indiana	L	Jurisdiction of Criminal Appeals Process	65	30	49	-19
1	Iowa	L	Call for Constitutional Convention	33	37	61	-24
1	New Hampshire	L	Home Rule for Municipalities	48	46	62	-16
1	North Carolina	L	Higher Education Improvement Bonds	73	43	50	-7
1	North Dakota	L	Preservation of Hunting, Trapping, and Fishing	77	56	60	-4
1	West Virginia	L	Establish a Family Court	73	33	46	-13
1	Wisconsin	L	Voting Rights Extension	66	53	66	-13
1	Wyoming	L	Appointment of National Guard Officers	65	54	60	-6

Note: L = legislative referendum; I = citizens' initiative. VAP denotes percentage of voting age population voting on the item; PRES denotes percentage of voting age population marking the presidential ballot; drop-off is the difference between the two.
Sources: Initiative and Referendum Institute (http://www.iandrinstitute.org); state government sites.

at the time of the US presidential election in November 2000. In all, 205 propositions appeared on the ballot on that date in 41 states. Twenty-six propositions, dealing with such subjects as a fund for war veterans, tobacco settlement issues, gun control, campaign finance reform, and utility rates appeared on the ballot in Oregon alone. But while Oregon has in recent years used the initiative process the most extensively (and controversially), California, more than any other state, has set the standard for direct democracy in the United States. With the election of a Progressive governor, Hiram Johnson, in 1910, populist devices such as the initiative, referendum, and recall came early to California politics. Although usage of these instruments declined somewhat in the middle part of the twentieth century, their frequency has exploded over the past two decades. Since 1970 nearly 800 initiative petitions have been filed with the California secretary of state, and of these 135 qualified for the ballot. Although many of these proposals failed to win approval by the voters, they have nevertheless exercised great influence in the state's politics and have often spilled over onto the national political scene in the United States, because of California's size and importance.[18] One of the most famous California initiatives, the 1978 tax-limitation proposal known as Proposition 13, had profound effects on state finances and has effectively rearranged the political landscape in California. By prohibiting governments from raising property taxes without resorting to further referendums, Proposition 13 and its successors forced extensive cutbacks in spending for a wide array of public services, notably education. Peter Schrag (1998) argues that the ripple effects of Proposition 13 and subsequent tax-limitation amendments in California and other states have been as "profound and lasting as the New Deal" in reshaping the American political agenda.

One source of the variation in the use of initiatives among the fifty states is the stringency of the requirements for placing an issue on the ballot. California is fairly typical. To qualify for placement on the ballot, a proposed constitutional amendment requires the signatures of a number of registered voters equal to 8 per cent of the total votes cast for the office of governor in the preceding election. For a statutory proposal, the required number is 5 per cent. These signatures must be collected over a period no greater than 150 days and must be certified as valid by the secretary of state. Other states have similar requirements, but both the number of required signatures and the period within which they must be collected and certified varies widely. In Arizona, a higher proportion of signatures is required (15 per cent and 10 per cent respectively), but the period within which they must be collected is longer (20 months). In Colorado, the time limit is similar to California's (6 months), but the threshold is lower (5 per cent for both constitutional and statutory proposals).

It is not an easy task to meet the legal requirements for placing a measure on the ballot in most states. In California, because more than eight million votes were cast for the office of governor in 1998, it was necessary to collect and verify more than six hundred thousand signatures in order to qualify a constitutional proposal for the 2000 ballot, or four hundred thousand for a statutory proposal. But in spite of such relatively high thresholds, the number of proposals filed has increased dramatically in recent years in California and in many other states (see Figure 6C1). As Table 6C1 confirms, many of these proposals do make it through to the ballot. The patterns suggested in Table 6C1 are fairly typical, although there is, of course, considerable variation from state to state and from one election year to another. California had only eight proposals on the 2000 ballot, but it had twelve in 1998 and seventeen in 1996. Oregon, with its high of twenty-six proposals on the ballot in 2000, had nine in 1998 and sixteen in 1996.[19] One reason why so many proposals manage to reach the ballot is that groups and individuals with an interest in promoting an issue increasingly employ professional firms to collect the required number of signatures. This trend has spurred the growth of what Magleby (1984) calls the "initiative industry" and has greatly increased the role that money plays in many initiative campaigns. From collecting signatures to organizing and running campaigns, the initiative process in America, particularly in large states such as California, has come to require what Donovan et al. (2001) refer to as "extraordinary sums of money."

In addition to money, minority rights have become an important issue in the debate over the initiative and referendum process, because some of the initiatives on American ballots in recent years seem to target particular groups or to promote issues that appear threatening to minorities. California's controversial Proposition 63, for example, which was adopted in 1986, established English as "the official language of the state." Although couched in innocent-sounding language, this proposal was clearly perceived as an attack on California's growing Hispanic community and as a device that might be used to kill bilingual programs of education and other state services. Eight years later, California voters approved an even more controversial measure (Proposition 187), which would effectively deny education and health and social services to illegal immigrants in the state.[20] In the same category was Colorado's notorious Amendment 2, adopted in 1992, which would have overturned various state and local laws that prohibited discrimination based on sexual orientation in areas such as employment and housing. Although Amendment 2 was struck down as unconstitutional by the courts, other such initiatives challenging gay rights soon appeared on the ballot in other states.[21] In the past decade, it has become clear that the initiative process at both the state and the local level could indeed be used to "put civil rights to a popular vote" (Gamble, 1997).

Another common concern arises from the increasing number and complexity of ballot propositions. Oregon voters might well have balked at being confronted with twenty-six propositions on an already long presidential ballot. Voters might also feel that they do not have sufficient information to vote on such a wide array of proposals, or they may sometimes find the campaigns mounted by various groups misleading. Such criticisms are not new, although the intensity of the critique has grown in recent years along with the number of proposals. Yet these institutions of direct democracy remain generally popular in states such as California where they have long been established. While low voting turnout remains a concern, there is considerable evidence that voters can and do use the various sources of information available to them in voting on these propositions (Bowler and Donovan 1998a; Lupia 1992, 1994). They can, in the words of Lupia and McCubbins (1998) "learn what they need to know."

Nevertheless, the widespread and growing use of initiatives and referendums raises several difficult questions about democracy in America. When used to target vulnerable minorities, the initiative appears as a modern-day example of Madison's "tyranny of the majority." In the hands of powerful and well-financed interest groups, such devices might be used to undermine the regulatory powers of the state. But the wide variety of subjects treated in American ballot proposals makes such generalizations difficult. Although the initiative process in particular has sometimes been viewed as the tool of right-wing groups interested in limiting the scope of government, it remains relatively eclectic as a political device. A survey of the subject matter of recent ballot proposals in the various states shows that they continue to provide a means to raise and debate issues at the cutting edge of politics—questions concerning school vouchers, euthanasia, the legalization of drugs, environmental protection, and campaign-finance reform. Even when a proposal succeeds in winning approval, the referendum is not necessarily the final answer on such issues, since the courts and legislatures continue to be engaged in the process. As the early populists intended, citizen initiatives continue to provide a means of raising issues outside the partisan and legislative arenas and forcing them into the political discourse. Nevertheless, the debate over the merits of the "California model" appears likely to continue. To some, it represents democracy at its best — placing power directly in the hands of the voters in a way that other political institutions do not. To others, it has indeed become "democracy derailed" (Broder 2000).

D. Switzerland: Government by Referendum?

Switzerland is the one country where the referendum is truly the centrepiece of the political system (Treschel and Kriesi 1996). There is literally no comparison between the number of referendums held in Switzerland over the twenty-five-year period surveyed earlier in this book (see Table 1.1) and the pattern found in any other country. During that period (1975-2000), Switzerland held 72 referendums on 222 separate issues. As is the case in other countries, the use of the referendum in Switzerland also appears to be on the increase. The number of separate referendum voting decisions made by the Swiss during this time is more than double that for the comparable preceding period.[22] Like Californians, Swiss voters are being called upon more often to express their judgment on a wider array of political issues. At the cantonal level, the referendum is used even more extensively.

An issue can find its way to a national referendum in Switzerland in any one of four ways:

- As in Australia (see Chapter 3, section D), constitutional changes proposed by the federal assembly require a mandatory referendum.[23] Constitutional amendments must be approved by a majority of the voters in the country as a whole *and* by majorities in more than half the twenty-six cantons.[24]

- A special constitutional provision (article 89) covers the procedure for ratifying international treaties.[25]

- Switzerland also has provisions for rejective, or "facultative," referendums, in which an ordinary law adopted by the federal assembly may be submitted to a referendum upon petition by fifty thousand citizens or eight cantons within ninety days of its publication. To take effect, the law must be approved in the referendum by a simple majority of voters (a double majority is not required in this instance). A similar provision applies to federal decrees.

- Swiss law also provides for referendums on proposed constitutional changes initiated by a petition of citizens. To trigger this process, the signatures of one hundred thousand eligible voters collected over a period of no more than eighteen months are required. A double majority is then required for approval of the proposed change.

Ironically, Switzerland has no provision for non-binding consultative referendums initiated by the government—the type of referendum that is common in many of the other countries discussed in this book. About half of the popular votes that have taken place in Switzerland over the course of its modern history have been mandatory constitutional referendums. The balance have divided about evenly between facultative referendums and citizen initiatives.[26] Table 6D1 lists the type and subject matter of referendums that took place between 1990 and 2000. During this period, Swiss voters were asked to consider 115 separate issues in 33 referendums. The subject matter was diverse, ranging from constitutional matters such as lowering the voting age (March 1991) to citizen initiatives that would ban alcohol and tobacco advertising (November 1993) or prohibit the export of weapons (June 1997). Several dealt with international commitments, such as joining the World Bank and the International Monetary Fund (May 1992) or participating in UN peacekeeping operations (June 1994).

Participation in Swiss referendums varies widely, depending in part on the ability of a particular issue to engage the attention of voters and also on the mobilizing activities of interested groups. As is seen in Table 6D1, voting turnout in referendums over this three-year period varied from a high of 78 per cent in the December 1992 referendum on Swiss membership in the European Economic Area to a low of 31 per cent in the March 1991 referendums on lowering the voting age and transferring

Table 6D1
Referendums in Switzerland, 1990–2000

Date	Turnout (%)	Type	Subject	Result
1990 04 01	41	initiative	Stop all new road construction	
		initiative	Ban of autoroute N1	
		initiative	Ban of autoroute N4	
		initiative	Ban of autoroute N5	
		facultative	Viticulture regulations	
		facultative	Judicial organization	
1990 09 23	41	initiative	Ban nuclear energy	
		initiative	Moratorium on nuclear plants	*
		mandatory	Energy policy	*
		facultative	Traffic regulation	*
1991 03 03	31	mandatory	Lower voting age to 18	*
		initiative	Increased funding for public transport	
1991 06 02	33	mandatory	Federal VAT to replace corporate tax	
		facultative	Decriminalize conscientious objection	*
1992 02 16	44	initiative	Health insurance subsidy	
		initiative	Limit animal experiments	
1992 05 17	38	facultative	IMF and World Bank membership	*
		facultative	Conditions of IMF and World Bank membership	*

Date	No.	Type	Issue	
1992 09 27	46	initiative	Water conservation	*
		counterproposal	Regulate genetic technology	*
		mandatory	Civilian service for conscientious objectors	*
		facultative	Decriminalize sexual practices	*
		facultative	Water conservation	*
		facultative	Construction of cross-alpine railway	*
		facultative	Procedures for publication of laws	*
		facultative	Change in banking stamp tax	*
		facultative	Regulations concerning inheritance of farms	*
		facultative	Increase salaries of deputies	
		facultative	Improve administrative services for deputies	
1992 12 06	78	mandatory	European Economic Area membership	
1993 03 07	51	facultative	Increase gasoline tax	*
		mandatory	Legalize casino gambling	*
		initiative	Ban animal experiments	
1993 06 06	55	initiative	Stop purchase of FA-18 military aircraft	
		initiative	Limit number of military bases	
1993 09 26	39	mandatory	Restrictions on weapons	*
		mandatory	Municipal annexation	*
		initiative	Creation of federal holiday	*
		facultative	Limit increases in health insurance costs	*
		facultative	Revisions of unemployment insurance	*

Date	Turnout (%)	Type	Subject	Result
1993 11 28	44	mandatory	Financial system regulations	*
		mandatory	Impose federal VAT	*
		mandatory	Rate of VAT	*
		mandatory	Social insurance provisions	*
		initiative	Ban alcohol advertising	
		initiative	Ban tobacco advertising	
1994 02 20	41	mandatory	Transport regulations	*
		mandatory	Transport regulations	*
		mandatory	Transport regulations	*
		initiative	Ban on road freight transit	*
		facultative	Air navigation legislation	*
1994 06 12	47	mandatory	Promotion of culture	
		mandatory	Citizenship laws	
		facultative	Participation in UN Peacekeeping	
1994 09 25	46	mandatory	Wheat subsidies	*
		facultative	Anti-racism law	*
1994 12 04	44	facultative	Health insurance	*
		initiative	Health insurance	
		facultative	Immigration	
1995 03 12	38	counterproposal	Agriculture	*
		facultative	Agriculture	

Date	No.	Type	Topic	
1995 06 25	40	facultative	Agriculture	*
		mandatory	Public spending	*
		facultative	Retirement age	
		initiative	Social security contributions	
		facultative	Foreign ownership of property	*
1996 03 10	31	mandatory	Language rights	*
		mandatory	Municipal annexation	*
		mandatory	Military supply	
		mandatory	Liquor taxes	*
		mandatory	Federal railway station subsidy	*
1996 06 09	31	counterproposal	Agriculture	
		facultative	Government organization	
1996 12 01	47	initiative	Illegal immigration	
		facultative	Workplace regulations	
1997 06 08	35	initiative	European Union negotiations	
		initiative	Export of armaments	
		mandatory	Drug laws	*
1997 09 28	41	facultative	Unemployment benefits	
		initiative	Drug laws	
1998 06 07	41	mandatory	Balanced budget	*
		initiative	Genetic research	
		initiative	Law enforcement	

Date	Turnout (%)	Type	Subject	Result
1998 09 27	52	facultative	Heavy vehicle regulations	*
		initiative	Natural foods	
		initiative	Retirement age	
1998 11 29	38	mandatory	Public transport	*
		mandatory	Food regulations	*
		initiative	Drug policies	
		facultative	Workplace regulations	*
1999 02 07	38	mandatory	Candidate qualifications	*
		mandatory	Organ transplants	*
		initiative	Housing rights	
		facultative	Territorial adjustment	*
1999 04 18	36	mandatory	Constitutional amendment	*
1999 06 13	44	facultative	Refugee policy	*
		facultative	Refugee policy	*
		facultative	Medical prescription of heroin	*
		facultative	Disability insurance	
		facultative	Maternity leave	
2000 03 12	44	mandatory	Reform of the justice system	*
		initiative	Expediting initiatives	
		initiative	Equal representation of women	
		initiative	Human reproduction	

Date		Type	Issue	
		initiative	Reduction of road traffic	*
2000 05 21	48	facultative	Economic ties with European Union	
2000 09 24	45	initiative	Solar energy	
		counterproposal	Energy and environment	
		initiative	Immigration	
		initiative	Initiative procedures	
		initiative	Retirement age for women	
2000 11 26	42	initiative	Retirement age	
		initiative	Defence spending	
		initiative	Students' health expenses	
		facultative	Federal employment policies	*

Sources: University of Geneva Center for the Study of Direct Democracy (http://c2d.unige.ch/start.en.msql); Government of Switzerland site (http://193.5.216.31/ch/f/pore/va/19990613/index.html); Kobach (1994).

* Denotes passage of proposal.

federal funds from road construction to public transport. The average for the period was only 43 per cent, a level of participation roughly comparable to that found in Swiss elections.[27] Franklin (1996) argues that the frequency of referendums may itself partly account for low electoral turnout, since the ability to make important political decisions directly through referendums reduces the significance of elections. Kobach (1994), on the other hand, thinks low participation rates indicate a general satisfaction with Swiss democracy, arguing that the referendum allows citizens to redress political grievances in a way that elections do not. The danger that low turnout rates might empower interested minorities is of course significantly reduced by the double-majority requirement. Over time, the success rate for citizen initiatives has been only about 10 per cent, while that for constitutional proposals put forward by the government has been much higher (about 65 per cent). On the other hand, Swiss voters have not hesitated to use the mechanism of the facultative referendum to challenge or overturn government legislation. Of the 122 laws that had been brought to a popular vote until 1995, exactly half were confirmed and half rejected by the voters (Treschel and Kriesi 1996).

The referendum has come to occupy a central role in Swiss democracy, but its centrality can easily be overstated. Most legislation adopted by the federal assembly never comes before the people in a referendum. Kobach (1994) notes that only about 7 per cent of all federal legislation is challenged in this way. Of the challenges to legislation that are brought forward under the facultative referendum provisions of the constitution, only a small fraction carry through to the final step of coming to a popular vote. Thus, in Switzerland representative government proceeds much as it does in other democracies. Yet the mere existence of the facultative referendum provides an important check on the powers of government. The option of the facultative referendum forces legislators to seek the broadest possible coalition of support in the assembly because a parliamentary majority alone cannot guarantee success in a referendum if a law is challenged (Kobach 1993b). Similarly, the citizen initiative undoubtedly has a much greater impact on Swiss political culture than the statistics measuring its rate of success alone would tend to suggest, because the very act of organizing an initiative campaign may bring pressure to bear on the authorities to deal with a particular policy matter.

In Switzerland the referendum in all its variations is much less a tool of government and more truly the "recourse of the citizens" than could be said to be the case in any other country. In recent years it has also become a favoured tool of some of the smaller political parties, who find it opens channels of political activity that are not available to them in parliamentary or electoral politics. Setälä (1999) observes that in Switzerland the institutions of direct democracy compensate to some degree for the relative lack of competition found in Swiss elections. The referendum also provides opportunities for political expression to parties and groups who find themselves outside the governing coalition, and it affords social movements outside the party system a means of influencing the political agenda (Kriesi and Wisler 1996). While elsewhere the referendum has sometimes been seen as a blunt instrument of majoritarian rule, in Switzerland it has gradually become blended with consociational institutions to create a uniquely Swiss style of democracy.

NOTES

1. The practice ended in 1987. However, New Zealand has since adopted provisions for citizen-initiated referendums. See Parkinson (2001).

2. In Switzerland, 50,000 electors or 8 cantons may petition for a "rejective" vote within 90 days of the formal publication of a bill passed by the Federal Assembly. In Italy, 500,000 voters or 5 regional councils may initiate such a process, and it may be directed toward repeal of any law currently in effect. The Irish constitution provides that a majority of the members of the Seanad and one-third of the members of the Dáil may petition the president for a referendum on a bill passed by the Dáil. Rejective or abrogative referendums are commonplace in Switzerland and Italy, but the provision has never been used in Ireland. See Pier Vincenzo Uleri, "Italy: Referendums and Initiatives from the Origins to the Crisis of a Democratic Regime," Alexander Treschel and Hanspeter Kriesi, "Switzerland: The Referendum and Initiative as a Centerpiece of the Political System," and Michael Gallagher, "Ireland: The Referendum as a Conservative Device," all in Gallagher and Uleri (1996).

3. Turnout in the 1979 general election six months earlier was 90 per cent.

4. In the 1988 election, the Centre Party vote declined to 11 per cent of the total vote and 42 seats in the 349-member Riksdag. By 1991, it was down to 8 per cent of the vote and 31 seats.

5. Swedish electoral law provides that only parties that receive 4 per cent of the total votes cast nationally or 12 per cent in an electoral region obtain seats in the Riksdag.

6. The constitution was approved by 56 per cent of those voting in the referendum of July 1, 1937. The most recent referendums in Ireland have dealt with approval of the International Criminal Court, prohibition of the death penalty, and ratification of the Nice Treaty (all June 2001) and a third referendum on abortion (June 2002).

7. The Nice Treaty was rejected by Irish voters in the June 7, 2001, referendum by a vote of 46 per cent YES to 54 per cent NO. The turnout was an exceptionally low

35 per cent. All other European treaties to date have been approved by wide margins, including a second referendum on Nice held on October 19, 2002 , in which 63 per cent voted YES. Turnout in the 2002 referendum was 48 per cent.

8. This largely symbolic provision was removed from the constitution in a relatively noncontroversial referendum held on July 10, 1972. The proposal to delete article 44 of the constitution, which contained the reference to a "special position" of the Church as "guardian of the faith" was backed by all political parties, and the Church itself offered no opposition. In the referendum, removal of article 44 was endorsed by 84 per cent of voters. At the same time, Irish voters approved lowering the voting age from twenty-one to eighteen by a margin of 85 per cent to 15 per cent.

9. The text of the amendment read as follows: "The State acknowledges the right to life of the unborn and, with due regard to the equal right to life of the mother, guarantees in its laws to respect and, as far as practicable, by its laws to defend and vindicate that right."

10. Compare, for example, the turnout of 75 per cent in the November 1982 general election.

11. The protocol specified that "Nothing in the Treaty on European Union or in the treaties establishing the European communities, or in the treaties or acts modifying or supplementing those treaties, shall affect the application in Ireland of article 40.3.3 of the Constitution of Ireland."

12. The Maastricht treaty was endorsed by a vote of 69 per cent to 31 per cent in the June 18, 1992, referendum. Turnout was 57 per cent.

13. The text of the substantive amendment was as follows: "It shall be unlawful to terminate the life of an unborn unless such termination is necessary to save the life, as distinct from the health, of the mother where there is an illness or disorder of the mother giving rise to a real and substantial risk to her life, not being a risk of self destruction."

14. The referendum proposed to entrench the Protection of Human Life in Pregnancy Act in article 40 of the constitution, stating that "the life of the unborn in the womb shall be protected in accordance with the Protection of Human Life in Pregnancy Act of 2002." But the language of the act itself, in giving discretion to doctors "to undertake any treatment necessary to protect the life of pregnant women," was seen by some pro-life campaigners as creating new loopholes that might encourage abortions, rather than prohibit them.

15. In some respects the relatively uncontroversial removal of the "special position" of the Catholic Church from the constitution in 1972 had been seen by some as the first step in a longer-term program of constitutional secularization and modernization. The entry into the European Community in the same year likewise spurred these efforts. In the early 1980s the desire to secularize the constitution was also driven partly by the Northern Ireland agenda, since the objections of the Protestant/Unionist community in that province of the United Kingdom to closer ties with the Irish republic stemmed in part from its resistance to the influence of the Catholic church.

16. The circumstances included a five-year period of separation and demonstrated lack of any possibility of reconciliation.

17. For a discussion of some of these issues, see Broder (2000), Haskell (2001), and Sabato et al. (2001).

18. The average approval percentage for California initiatives that qualified for the ballot is about 34 per cent (Bowler and Donovan 2000; Initiative and Referendum Institute). This is roughly equivalent to the percentage calculated for all states in an earlier period by Magleby (1984). However, among the states that frequently use initiatives, his calculations show that the success rate varied from a high of 61 per cent in Montana to 12 per cent in South Dakota over the 1898-1979 period.

19. The requirements for a proposal to qualify for the ballot in Oregon are the same as California's.

20. Although it passed with 59 per cent of the vote, a court injunction against enforcement of Proposition 187 was obtained shortly after its passage. In subsequent years, further decisions by the courts effectively ruled most of Proposition 187 unconstitutional (Allswang 2000).

21. *Evans v. Romer* (1993).

22. During the period 1950-75, the Swiss electorate voted on 104 items in 69 separate referendums.

23. A slightly different procedure applies if a "total revision" of the constitution is called for. The request for total revision is itself submitted to a referendum, in which it must be approved by a double majority. If this occurs, then the federal assembly is dissolved, and elections are held for a new legislature, which sits as a constitutional assembly. Any new constitutional document drafted by such an assembly is then submitted to the people in a second referendum, in which a double majority is again required for approval. Calls for total revision of the constitution have been put forward to a referendum only twice in Swiss history, the last such instance occurring with the adoption of the new constitution in 1874.

24. Six of the twenty-six cantons are weighted as half units for this purpose. See Kobach (1993a).

25. Fifty thousand voters or eight cantons can request a referendum on a treaty that does not otherwise involve a constitutional amendment. Only a simple majority of voters (not a double majority) is required to confirm the treaty.

26. Swiss law also presents the opportunity for the government to offer a "counterproposal" to a citizen constitutional initiative that qualifies for the ballot. Before 1987, counter proposals were sometimes put forward as a tactic primarily intended to defeat an initiative that the government opposed. A change in the voting rules in that year to permit a YES vote on both of two competing proposals has now made this practice less common. However, when a citizen initiative qualifies for the ballot, the government still has the opportunity to endorse it, recommend rejection, or offer a counterproposal of its own.

27. Turnout in the Swiss parliamentary election of October 20, 1991, for example, was 46 per cent, while that in the election of October 22, 1995, was 42 per cent.

7
Citizens, Parties, and Voters

Referendums provide opportunities for citizens to participate directly in the political process in ways that elections and other more conventional political processes do not. But they present a different set of choices to the voter than does an election. In a referendum, unlike an election, no political party or candidate names appear on the ballot. Voters often must choose among unfamiliar alternatives that perhaps lack reliable voting cues. Yet at least some of the factors that political scientists are accustomed to considering in studies of elections—ideology, parties, and partisanship; the images of political leaders; the issues underlying the ballot question; the impact of campaign strategies and advertising; the role of the media—can affect the outcome of a referendum in much the same way as in elections. We might expect to find greater volatility and uncertainty in referendum voting than is typically found in an election, because referendums are often unique political events and the circumstances under which they take place can vary considerably.

One would not expect as much volatility in a referendum such as the 1995 Quebec sovereignty vote, where the ballot question was rooted in long-standing divisions reflected in the polarized structure of the Quebec party system. Likewise, in Ireland we might have expected that votes on moral questions like divorce and abortion would tend to reflect relatively strong religious feelings, which would not be as subject to sudden change over a short electoral campaign, as was the case in some Irish referendums on these issues (Chapter 6, section B). By contrast, only those who followed politics very closely in Australia might have been expected to be conversant with the complex packages of constitutional issues put before the voters in the 1988 referendum in that country. Similar circumstances were seen in many of the California-style ballot propositions, where the campaign is often the sole source of information for the voter. The several European votes on the Maastricht Treaty involved a range of different attitudes, some of which could shift rapidly, others more slowly. Some voters hold strong views on the structure and institutions of the "new" Europe, others less so. But only a few are truly knowledgeable about the specifics of a newly negotiated treaty such as Maastricht, Amsterdam, or Nice.

As we have seen in some of the cases discussed here, referendums can be highly partisan contests, even without the appearance of party or candidate names on the ballot. If the positions of parties on an issue are well known or if the referendum debate follows clearly understood ideological lines, voting behaviour may tend to conform to familiar and relatively predictable patterns. In such situations, the voting choice may be driven by partisan or ideological cues or by familiarity with one or more of the issues in a long-standing political debate. On the other hand, the 1994 Nordic referendums on European Union membership or the 1992 Canadian constitutional referendum found political parties who regularly oppose each other in elections campaigning together on the same side of an issue, thus providing mixed cues to their electorates. In some other instances parties that might normally provide their supporters with reliable voting cues are internally divided. In the 1992 French Maastricht referendum, for example, or the 1980 Swedish nuclear power referendum prominent figures from the same political party actively campaigned on opposite sides of the issue.

Referendum campaigns can also become entangled with other political issues above and beyond the actual question presented on the referendum ballot. Examining the 1992 Danish and French referendums on Maastricht, Franklin et al. (1994, 1995) concluded that shifting attitudes towards domestic political actors or the relative popularity or unpopularity of the government of the day can sometimes provide a more plausible explanation of shifts in voter sentiment than feelings about the referendum issue itself. Seemingly unrelated matters such as prevailing economic conditions may also play a role in the outcome. Some types of issues may be less susceptible to such short-term influences than others. For some voters, opinions on Quebec sovereignty or on European integration may reflect their fundamental beliefs about the nation or their sense of political identity. For others, such attitudes may be less the product of deeply held beliefs than a simple electoral decision based on the persuasive arguments of an advertising campaign, apprehensions about the state of the economy, or judgments about the relative credibility of those delivering the message.

Why Governments Call Referendums

Referendums arise under various legal forms, but they do not just happen. Any referendum nearly always originates in a conscious political decision taken by a party, organization, or group. Even in the case of citizen-initiated referendums, the undertaking generally requires the political and financial resources of a well-organized group in order to collect the thousands of signatures needed to get a proposed measure onto the ballot. In most countries it will generally be the governing party, or parties, that is in a position to organize a referendum. Thus, to better understand the varying political circumstances under which referendums occur, it is necessary to first examine how and why they come about.

As noted in Chapter 2, referendums most often take place as the recourse of the parties rather than of princes or citizens. This simple observation covers a wide range of possibilities. Smaller political parties sometimes find that initiatives and referendums enable them to gain greater leverage in the political system than is possible through parliamentary or electoral channels.[1] But parties in government also find such devices useful. A governing party or coalition might opt for a referendum for many different reasons. Sometimes the governing party or parties have concluded that a particular political agenda requires demonstrated public support to carry it through. No British government today would risk joining the European Monetary Union without obtaining the public's approval in a referendum, even though such a course is not legally required. Similarly, in 1994 none of the governments of the Nordic countries were willing to undertake the historic decision to join the European Union without the concurrence of their citizens (see Chapter 4, section C). The ten countries scheduled to enter the European Union in 2004 are all likely to hold referendums on the matter—votes initiated by their governments, whether they are constitutionally required or not. In choosing this course, they are following the example set by other recent entrants. To do otherwise would invite criticism from political opponents at home that they were behaving "undemocratically."

Governing parties also commonly organize referendums because of divisions within the party on a sensitive issue (Morel 1993). By passing the responsibility for taking a decision to the electorate, party leaders may hope to quell dissent within the party on a divisive issue. The decision by the British Labour Party to hold a referendum on the issue of EC membership shortly after coming to power in 1974 provides one good example of this strategy. Knowing that his own party was divided on the issue of EC membership, Harold Wilson found that the referendum provided a means of managing the intraparty conflict that was certain to ensue. A similar strategy was followed by the prime ministers of Sweden and Norway in 1994, who knew that their parties were deeply divided on the issue of EU membership. The Swedish and Austrian referendums on the divisive issue of nuclear power provide other examples in which a popular vote was used by party leaders to prevent an issue from tearing their parties apart (see Chapter 6, section A).

A referendum may also be a strategic part of a larger political objective. The 1992 Irish abortion referendum took place because of the government's desire to separate the abortion issue from the debate on the Maastricht Treaty, thereby ensuring its ratification. The decision by the British and Irish governments to put the 1998 Northern Ireland peace agreement to referendum in both the North and the South was designed to bring greater pressure on the factions in the North to consent to the terms of the agreement. Following the decisive results of that referendum, leaders of various groups were placed in the position of seeming to defy the will of the people if they hesitated to sign on. In addition to bringing pressure on the leaders, the referendum also helped to build momentum for the agreement in the minds both of the elites and of the public at large.

In each of these instances and in dozens of others that might be mentioned, the political chain of events that led up to the decision to hold a referendum can be easily reconstructed. However, it should be noted that the mere fact that a referendum was held on a particular issue in one case does not ensure that one will be held on the same issue elsewhere. The Parti Québécois, for example, might have decided to pursue its sovereignty agenda without a referendum, as indeed some groups within the party would have preferred. But it made a calculation in the course of devising its 1976 election campaign strategy that the commitment to conduct a referendum on the issue would allow it to decouple the sovereignty question from other election issues. Once it had made such a commitment, it would have been politically impossible to reverse it later. Slovakia, in contrast, pursued its path to independence without a referendum, and the "velvet divorce" of 1993 occurred without the benefit of any direct vote of either the Czech or Slovak people.

When a governing party opts for a referendum strategy, it generally does so in the expectation that it will win, or that its position on a particular issue will be sustained. While a party may sometimes find itself trapped into a prior commitment to hold a referendum, as, for example, the New Zealand government was on the electoral reform issue in 1992, political leaders rarely stumble blindly into a referendum on an important political question. Even when a party is internally divided, it is generally possible to discern the preferred outcome of the party leaders who plan and organize the referendum strategy. Hence, Harold Wilson saw the referendum as a means of sustaining British membership in the European Community in 1975, even though many prominent members of his party continued to oppose it. Similarly, Felipe Gonzàlez used the 1986 Spanish referendum on NATO membership to quell opposition to NATO involvement within his own governing party and to move the country forward towards membership in the EU (Chapter 4, section A). Such strategies can easily fail, however, because the volatility and uncertainty of a campaign may place at risk even the most carefully thought out postreferendum strategy. The 1986 Irish referendum on divorce was part of a coherent plan to "secularize" the constitution, and it is clear that Garret FitzGerald timed the referendum to take advantage of perceived public support for removal of the constitutional ban on divorce. He could not have anticipated that the voters, following a short campaign, would deliver a stunning defeat to the proposal. Neither did Canadian political leaders, having committed themselves to a referendum following the 1992 constitutional agreement, anticipate that the electorate would ultimately reject their carefully balanced package of reforms. While the political strategy behind calling a referendum may be clear, the outcome of the venture, once undertaken, becomes much more uncertain.

Participation and Voter Turnout

Although proponents of direct democracy argue that referendums are a superior device for democratic citizen participation, the evidence shows

Table 7.1

Selected Turnout Comparisons, Referendums and General Elections

		Turnout (%)	Change*
Australia	1988 constitutional amendments	92	-2
	1998 federal election	95	
	1999 republic/preamble	95	0
Canada	1992 constitutional referendum	75	+5
	1993 federal election	70	
Denmark	1992 Maastricht Treaty	83	0
	1993 Edinburgh Agreement	86	+3
	1998 general election	87	
	2000 European currency referendum	89	+2
France	1992 Maastricht Treaty	70	+1
	1993 national assembly election	69	
	1995 presidential election (second round)	75	
Ireland	1992 parliamentary election	69	
	1992 abortion laws	65	-4
	1995 divorce amendment	62	-7
New Zealand	1992 electoral system referendum	55	-28
	1993 general election and referendum	83	0
Norway	1993 general election	76	
	1994 EU referendum	89	+13
Puerto Rico	1993 political status plebiscite	74	-9
	1996 gubernatorial election*	83	
	1998 political status plebiscite	71	-12

that voter participation can vary much more widely in referendums than it does in elections. In Switzerland, where referendums are commonplace, turnout is generally below 50 per cent and can sometimes be much lower. It can, however, rise to higher levels when a particular issue engages wider voter interest or when an intensive campaign is waged by interested groups.[2] In US state referendums turnout is notoriously low and may be subject to even more extreme fluctuations. Butler and Ranney (1994)

Table 7.1 (continued)		Turnout (%)	Change*
Quebec	1980 sovereignty referendum	86	+3
	1993 federal election (Quebec)	77	
	1994 provincial election*	82	
	1995 sovereignty referendum	94	+12
Russia	1993 economic reforms, presidency	65	+12
	1993 constitutional referendum	58	+5
	1993 Duma election	53	
	1996 presidential election (2nd round)	69	
Scotland	1997 devolution referendum	60	-11
	1997 UK election (Scotland)	71	
	1999 Scottish parliament	59	
Spain	1986 NATO referendum	59	-11
	1986 general election	70	
Sweden	1980 nuclear power referendum	76	-15
	1994 EU referendum	83	-4
	1994 general election	87	
Switzerland	1991 (March) transport policy, voting age	31	-15
	1992 (May) IMF, World Bank, water reservoirs, genetic technology	36	-10
	1992 (December) EEA membership	78	+32
	1993 (March) casino gambling, gasoline taxes, animal experiments	51	+5
	1994 (June) citizenship, culture, UN peace-keeping participation	46	+4
	1995 federal election	42	
Uruguay	1992 privatization referendum	77	-12
	1994 education, social security	90	+1
	1994 general election	89	
Wales	1997 devolution referendum	50	-23
	1997 UK election (Wales)	73	
	1999 assembly	46	

* Comparison is with nearest parliamentary election unless otherwise noted.

found that turnout over a large number of referendum cases in various nations averaged fifteen percentage points lower than the turnout found in general elections in the same countries. Thomas Cronin (1989) found a comparable rate of "drop-off"—i.e., the difference between voting for a candidate and voting in the propositions sections of the ballot—in American state referendums. However there is no reason to believe that turnout in referendums is necessarily lower than the turnout in elections, although it may vary more widely from case to case. The turnout in some of the more important European referendums has generally been quite comparable to the turnout in national elections, and turnout in the 1995 Quebec sovereignty referendum registered an astonishing 94 per cent, higher than in any provincial or federal election (Table 7.1). Other important referendums in which turnout was higher than in a comparable election are the 1992 Canadian constitutional referendum, the 1994 Norwegian EU membership referendum, and the 2000 Danish referendum on the Euro. But clearly, a referendum held separately on a less salient issue runs the risk of lower voter participation. The 1992 New Zealand referendum on electoral reform, the 1980 Swedish nuclear power referendum, and the 1992 Uruguayan referendum on privatization of state industries are examples in which turnout registered significantly below that of the most nearly comparable election.

To combat low turnout, some countries hold referendums at the same time as a general election.[3] However, while this strategy may boost voter participation, it may also cause the referendum to be ignored by the voters, or it may allow the referendum issue to become engulfed in the partisan politics of the election. Minimum-participation requirements or specific thresholds for a referendum to be considered valid are also sometimes used to prevent low turnout from producing a distorted result. Italy, for example, requires a minimum turnout of 50 per cent plus one of all eligible voters for a referendum to be considered valid. However, these strategies sometimes simply make it more difficult for a referendum proposal to pass, even when it may be favoured by a majority of the voters in the referendum.

Campaigns

Campaigns are almost always important in determining referendum outcomes, just as they are in elections. For some reason, however, this fact is not as readily recognized in many studies of referendums as it is in the literature on elections.[4] Between the time that a referendum is called and the day that the result is announced, there usually stands a hard fought campaign lasting several weeks or months. Over the course of that campaign, public opinion on the central issues of the referendum can sometimes shift dramatically. The dynamics of a referendum campaign can often be hard to anticipate, and the full participation of the electorate cannot always be assumed. It follows, therefore, that the outcome of many referendums is not easily predicted. In a study of the 1986 Irish referendum on the divorce amendment, Darcy and Laver (1990) found that the result had more to do with the dynamics of the campaign than with the actual beliefs of Irish voters on the issue of divorce. In many of the cases examined in this book, public opinion polls taken in advance of the campaign would have suggested quite different results from those that actually occurred. While longer-term factors such as partisanship or ideology may also be important, the short-term impact of opposing campaign strategies and tactics can easily make the critical difference in determining the outcome of a referendum.

Shaun Bowler and Todd Donovan (1998) note that voters draw upon various sources in forming opinions about the sometimes complex and confusing initiatives that appear on some US state ballots. Among the most frequently mentioned are campaign pamphlets, newspaper and television editorials, and direct mailings from various campaign organizations. Voters in such situations take cues from these and other sources. Hence, the knowledge that the prominent consumer advocate Ralph Nader backed a 1988 California proposal on auto insurance and opposed several competing proposals put forward by business groups was instrumental in shaping opinion on five insurance propositions that appeared together on the ballot (Lupia 1994). Similarly, knowledge that the tobacco industry was behind a 1994 proposal to loosen local smoking restrictions led to its defeat (Bowler and Donovan 1998). A referendum that involves a cleavage or ideological issue, or in which political parties take well-known and predictably opposite positions, ought to see the least volatility (Tonsgaard 1992). One that involves a new or previously undiscussed issue or one in which parties line up in a nontraditional manner is more likely to lead to greater volatility during the campaign and greater uncertainty about the outcome (LeDuc 2001b).

Table 7.2

Reported Time of Vote Decision in Eight Referendums (Percentages)

		Long Before	At Call	During Campaign	Final Week
Quebec[a]	1995	70	5	14	11
France[b]	1992	60		20	20
Norway[c]	1994	59		24	17
Sweden[c]	1994	58		17	25
Australia[d]	1999	42	19	20	19
Scotland[e]	1997	40	21	16	24
Wales[e]	1997	32	20	16	33
Canada[f]	1992	–	38	33	29

[a] 1995 Carleton ISSP Study (LeDuc and Pammett 2001).
[b] SOFRES/ Le Figaro (Franklin et al. 1995).
[c] Comparative Nordic Referendums Study (Pesonen 1998).
[d] 1999 Australian Constitutional Referendum Study (McAllister 2000).
[e] 1997 CREST surveys (Taylor and Thomson 1999).
[f] 1992 Carleton Referendum Study (LeDuc and Pammett 1995).

John Zaller's (1992) model of opinion formation is particularly well suited to the study of public opinion and voting behaviour in referendums. As he argues, any process of opinion formation proceeds from an interaction of *information* and *predisposition*. If the issues of a referendum are entirely new to the voter, the learning process of the campaign becomes more important in providing the information needed to come to a decision. In other situations, however, voters may be able to make up their minds more quickly on the basis of partisan or ideological cues or familiarity with one or more of the issues in a long-standing political debate. The more widely anticipated a future referendum is, the more likely it is that a high proportion of voters will hold a predisposition or perhaps have already decided how they will vote. Strong supporters of the Parti Québécois, for example, would hardly have needed a campaign in order to make up their minds about how to vote in the 1995 Quebec sovereignty referendum. However, when parties are split or when the ideological alignment is unclear, voters might be expected to depend more on the campaign and to require more time to reach a decision. The events of the campaign under these circumstances thus become more critical to the outcome. The absence of strong party or leadership cues may also render the voting decision more difficult and thus more uncertain.

When voters clearly need the campaign in order to form an opinion on the issue(s) of the referendum, voting decisions tend to be made later in the campaign, after a sufficient amount of information has become available about the issue. Conversely, if voters are able to make up their minds on the basis of clear partisan or ideological cues or if there is a high degree of prior familiarity with the issue(s), voting decisions may be made earlier. Survey data on the reported times of voting decisions for several of the referendums examined in this book confirm this general pattern (Table 7.2).[5] In the 1992 Canadian constitutional referendum, voters could not have been expected to have had a high degree of prior knowledge of the content of a constitutional agreement that was negotiated in closed sessions. Not surprisingly, therefore, nearly two-thirds of the voters in that referendum made their decisions over the course of the campaign, and a substantial number did so as late as the final week. By contrast, voters in the 1995 Quebec sovereignty referendum were able to come to a decision much more quickly on the issue, in part because the subject matter of that referendum was well known but also because the campaign provided strongly reinforcing partisan cues for many voters. While the campaign was still important to the outcome, in part because of the closeness of the result, fewer voters needed the additional information provided by the campaign in order to reach a decision. Three-quarters of the Quebec electorate had already made up their minds how to vote when the referendum was called. Voters in the EU referendums may also have had a high degree of knowledge of the underlying issues but would still have needed the campaign in order to assess the arguments regarding the specific treaties or agreements. The fact that some parties that are normally opponents in election campaigns were campaigning together on the same side in some of these referendums would also have presented voters with "new" information. In Sweden divisions among the governing Social Democrats spilled over into the 1994 referendum campaign, with the government actively supporting the YES side but some of its own partisans campaigning against it under the umbrella group Social Democrats Against the EU (see Chapter 4, section C). These circumstances presented a quite different picture from the 1995 Quebec case, in which parties with well-known and strongly held positions on sovereignty were putting forward highly familiar arguments right from the beginning and mobilizing their traditional supporters in support of a cause to which they could be expected to have a strong prior commitment.

The positions that political parties take, either during the evolution of the referendum issue or during the campaign itself, provide strong information cues to voters. When these cues are present, voters are often able to find their own positions fairly quickly. When they are absent, other short-term elements tend to become more powerful, or alternative groups, organizations, or individuals may intervene to provide voters with the same types of shortcuts that political parties would otherwise provide (Lupia 1992, 1994; Bowler and Donovan 1998). Ideology may provide a similar anchor for some types of referendum issues. If voters are easily able to locate an issue on a left-right spectrum, they might more readily form their own opinions on the issue, particularly in countries where party politics arrays itself along clearly defined ideological lines.

Parties and Leaders

In referendums, as in elections, the messengers often matter as much as the message. Although no candidates' names or party affiliations appear on the ballot, the arguments that are put before the voters over the course of a referendum campaign are frequently interpreted and delivered by participants who are already well known to the voters—namely, the established political parties and their leaders. While the specific question of the referendum may or may not be new to the political scene, the parties and leaders who convey information to the public are almost always familiar figures about whom voters invariably already have opinions. There is considerable evidence that the relative popularity or unpopularity of individual political leaders and attitudes toward the government and particular political parties can affect the outcome of a referendum. Franklin et al. (1995) argue that the unpopularity of the Liberal-Conservative coalition government contributed to the defeat of the Maastricht Treaty in Denmark in the 1992 referendum and that a change of government to a coalition including the Social Democrats paved the way for the victory of the Edinburgh Agreement in another referendum held one year later.[6] In Britain an unpopular Labour government, itself headed for electoral defeat, was unsuccessful in winning support in Scotland and Wales for its devolution proposals in the 1979 referendums.[7] Nearly twenty years later, a newly elected Labour prime minister, Tony Blair, made the establishment of Scottish and Welsh assemblies his first policy priority. In the referendums that followed, the popularity of the new prime minister and the momentum provided by Labour's electoral majority undoubtedly contributed towards the victories (Heath and Taylor 1999). While this may have made only a small difference in Scotland, where the 1997 proposals enjoyed wide support, it may well have been critical to the narrow victory in Wales, where exhortations to "Back Blair" proved to be the single most effective campaign tactic of the YES side in winning over a skeptical electorate (see Chapter 5, section C).

There are other examples, both positive and negative, of the impact of political leaders on referendum votes. President Mitterrand's unpopularity and the widespread discontent in France with the political class more generally certainly contributed to the erosion of public support for the Maastricht Treaty in 1992 (Chapter 4, section B). The 1992 Canadian constitutional referendum is yet another example of a referendum in which a proposal may have been lost partly because of the unpopularity of the prime minister who led the campaign and of the government that he represented. On the other hand, the ability of the Spanish government to reverse its earlier position and sustain Spanish membership in NATO was due as much to the personal popularity of Felipe Gonzàlez as to any feelings about the merits of NATO membership itself (Chapter 4, section A).

Cases in which political parties are internally divided or in which support for or opposition to a proposal does not align along familiar party lines present a somewhat different picture to the voter. One might think that a campaign in which all the major political parties are aligned on the same side of an issue would tend to produce a very one-sided result. But examples such as the 1992 Danish and French referendums on Maastricht, the 1992 Canadian constitutional referendum, and the 1994 Norwegian and Swedish referendums on European Union membership demonstrate clearly that such is not necessarily the case. In those instances, voters simply took their cues from sources other than the mainstream parties, in many instances going directly against the position of a party that they would subsequently support in an election. In these cases, information coming from prominent figures in the campaign, from the media or other interested groups, or sometimes even from actors outside the normal partisan political arena were as likely to influence the outcome as any cues provided by established parties. When this occurs, the result is often greater volatility or uncertainty than would be found in a referendum campaign fought along more conventional partisan lines.

Ola Listhaug et al. (1998) concluded that partisanship played an important role in the voting in the 1994 EU referendums in all three Nordic countries, but they also found that the strength of this relationship varied significantly both between countries and between parties. In Norway, for example, the relationship between the vote and identification with the Labour and Conservative Parties, both of which campaigned actively in support of EU membership, was moderately strong and positive. Yet the Conservatives managed to deliver a much higher percentage of their supporters to the YES side in that referendum than did the governing Labour Party, even though both parties campaigned for the YES side. Supporters of the Centre Party, on the other hand, which campaigned vigorously against membership, voted almost entirely NO. In Finland, the relationships between party feelings and voting were generally much weaker. Yet several of the parties that campaigned for a YES vote delivered high percentages of their supporters.

The voting patterns found in Sweden in the 1994 referendum were somewhat different from those in the other two countries, in part reflecting the deep divisions among the governing Social Democrats (see Chapter 4, section C). Listhaug et al. (1998) show that the party was able to win back at least some of its supporters to the YES side over the course of the campaign, perhaps making the difference between victory and defeat for the proposal. In the end, Social Democratric supporters split nearly evenly, with 48 per cent voting for the YES option in the referendum. Moderate party (conservative) supporters, on the other hand, voted heavily for the YES, in part reflecting the more strongly positive feelings toward Europe held by supporters of that party. The strong campaign waged by the Greens in Sweden against EU membership was also reflected in the low percentage of Green supporters who voted YES (19 per cent). In Finland, by contrast, there was little relationship between support for the Greens and either feelings about Europe or voting behaviour in the referendum (Aardal et al. 1998).

The 1999 Australian constitutional referendum involved an entirely different type of issue in which linkages between party feelings and attitudes toward the underlying issue were fairly weak. Nevertheless, some fairly clear partisan voting patterns were in evidence, at least on the central issue

Figure 7.1
Elements Leading towards Stability or Volatility in Referendum Voting

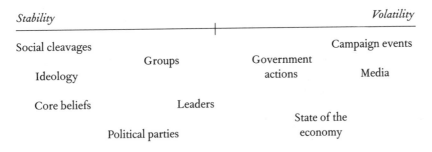

of the referendum involving replacement of the monarchy, with 60 per cent of Labor partisans voting YES on that issue, compared to only 34 per cent of Liberals and 24 per cent of National voters (McAllister 2000). In general, the partisan patterns that did exist reflected the effectiveness of the campaign strategies followed by the NO side more than the existence of an underlying party/issue cleavage (Luskin et al. 2000). Had the referendum itself been either a straight party fight or a contest driven entirely by public opinion on the underlying issues, the outcome might very well have been different. In reality, it was neither of these. Rather, it was a contest in which campaign tactics mattered a great deal and in which a short-term movement in public opinion was sufficient to overcome, at least temporarily, partisan, ideological, or issue cleavages that may have existed before the beginning of the referendum campaign.

In these and other cases, a key point to note is that referendums are not, as is sometimes thought, nonpartisan. As Ian Budge (1996) points out, political parties and their leaders are most often the central actors in referendum campaigns, a view that is easily confirmed by the survey of cases treated in chapters 3 to 6 of this book. If American state referendums sometimes appear to constitute a partial exception to this observation, it is as much due to the weakness of American parties as to anything inherent in the referendum process itself. Where parties govern, referendums tend to be partisan or party-led contests for voter support.

Voting Behaviour and Outcomes

Because there is no long-term basis of opinion on many of the issues put before the voters in referendums, there is often greater uncertainty about the outcome than would typically be found in an election. Yet many of the variables that account for voting choice in referendums are similar to those typically found in studies of elections (Jenssen et al. 1998; LeDuc and Pammett 1995). Sometimes voters are able to make up their minds on the basis of party identification, ideological leanings, or familiarity with the arguments on different sides of a well-known or previously debated political issue. These factors provide operational examples of Zaller's (1992) "predispositions." Figure 7.1 summarizes a number of the relevant variables, which are arranged to fit the context of referendum voting as it might vary from issue to issue or case to case. The closer a particular referendum comes to involving elements at the left-hand side of the diagram, the more its outcome is likely to be driven by predispositions and the more limited (or reinforcing) will be the effects of the campaign. When a referendum involves elements towards the right-hand side of the diagram, on the other hand the potential for movement over the course of the campaign increases and the outcome becomes more uncertain. Many strongly Catholic voters in Ireland, for example, might have taken their cues on an issue such as divorce or abortion from the Church rather than from the rhetoric of a campaign. But this is only a beginning point for estimating the potential for opinion change on a referendum issue. Often, an important part of the dynamic of a referendum campaign involves changing and redefining the subject matter through the discourse of the campaign. There are some instances, of course, where the issues in a referendum will be completely unfamiliar to the average voter. Even when voters must form their opinions entirely from information acquired over the course of a short campaign, that information is not written on a blank slate. Cues are often provided by political leaders, parties, groups, or personalities, about whom at least some voters already hold strong opinions.

The processes by which voters make decisions in referendum campaigns are not inherently different from those found in elections (LeDuc and Pammett 1995, 2001). The specific way in which these various elements fit together can vary considerably, however, and the sources of information available are sometimes more constrained and less accessible to voters than the ones that they rely upon in partisan elections. Only through the various sources that are available over the course of the campaign will voters be able to form opinions on new political questions that are presented to them or to properly assess unexpected positions taken by political parties or leaders. As noted earlier, in some referendums voting decisions tend to be made fairly late in a campaign, after a sufficient amount of information has been absorbed from a variety of sources.

The referendum appeals to both political practitioners and theorists alike because they believe it provides a democratic process by which a difficult or complex issue that might otherwise be irresolvable can be brought to closure. The reality of direct democracy, however, suggests that such is not always the case. Referendum outcomes are often only one part of a larger debate on many political issues, and they may provide only a temporary resolution. Thus, the Danish votes on the Maastricht (1992-93) and Amsterdam (1998) Treaties and on the European currency resolved those specific matters, but they also exposed deeper divisions in the country over the issue of European political and economic integration more generally. The Danish outcome of 1992 is particularly instructive. The rejection of the Maastricht Treaty by Danish voters did not end the debate but instead ushered in a hectic period of political and diplomatic activity leading to another referendum a year later (Siune et al. 1994). A similar story unfolded when Irish voters unexpectedly rejected the Nice treaty, which paved the way for EU enlargement, in a 2001 referendum. This outcome did not, as some feared, bring a halt to the European enlargement project. Rather, it led to a second referendum on the issue a year later, a referendum held under enormous pressure from both Irish and European elites who were strongly committed to carrying through the enlargement of the EU, which they had been instrumental in negotiating.

Similarly, many of the issues that American voters consider in state referendums are only partially or temporarily resolved in any given vote. Some further examples are provided by the many ballots that took place during the earlier part of the twentieth century on prohibition or liquor controls in many of the US and Australian states and in New Zealand. Between 1911 and 1987, New Zealanders voted in every national election on liquor licensing issues—a total of twenty-four such votes. Quebec voters have been consulted twice by their provincial government on sovereignty proposals and may well vote on the matter again at some future date. Likewise, Irish voters twice rendered a verdict on the contentious issue of abortion in 1983 and 1992, but neither vote brought closure to the issue. Interested groups continued to actively lobby for a third referendum, and the vote that finally took place in 2002 revealed an electorate still deeply divided over the issue.[8]

The referendum cases discussed in this book took place in a range of different contexts that were surely wider and more diverse than would be found in comparing several elections over time within the same set of countries. The nature of the referendum issue, the manner in which it arises, the appeal of leaders, the positioning of the parties, and the involvement of other nonparty organizations or groups may, over time, introduce different dynamics, even in different referendum contexts in the same countries. In the few polities where referendums are more commonplace events, this variation in electoral context is more readily observed. The Irish referendums on divorce, abortion, European issues, and other constitutional matters, for example, display several distinctive patterns with respect to voting turnout, the positioning of the parties, the dynamics of the campaign, and the outcome of the referendum. In the 2000 Danish referendum on the European currency (Chapter 4, section D), voting patterns were similar in some ways to the patterns in the five previous votes on other European issues, but there were also some important differences. Danish politicians were not surprised by the result, but the contest was nevertheless hard-fought and the outcome uncertain until well into the campaign. The two Quebec referendums, separated by fifteen years, likewise do not display exactly the same electoral patterns, even though they involved essentially the same issue. While a third referendum may exhibit many similarities to the previous two, it is also likely to be different in a number of ways that are not readily predictable before the campaign actually begins (LeDuc 2001a). Different leaders, different questions, and a potentially different political context invariably combine to introduce key elements of uncertainty and uniqueness. Theories of direct democracy tend to presume that referendum voters always vote on issues. But research on referendum voting, like that on elections, teaches us that attitudes toward issues comprise only one of the variables affecting voting choice and not always the most important one in determining outcomes.

NOTES

1. This use of citizen initiatives or abrogative referendums is common among smaller parties in several European countries, particularly Italy and Switzerland. See Gallagher and Uleri (1996).

2. For example, turnout in the December 1992 referendum on Swiss membership in the European Economic Area was 78 per cent. But turnout in the March 1991 referendum, which included votes on lowering the voting age to eighteen and transferring funds from road construction to public transport, was only 31 per cent. Other turnout comparisons for Swiss referendums are found in Table 7.1, and in Chapter 6, Table 6D1.

3. Such a test is provided by the 1992 and 1993 referendums on electoral reform in New Zealand (Chapter 3, section C). The first of these, in which the referendum question was the only item on the ballot, drew a turnout of 55 per cent. In the second, which was held to coincide with the 1993 general election, the turnout was 83 per cent.

4. But see Johnston et al. (1996) and Darcy and Laver (1990) on the dynamics of referendum campaigns.

5. The categories in some of the surveys do not always coincide perfectly with the labels employed in Table 7.2. In the CREST surveys in Scotland and Wales, for example, the categories were as follows: before the general election (i.e., before May 1, 1997); between the general election and the referendum; in the month before; in the week before. The category of when the referendum was called was not used in the SOFRES or the Nordic countries surveys, but the other categories used in those instances were similar to the categories shown in the table.

6. See Siune et al. (1994) for another interpretation of these results. Maastricht was defeated in Denmark by a margin of 49.3 per cent to 50.7 per cent in the 1992 referendum. In 1993 the Edinburgh agreement was approved by a margin of 56.7 per cent to 43.3 per cent. Turnout was slightly over 3 per cent higher in the 1993 referendum.

7. In Scotland the question actually passed, but because the turnout was only 64 per cent, the measure failed to achieve the threshold of 40 per cent of the entire electorate that had been specified in the legislation. In Wales the 1979 proposal was overwhelmingly defeated in the 1979 referendum. See Chapter 5, section C.

8. The proposal to entrench the Protection of Human Life in Pregnancy Act in article 40 of the Irish constitution was rejected by a narrow majority of voters (50.4 per cent) in the June 2002 referendum. See Chapter 6, section C.

8

The Present and Future
of Direct Democracy

The referendum has been associated in one way or another with some of the truly momentous political events of the late twentieth century. Mikhail Gorbachev's all-union referendum of March 1991, although it failed in its objectives, ultimately became an instrumental part of the process of political change in the former USSR. In the end, it led to the independence of Ukraine and other former Soviet republics (Chapter 5, section B), and to the processes of political and economic reform that were set in motion in Russia and the Baltic states. The 1992 referendum in South Africa advanced the process of dismantling apartheid and set the stage for the election of a multiracial democratic regime and the presidency of Nelson Mandela.[1] Referendums brought about the enlargement of the European Union from its original membership of six countries to a projected twenty-five in 2004. Referendums have been an integral part of the process of economic and political integration in Europe, which has been achieved through such landmark agreements as the Single European Act (1986) and the Maastricht (1992), Amsterdam (1998), and Nice (2000) Treaties. It would be easy to expand this list of political milestones to include the transitions to democracy in Poland and Chile, the search for a settlement in Northern Ireland, and the remaking of representative institutions in Italy. The referendum has been an important device for bringing about political change in many nations in recent decades.

One might argue of course that many of these events could well have taken place without a referendum. The process of peacefully dismantling the apartheid regime in South Africa was long and complex, and the referendum was only one part of that process. Yet without it, the sense of democratic legitimacy that President de Klerk obtained for this momentous policy shift would not have been achieved, and the course of change in South Africa might well have become more protracted and violent. Similarly, although not all the countries of the European Union have put major European issues to a popular vote, those that have done so have often been able to better manage some of the sharp divisions within political parties and among voters that have been precipitated by the European project—a project that has been pursued largely by elites. Once a precedent is set in a particular country for holding a referendum on issues involving major political change, it becomes unlikely that further changes of similar magnitude will be attempted without again consulting the people, even when such consultation is not constitutionally mandated. Thus, we can be certain that referendums on major constitutional questions, political and economic integration, or significant institutional changes lie in the future of many of the countries that have been discussed in this book and perhaps of some others that will use processes of direct democracy to address new political issues in the future.

As we have seen throughout this book the referendum has not been employed only to deal with extraordinary issues of regime change or constitutional reform. In some countries it has become embedded in the political culture to the extent that it has become a normal part of the process of government. The number of such cases could well increase in the future, as democratic polities search for ways to improve the quality of their democracy and to satisfy the demand of modern electorates for a greater participatory voice in the processes under which they are governed. Advancing technology, wider and more rapid dissemination of information, and improved methods of communication could do much to accelerate this trend toward more participatory forms of democracy. While I do not foresee a sudden shift from conventional political processes to "electronic democracy," many observers believe that some forms of political participation that might have seemed unrealistic only a few years ago are now becoming more feasible. Such developments, if they do occur, could begin to remove one of the traditional arguments against the wider use of direct democracy, namely, its seeming impracticality.

These trends will not necessarily be welcomed, even by many who in principle support the concept of a more directly democratic form of politics. While the referendum is no longer associated, as it once was, with the manipulations of authoritarian rulers, it nevertheless continues to engender skepticism in some circles about its ability to deliver a genuinely better quality of democracy. The trend in some US states where popular votes on certain types of issues increasingly appear capable of threatening the civil rights of vulnerable minorities is particularly worrisome (Gamble 1997). The tendency of well-funded interest groups in the United States to use the initiative process to promote narrow political causes also concerns some observers of these trends in that country (Sabato et al. 2001). A vigorous debate has developed in America over whether traditional forms of democracy have been enhanced by the growth of initiative and referendum processes or whether democracy itself is being "derailed" by them (Broder 2000).

Bowler and Donovan (1998) find these concerns overstated, arguing that voters readily recognize and often correctly evaluate the sponsorship of ballot propositions and that the courts and legislatures already possess the tools necessary to curb excesses in most instances. In fact, they argue, the groups that are most threatened by the initiative process are those who are supposed to feel threatened by it—namely, the political elites. As Donovan and Bowler (1998) note hopefully, the growth of the initiative process in the US states "may bring about a different way of doing politics, in large part because the groups and policy entrepreneurs using the process are not part of the standard cast of characters found in state capitols."

The traditional concern that the referendum may reopen old conflicts in divided societies also does not appear as compelling today as it once did. Largely because of this danger, Belgium does not employ the referendum at the national level. Canada has also been wary of the referendum over much of its history for the same reason, as has the Netherlands.[2] But Switzerland, in spite of its historic linguistic, religious and territorial divisions, stands as a clear exception, leading many scholars to re-evaluate the role that more participatory democratic institutions might be able to play in plural societies. The Swiss success in blending consociational and participatory types of democratic institutions has led political scientists to look at this question somewhat differently than they have in the past. So, too, has the recent example of Northern Ireland, in which majorities of both Protestant and Catholic voters supported the Good Friday peace agreement in the May 1998 referendum.[3] These successful applications of direct democratic processes in societies where they might once have been greatly feared are gradually leading to a lessening of the traditional concern that direct votes on potentially divisive issues promote only rampant majoritarianism—catering to the prejudices of the majority without concern for the rights of minorities. Rather, more participatory democratic institutions may come to be seen in at least some instances as part of a creative solution to the political difficulties caused by long-standing ethnic, religious, or linguistic tensions. But such results cannot be assured. The UN-sponsored referendum conducted in East Timor in 1999 initially held out the hope that the conflicts that had consumed that part of Indonesia since 1976 might finally be resolved. But the violence that erupted in its aftermath served as a reminder that a referendum alone may not necessarily provide a solution to the deep-seated ethnic, regional, or racial conflicts that persist in many societies. While a referendum on self-determination is often advanced as a possible solution to the India-Pakistan dispute over Kashmir, for example, few observers believe that such a vote will actually take place or that, if it did, it could truly bring an end to this deeply embedded conflict.

Referendums have also had a number of implications for the traditional role of political parties in contemporary liberal democracies. In the North American context, initiatives and referendums have sometimes been seen as devices that could provide an alternative to parties or possibly reduce the role of parties in aggregating and channelling citizens' demands on governments. Indeed, as mentioned in Chapter 1, the rapid growth of initiative and referendum processes in the American states took place largely at the beginning of the twentieth century, in the era of populist reaction against the power exercised by partisan political machines. In conjunction with devices such as the open primary, the referendum was part of a broad and largely successful attack by reformers on the powers of entrenched party organizations. The European experience in this regard, however, is somewhat different. The political parties themselves initiated and organized many of the referendums we have considered here, and they have used them to advance their own policy goals or to address particular intraparty concerns. In this sense, then, the tools of direct democracy are at least as often tools of party government as they are instruments to be deployed against political parties. As I noted earlier, quoting Hamon (1995), in a modern democracy the referendum can be either the "recourse of the citizens" or the "recourse of the parties." Most likely, as Budge (1996) argues, the growing use of the referendum will act to complement party democracy, not to replace it. Rather than weakening parties, the selective use of the referendum to inform and legitimize important policy decisions may actually strengthen them (Seyd 1998).

One should not, however, be too sanguine about the growth of more participatory democratic institutions such as initiatives and referendums. While we might agree that some of the worst fears of their critics seem unfounded, such institutions may not be capable of fulfilling the high expectations of their most enthusiastic partisans. Too many of the issues that referendums have been intended to resolve remain unresolved even after a referendum has taken place. The Northern Ireland peace agreement remains stalled years after a seemingly decisive referendum on its provisions. The Quebec sovereignty debate continues, in spite of two previous referendums on the issue. Public opinion polls in Sweden and Denmark continue to register high levels of Euroskepticism. Abortion has not disappeared from the political agenda in Ireland. The danger clearly exists that referendums on these types of issues will lead, not to their resolution, but to more or less permanent and ongoing electoral campaigns and more frequent referendums. This pattern was found with regard to the prohibition of alcohol in some countries early in the twentieth century. Temperance groups continued to employ the institutions of direct democracy, where available, to promote their cause, and governments found it more expedient to hold repeated referendums on the issue than to deal more directly with the policy alternatives.

Referendums are much like elections in this regard. They hold the promise of delivering a more truly democratic form of politics, but in practice they can easily disappoint. Referendum campaigns, like election campaigns, are real political contests in which money, organization, and media all play an important role. Interested groups will seek to word the question, set the agenda, or define the rules, even before the actual campaign gets under way. The various groups involved, including the political parties, campaign to win, not merely to "let the people decide," a simple fact of politics that is often forgotten by some of the more idealistic proponents of direct democracy. Thus, the quality of "deliberation" in referendum campaigns is not always what theorists expect. The outcome of a referendum can turn as easily on the popularity of political leaders, the state of the economy at the time of the vote, or the power of an advertising blitz as on the fundamentals of the issue on the ballot. Purists often find this process disconcerting, but the reality is that referendum campaigns contain much of the same "messiness" that characterizes elections. At the conclusion of an election campaign conducted under conditions acknowledged to be free and fair, all participants generally accept the premise that "the people have spoken." Someone is almost always tempted to add, however, even if only in a hushed whisper, "But what did they say?" Just as an election might produce a minority government, an inconclusive result, or an unexpected policy reversal, so too a referendum cannot always be expected to provide a decisive answer to complex political questions that may contain more than a few possible permutations.

Referendums may also have unintended consequences. When Canadian voters rejected the Progressive Conservative government's proposed constitutional package in the 1992 referendum (Chapter 3, section A), the new Liberal government that took office the following year chose to interpret the outcome of that referendum as indicating that "Canadians don't want to talk about the constitution." As a result, the constitutional impasse which has done considerable harm to the Canadian polity over the years has been allowed to continue, and future governments will hesitate to undertake any new initiative unless they are forced by events to do so. The narrow outcome of the Swedish EU referendum in 1994 (Chapter 4, section C), while positive for Sweden's membership in the European Union, had the effect of keeping Sweden out of the monetary union, even though Swedish voters did not vote specifically on that issue. The victory of "none of the above" in the 1998 Puerto Rican statehood referendum (Chapter 5, section D) added to the uncertainty about the island's political future at a time when this long-standing issue seemed to be approaching resolution.

This lack of finality does not make the referendum any less democratic or any less useful as a tool of party government. Knowing that a particular issue will be put to a referendum often frames the political debate on that issue and ensures that governments will not venture too far away from the views of their electorates. It also reminds us that referendums in themselves are not a panacea for democracy and that they may sometimes deliver a great deal less than they seem to promise. Just as elections are no more than a beginning for a process of democratic governance, referendums only rarely deliver the last word on the complex political questions that they are called upon to address. More often than not, they are but one part of the larger democratic mosaic within which governments function.

Awareness of their limitations need not reduce the appeal of these institutions of direct democracy. The trends in political thought in many of the established democracies today suggest that the adoption and increased usage of these devices is likely to continue well into the foreseeable future.

However, it is also evident that such institutions function best when they are able to complement, rather than compete with, existing representative institutions. Like the Swiss, who have over their 150-year modern history found ways to blend many of the best attributes of representative, direct, and consociational democratic practices, citizens of many other nations will continue to look to these institutions as a way to enhance and improve the quality of their democracy.

NOTES

1. The referendum of March 17, 1992, was conducted by the former white regime of President F.W. de Klerk. The question put to white voters only was, "Do you support continuation of the reform process which the state president began on February 2, 1990, and which is aimed at a new constitution through negotiations?" Of those participating 69 per cent voted YES, in a turnout of 86 per cent of the eligible electorate. The first multiracial election took place in South Africa on April 27-29, 1994. Nelson Mandela was subsequently elected as state president by the new national assembly.

2. The traditional Canadian example is the 1942 conscription plebiscite, in which a majority of voters in English Canada voted in favour of military conscription, while a majority in Quebec voted against. In the Netherlands, the adoption of a new referendum law generated heated controversy and led to the collapse of the ruling three-party coalition.

3. The YES vote of 71 per cent in the referendum of May 22, with a turnout of 81 per cent, was large enough to indicate broad cross-sectarian support. On the same day, voters in the Republic of Ireland also approved the agreement and endorsed removing articles 2 and 3 of the constitution, which asserted a claim to the territory of Northern Ireland, by a vote of 94 per cent.

References

Chapters 1-2

Barber, Benjamin. 1984. *Strong Democracy: Participatory Politics for a New Age*. Berkeley, CA: University of California Press.

Boyer, Patrick. 1992a. *The People's Mandate: Referendums and a More Democratic Canada*. Toronto: Dundurn Press.

Boyer, Patrick. 1992b. *Direct Democracy in Canada: the History and Future of Referendums*. Toronto: Dundurn Press.

Bogdanor, Vernon. 1981. *The People and the Party System: The Referendum and Electoral Reform in British Politics*. Cambridge: Cambridge University Press.

Bowler, Shaun, and Todd Donovan. 1998. *Demanding Choices: Opinion, Voting, and Direct Democracy*. Ann Arbor, MI: University of Michigan Press.

Broder, David. 2000. *Democracy Derailed*. New York: Harcourt.

Budge, Ian. 1996. *The New Challenge of Direct Democracy*. Cambridge: Polity Press.

Butler, David, and Austin Ranney, eds. 1994. *Referendums around the World: The Growing Use of Direct Democracy*. London: Macmillan.

Catt, Helena, ed. 1999. *Democracy in Practice*. London: Routledge.

Center for the Study of Direct Democracy, University of Geneva. http://c2d.unige.ch/.

Clarke, Harold D., Jane Jenson, Lawrence LeDuc, and Jon H. Pammett. 1996. *Absent Mandate: Canadian Electoral Politics in an Era of Restructuring*. 3d ed. Toronto: Gage.

Dalton, Russell. 2002. *Citizen Politics: Public Opinion and Political Parties in Advanced Western Democracies*, 3d ed. Chatham, NJ: Chatham House.

Gallagher, Michael, and Pier Vincenzo Uleri, eds. 1996. *The Referendum Experience in Europe*. London: Macmillan.

Gamble, Barbara. 1997. "Putting Civil Rights to a Popular Vote," *American Journal of Political Science* 91: 245-69

Gerber, Elisabeth. 1999. *The Populist Paradox*. Princeton, NJ: Princeton University Press.

Hamon, Francis. 1995. *Le référendum: Étude comparative*. Paris: LGDJ.

Hayward, Jack, ed. 1996. *The Crisis of Representation in Europe*. London: Frank Cass.

Huntington, Samuel. 1991. *The Third Wave: Democratization in the Late Twentieth Century*. Norman, OK: University of Oklahoma Press.

Initiative and Referendum Institute, United States. http://www.iandrinstitute.org.

Institute for Democracy and Electoral Assistance. Sweden. http://www.idea.int/vt.

Jenssen, Anders Todal, Pertti Pesonen and Mikael Gilljam, eds. 1998. *To Join or Not to Join: Three Nordic Referendums on Membership in the European Union.* Oslo: Scandinavian University Press.

Keesing's Record of World Events. http://www.keesings.com.

Kobach, Kris. 1993. *The Referendum: Direct Democracy in Switzerland.* Aldershot, England: Dartmouth.

Kriesi, Hanspeter. 1993. *Citoyenneté et démocratie directe.* Zürich: Seismo.

LeDuc, Lawrence, Richard G. Niemi, and Pippa Norris, eds. 2002. *Comparing Democracies 2: New Challenges in the Study of Elections and Voting.* London: Sage.

Lupia, Arthur, and Matthew McCubbins. 1998. *The Democratic Dilemma: Can Citizens Learn What They Need to Know?* New York: Cambridge University Press.

McLean, Iain. 1989. *Democracy and New Technology.* Cambridge: Polity Press.

Magleby, David. 1994. "Direct Legislation in the American States," in David Butler and Austin Ranney, eds., *Referendums Around the World: The Growing Use of Direct Democracy.* London: Macmillan.

Mendelsohn, Matthew, and Andrew Parkin, eds. 2001. *Referendum Democracy: Citizens, Elites and Deliberation in Referendum Campaigns.* London: Palgrave.

Norris, Pippa, ed. 1999. *Critical Citizens: Global Support for Democratic Governance.* Oxford: Oxford University Press.

O'Mahony, Jane. 1998. "The Irish Referendum Experience," *Representation* 35: 225-36.

Parkinson, John. 2001. "Who Knows Best? The Creation of the Citizen-Initiated Referendum in New Zealand," *Government and Opposition* 36: 403-21.

Sartori, Giovanni. 1987. *The Theory of Democracy Revisited.* Chatham, NJ: Chatham House.

Setälä, Maija. 1999. *Referendums and Democratic Government.* New York: St. Martin's.

Simpson, Alan. 1992. *Referendums: Constitutional and Political Perspectives.* Victoria University of Wellington: Department of Political Science.

Suksi, Markku. 1993. *Bringing in the People: A Comparison of Constitutional Forms and Practices of the Referendum.* Dordrecht: Nijhoff.

Uleri, Pier Vincenzo. 1996. "Italy: Referendums and Initiatives from the Origins to the Crisis of a Democratic Regime," in Michael Gallagher and Pier Vincenzo Uleri, eds. *The Referendum Experience in Europe.* London: Macmillan.

———. 2002. "On Referendum Voting in Italy: Yes, No or Non-vote?: How Italian Parties Learned to Control Referenda," *European Journal of Political Research* 41: 863-83.

Chapter 3

CANADA

Blais, André, Richard Johnston, Elisabeth Gidengil, and Neil Nevitte. 1996. "La dynamique référendaire: Pourquois les Canadiens onts-ils rejecté l'accord de Charlottetown?" *Revue français de science politique* 46: 817-830.

Boyer, Patrick. 1992. *Direct Democracy in Canada: The History and Future of Referendums*. Toronto: Dundurn Press.

Cairns, Alan and Douglas Williams, eds. 1991. *Disruptions: Constitutional Struggles from the Charter to Meech Lake*. Toronto: McLelland and Stewart.

Clarke, Harold D., and Allan Kornberg. 1994. "The Politics and Economics of Constitutional Choice: Voting in Canada's 1992 National Referendum," *Journal of Politics* 56: 940-62.

Clarke, Harold D., Jane Jenson, Lawrence LeDuc, and Jon H. Pammett. 1996. *Absent Mandate: Canadian Electoral Politics in an Era of Restructuring*. 3d ed. Toronto: Gage.

Côté, Pierre F., et al. 1992. *Démocratie et référendum: La procédure référendaire*. Montreal: Quebec/Amerique.

Johnston, Richard, André Blais, Elisabeth Gidengil, and Neil Nevitte. 1996. *The Challenge of Direct Democracy: The 1992 Canadian Referendum*. Montreal: McGill-Queen's University Press.

LeDuc, Lawrence. 1993. "'A Great Big NO': Canada's Constitutional Referendum of 1992," *Electoral Studies* 12: 257-63

———. 2001. "Consulting the People: The Canadian Experience with Referendums," in Joanna Everitt and Brenda O'Neill, eds. *Citizen Politics: Research and Theory in Canadian Political Behaviour*. Toronto: Oxford University Press Canada.

LeDuc, Lawrence and Jon H. Pammett. 1995. "Referendum Voting: Attitudes and Behaviour in the 1992 Constitutional Referendum," *Canadian Journal of Political Science* 28: 3-33.

McRoberts, Kenneth. 1997. *Misconceiving Canada: The Struggle for National Unity*. Toronto: Oxford University Press Canada.

Pal, Leslie, and F. Leslie Seidle. 1993. "Constitutional Politics: 1990-92: The Paradox of Participation," in Susan Phillips, *How Ottawa Spends, 1993-94: A More Democratic Canada?* Ottawa: Carleton University Press.

Russell, Peter. 1993. *Constitutional Odyssey*. 2d ed. Toronto: University of Toronto Press.

Saint-Germain, Maurice, and Gilles Grenier. 1994. "Le parti québécois, le 'Non' à Charlottetown et le bloc québécois: Est-ce le même électorat?" *Revue québécoise de science politique* 26: 161-78.

RUSSIA

Ahdieh, Robert B. 1997. *Russia's Constitutional Revolution: Legal Consciousness and the Transition to Democracy, 1985-1996*. University Park, PA: Pennsylvania State University Press.

Brady, Henry, and Cynthia Kaplan. 1994. "Eastern Europe and the Former Soviet Union," in David Butler and Austin Ranney, eds., *Referendums around the World: The Growing Use of Direct Democracy*. London: Macmillan.

Brown, Archie. 1993. "The October Crisis of 1993: Context and Implications," *Post Soviet Affairs* 9: 183-95.

Colton, Timothy. 2000. *Transitional Citizens: Voters and What Influences Them in the New Russia*. Cambridge, MA: Harvard University Press.

Colton, Timothy, and Robert Tucker, eds. 1995. *Patterns in Post-Soviet Leadership*. Boulder, CO: Westview Press.

Duncan, Peter J. 1993. "The Democratic Transition in Russia: From Coup to Referendum," *Parliamentary Affairs* 46: 490-505.

Fish, Steven. 1995. *Democracy from Scratch: Opposition and Regime in the New Russian Revolution*. Princeton, NJ: Princeton University Press.

Marsh, Christopher. 2002. *Russia at the Polls*. Washington, DC: CQ Press.

Ordeshook, Peter. 1997. "Constitutions for New Democracies: Reflections of Turmoil or Agents of Stability?" *Public Choice* 90:55-72.

Rose, Richard, and Evgeny Tikhomirov. 1996. *Trends in the New Russia Barometer: 1992-95*. Glasgow: University of Strathclyde.

White, Stephen. 2000. "Russia, Elections, Democracy," *Government and Opposition* 35: 302-24.

White, Stephen, and Ronald Hill. 1996. "Russia, the Former Soviet Union, and Eastern Europe: The Referendum as a Flexible Political Instrument," in Michael Gallagher and Pier Vincenzo Uleri, eds., *The Referendum Experience in Europe*. London: Macmillan.

White, Stephen, Richard Rose, and Ian McAllister. 1997. *How Russia Votes*. Chatham, NJ: Chatham House.

Wyman, Matthew, William Miller, Stephen White, and Paul Heywood. 1994. "The Russian Elections of December 1993," *Electoral Studies* 13: 254-71.

NEW ZEALAND

Aimer, Peter. 1999. "From Westminster Plurality to Continental Proportionality: Electoral System Change in New Zealand," in Henry Milner, ed., *Making Every Vote Count*. Peterborough: Broadview Press.

Boston, Jonathan. 1987. "Electoral Reform in New Zealand: The Report of the Royal Commission," *Electoral Studies* 6: 108-112.

Levine, Stephen and Nigel Roberts. 1993. "The New Zealand Electoral Referendum of 1992," *Electoral Studies* 12: 158-67.

———. 1994. "The New Zealand Electoral Referendum and General Election of 1993," *Electoral Studies* 13: 240-53.

———. 1997. "MMP: the Decision," in Raymond Miller, ed., *New Zealand Politics in Transition*. Auckland, NZ: Oxford University Press.

McRobie, Alan, ed. 1993. *Taking It to the People: The New Zealand Electoral Referendum Debate*. Christchurch, NZ: Hazard Press.

Miller, Raymond, ed. 1997. *New Zealand Politics in Transition*. Auckland, NZ: Oxford University Press.

Milner, Henry, ed. 1999. *Making Every Vote Count*. Peterborough: Broadview Press.

Nagel, Jack. 1999. "The Defect of Its Virtues: New Zealand's Experience with MMP," in Henry Milner, ed. *Making Every Vote Count*. Peterborough: Broadview Press.

Parkinson, John. 2001. "Who Knows Best? The Creation of the Citizen-Initiated Referendum in New Zealand," *Government and Opposition* 36: 403-21.

Royal Commission on Electoral Reform. 1986. *Towards a Better Democracy*. Wellington: Government Printer.

Vowles, Jack. 1995. "The Politics of Electoral Reform in New Zealand," *International Political Science Review* 16: 95-115.

Vowles, Jack, and Peter Aimer, eds. 1994. *Double Decision: The 1993 Election and Referendum in New Zealand*. Victoria University of Wellington Press.

Vowles, Jack, Peter Aimer, Susan Banducci, and Jeffrey Karp, eds. 1998. *Voters' Victory? New Zealand's First Election under Proportional Representation*. Auckland: Auckland University Press.

AUSTRALIA

Galligan, Brian. 1990. "The 1988 Referendums and Australia's Record on Constitutional Change," *Parliamentary Affairs* 43: 497-506.

———. 1995. *A Federal Republic: Australia's Constitutional System of Government.* Cambridge University Press.

———. 2001. "Amending Constitutions through the Referendum Device," in Matthew Mendelsohn and Andrew Parkin, *Referendum Democracy: Citizens, Elites and Deliberation in Referendum Campaigns.* London: Palgrave.

Galligan, Brian, and J.R. Nethercote. 1989. *The Constitutional Commission and the 1988 Referendums.* Canberra: Centre for Research on Federal Financial Relations, Australian National University.

Government of Australia, referendum information web site. http://www.dpmc.gov.au/referendum/index.htm.

Higley, John and R. Case. 2000. "Australia: The Politics of Becoming a Republic," *Journal of Democracy* 3: 136-50.

Hughes, Colin. 1994. "Australia and New Zealand," in David Butler and Austin Ranney, *Referendums around the World: The Growing Use of Direct Democracy.* London: Macmillan.

Luskin, Robert C., James S. Fishkin, Ian McAllister, John Higley, and Pamela Ryan. 2000. "Information Effects in Referendum Voting: Evidence from the Australian Deliberative Poll." Paper presented to the World Congress of the International Political Science Association, Quebec.

McAllister, Ian. 2001. "Elections without Cues: The 1999 Australian Republic Referendum," *Australian Journal of Political Science* 36: 247-69.

Miles, Richard. 1998. "Australia's Constitutional Referendum: A Shield Not a Sword," *Representation* 35: 237-46.

Uhr, John. 1998. *Deliberative Democracy in Australia.* Melbourne: Cambridge University Press.

———. 2000. "Testing Deliberative Democracy: The 1999 Australian Republic Referendum," *Government and Opposition* 35: 189-209.

Chapter 4

Baun, Michael. 1996. *An Imperfect Union: The Maastricht Treaty and the New Politics of European Integration.* Boulder, CO: Westview Press.

Best, Edward. 1994. "The Maastricht Treaty: What Does It Actually Say and Do?" in Finn Laursen and Sophie Vanhoonacker, eds., *The Ratification of the Maastricht Treaty: Issues, Debates and Future Implications.* Dordrecht: Nijhoff.

Franklin, Mark, Cees van der Eijk, and Michael Marsh. 1995. "Referendum Outcomes and Trust in Government: Public Support for Europe in the Wake of Maastricht," *West European Politics* 18: 101-17.

Gallagher, Michael. 1996. "Ireland: The Referendum as a Conservative Device," in Michael Gallagher and Pier Vincenzo Uleri, eds., *The Referendum Experience in Europe.* London: Macmillan.

Hamon, Francis. 1995. *Le référendum: Étude comparative.* Paris: LGDJ.

Hayward, Jack, ed. 1995. *The Crisis of Representation in Europe.* London: Frank Cass.

Laursen, Finn, and Sophie Vanhoonacker, eds. 1994. *The Ratification of the Maastricht Treaty: Issues, Debates and Future Implications.* Dordrecht: Nijhoff.

Qvortrup, Mads. 2001. "How to Lose a Referendum: The Danish Plebiscite on the Euro," *Political Quarterly* 72: 190-6.

Rourke, John T., Richard P. Hiskes, and Cyrus Zirakzadeh. 1992. *Direct Democracy and International Politics: Deciding International Issues through Referendums*. Boulder, CO: Lynne Rienner.

Wallace, William, and Julie Smith. 1995. "Democracy or Technocracy? European Integration and the Problem of Popular Consent," *West European Politics* 18: 137-57.

SPAIN

Boix, Carles and James Alt. 1991. "Partisan Voting in the Spanish 1986 NATO Referendum: An Ecological Analysis," *Electoral Studies* 10: 18-32.

Canals, R., F. Pallares, and J. Vallés. 1986. "The Referendum of March 12, 1986, on Spain's Remaining in NATO," *Electoral Studies* 5: 305-11.

Gillespie, Richard. 1989. *The Spanish Socialist Party*. Oxford: Clarendon.

Gooch, Anthony. 1986. "A Surrealistic Referendum: Spain and NATO," *Government and Opposition* 21: 300-316.

Gunther, Richard. 1986. "The Spanish Socialist Party: From Clandestine Opposition to Party of Government," in S.G. Payne, ed. *The Politics of Democratic Spain*. Chicago: Chicago Council on Foreign Relations.

Gunther, Richard, Giacomo Sani and Goldie Shabad. 1986. *Spain after Franco: The Making of a Competitive Party System*. Los Angeles: University of California Press.

Lopez Piña, Antonio, and Peter McDonough. 1984. "Cleavages in Spanish Politics: Regionalism, Religiosity and Social Class," in Russell Dalton, Scott Flanagan, and Paul Allen Beck, eds., *Electoral Change in Advanced Industrial Democracies*. Princeton: Princeton University Press.

Payne, S. G., ed. 1986. *The Politics of Democratic Spain*. Chicago: Chicago Council on Foreign Relations.

Prevost, Gary. 1986. "Spain's NATO Choice," *The World Today* 42: 129-32.

FRANCE

Appleton, Andrew. 1992. "Maastricht and the French Party System: Domestic Implications of the Treaty Referendum," *French Politics and Society* 10: 1-18.

Best, Edward. 1994. "The Maastricht Treaty: What Does It Actually Say and Do?" in Finn Laursen and Sophie Vanhoonacker, eds., *The Ratification of the Maastricht Treaty: Issues, Debates and Future Implications*. Dordrecht: Nijhoff.

Bogdanor, Vernon. 1994. "Western Europe," in David Butler and Austin Ranney, eds., *Referendums around the World: The Growing Use of Direct Democracy*. London: Macmillan.

Criddle, Byron. 1993. "The French Referendum on the Maastricht Treaty," *Parliamentary Affairs* 46: 228-38.

Dubois, Nicholas, and Phillipe Keraudren. 1994. "France and the Ratification of the Maastricht Treaty," in Finn Laursen and Sophie Vanhoonacker, eds., *The Ratification of the Maastricht Treaty: Issues, Debates and Future Implications*. Dordrecht: Nijhoff.

Franklin, Mark, Cees van der Eijk, and Michael Marsh. 1995. "Referendum Outcomes and Trust in Government: Public Support for Europe in the Wake of Maastricht," *West European Politics* 18: 101-17.

Habert, Phillipe. 1992. "Le choix de l'Europe et la décision de l'électeur," *Commentaire* 60.

Hartley, Anthony. 1992. "Maastricht's Problematical Future," *The World Today* 48: 179-82.

Morel, Laurence. 1993. "Party Attitudes toward Referendums in Western Europe," *West European Politics* 16: 225-44.

———. 1996. "France: Towards a Less Controversial Use of the Referendum," in Michael Gallagher and Pier Vincenzo Uleri eds., *The Referendum Experience in Europe*. London: Macmillan.

Wallace, William, and Julie Smith. 1995. "Democracy or Technocracy? European Integration and the Problem of Popular Consent," *West European Politics* 18: 137-57.

FINLAND, NORWAY, SWEDEN

Arter, David. 1995. "The EU Referendum in Finland on 16 October 1994: A Vote for the West, Not for Maastricht," *Journal of Common Market Studies* 33: 361-87.

Bjørklund, Tor. 1996. "The Three Nordic 1994 Referenda Concerning Membership in the EU," *Cooperation and Conflict* 31: 11-36.

Eddie, Graeme. 1994. "Sweden: Into Europe with the Social Democrats," *The World Today* 50: 203-5.

Fitzmaurice, John. 1995. "The 1994 Referenda on EU Membership in Austria and Scandinavia," *Electoral Studies* 14: 226-32.

Jahn, Detlef, and Ann-Sofie Storsved. 1995. "Legitimacy through Referendum: The Nearly Successful Domino Strategy of the EU Referendums in Austria, Finland, Sweden and Norway," *West European Politics* 18: 18-37.

Jenssen, Anders Todal, Pertti Pesonen and Mikael Gilljam, eds. 1998. *To Join or Not to Join: Three Nordic Referendums on Membership in the European Union*. Oslo: Scandinavian University Press.

Midtbø, Tor and Kjell Hines. 1998. "The Referendum-Election Nexus: An Aggregate Analysis of Norwegian Voting Behaviour," *Electoral Studies* 17: 77-94.

Pettersen, Per Arnt, Todal Jenssen and Ola Listhaug. 1996. "The 1994 EU Referendum in Norway: Continuity and Change," *Scandinavian Political Studies* 19: 257-30.

Pierce, Roy, Henry Valen, and Ola Listhaug. 1983. "Referendum Voting Behavior: The Norwegian and British Referenda on Membership in the European Community," *American Journal of Political Science* 27: 43-63.

Ruin, Olof. 1996. "Sweden: The Referendum as an Instrument for Defusing Political Issues," in Michael Gallagher and Pier Vincenzo Uleri, eds., *The Referendum Experience in Europe*. London: Macmillan.

Sogner, Ingrid, and Clive Archer. 1995. "Norway and Europe: Then and Now," *Journal of Common Market Studies* 33: 389-410.

Suksi, Marku. 1996. "Finland: the Referendum as a Dormant Feature," in Michael Gallagher and Pier Vincenzo Uleri, eds., *The Referendum Experience in Europe*. London: Macmillan.

Wyller, Thomas Chr. 1996. "Norway: Six Exceptions to the Rule," in Michael Gallagher and Pier Vincenzo Uleri, eds., *The Referendum Experience in Europe*. London: Macmillan.

DENMARK

Downs, William M. 2001. "Denmark's Referendum on the Euro," *West European Politics* 24: 222-6.

Franklin, Mark, Michael Marsh and Christopher Wlezien. 1994. "Attitudes toward Europe and Referendum Votes: A Response to Siune and Svensson," *Electoral Studies* 13: 117-21.

Gallagher, Michael. 1996. "Ireland: The Referendum as a Conservative Device," in Michael Gallagher and Pier Vincenzo Uleri, eds., *The Referendum Experience in Europe*. London: Macmillan.

Gundelach, Peter, and Karen Siune, eds. 1992. *From Voters to Participants*. Aarhus: Institute for Political Science, University of Aarhus.

Marcussen, Martin, and Mette Zølner. 2001. "The Danish EMU Referendum 2000: Business as Usual," *Government and Opposition* 36: 379-401.

Qvortrup, Mads. 1998. "Voter Knowledge and Participation: A Comparative Study of Referendums in Denmark and Switzerland," *Representation* 35: 255-64.

———. 2001. "How to Lose a Referendum: The Danish Plebiscite on the Euro," *Political Quarterly* 72: 190-96.

Siune, Karen, and Palle Svensson. 1993. "The Danes and the Maastricht Treaty: The Danish EC Referendum of June 1992," *Electoral Studies* 12: 99-111.

Siune, Karen, Palle Svensson, and Ole Tonsgaard. 1994. "The European Union: Why the Danes Said No in 1992 but Yes in 1993," *Electoral Studies* 13: 107-15.

Svensson, Palle. 1994. "The Danish Yes to Maastricht and Edinburgh," *Scandinavian Political Studies* 17: 69-82.

———. 1996. "Denmark: The Referendum as Minority Protection," in Michael Gallagher and Pier Vincenzo Uleri, eds., *The Referendum Experience in Europe*. London: Macmillan.

———. 2002. "Five Danish Referendums on the European Community and Union: A Critical Assessment of the Franklin Thesis," *European Journal of Political Research* 41: 733-50.

Chapter 5

QUEBEC

Bedlington, Stanley. 1978. *Malaysia and Singapore*. Ithaca, NY: Cornell University Press.

Blais, André, and Richard Nadeau. 1984. "La clientèle du oui," in Jean Crête, eds., *Le comportement électoral au Québec*. Chicoutimi, QC: Gaetan Morin.

———. 1992. "To Be or Not to Be Sovereignist: Quebeckers' Perennial Dilemma," *Canadian Public Policy* 28: 89-103.

Chan Heng Chee. 1971. *Singapore: The Politics of Survival 1965-67*. Oxford: Oxford University Press.

Clarke, Harold D., and Allan Kornberg. 1994. "The Politics and Economics of Constitutional Choice: Voting in Canada's 1992 National Referendum," *Journal of Politics* 56: 940-62.

———. 1996. "Choosing Canada? The 1995 Quebec Sovereignty Referendum," *PS* 26: 676-82.

Clarke, Harold D., Jane Jenson, Lawrence LeDuc and Jon H. Pammett. 1996. *Absent Mandate: Canadian Electoral Politics in an Era of Restructuring*, 3d ed. Toronto: Gage.

Cloutier, Edouard, et Le Centre de Recherches sur l'Opinion Publique. 1979. *Sondage sur la perception des problemes constitutionnels Québec-Canada par la population du Québec*. Quebec: Government of Québec, Ministry of Intergovernmental Affairs.

Cloutier, Edouard, Jean H. Guay, and Daniel Latouche. 1992. *Le Virage: L'évolution de l'opinion publique au Québec depuis 1960*. Montreal: Quebec/Amerique.

Crête, Jean, ed. 1984. *Le comportement électoral au Québec*. Chicoutimi, QC: Gaetan Morin.

Dion, Stephane. 1996. "Why is Secession Difficult in Well-Established Democracies?" *British Journal of Political Science* 26: 269-83.

Drouilly, Pierre. "Le référendum du 30 octobre 1995: Une analyse des résultats," http://www.cam.org/~pac/drouilly10.html.

Eggleston, Wilfrid. 1974. *Newfoundland: The Road to Confederation*. Ottawa: Information Centre.

Everitt, Joanna, and Brenda O'Neill. eds. 2002. *Citizen Politics: Research and Theory in Canadian Political Behaviour*. Toronto: Oxford University Press.

Kornberg, Allan and Harold D. Clarke, eds. 1983. *Political Support in Canada: The Crisis Years*. Durham, NC: Duke University Press.

LeDuc, Lawrence. 1997. "The Sovereignty Generation: A Cohort Analysis of the Quebec Electorate." Paper presented to the annual meeting of the Canadian Political Science Association, St. John's, Newfoundland.

———. 2001. "What Can Comparative Research Tell Us about the *Next* Quebec Referendum?" Paper presented to the annual meeting of the Canadian Political Science Association, Québec.

Leff, Carol Skelnik. 1997. *The Czech and Slovak Republics: Nation vs. State*. Boulder, CO: Westview Press.

Lindgren, Raymond. 1959. *Norway-Sweden: Union, Disunion, and Scandinavian Integration*. Princeton, NJ: Princeton University Press.

Linz, Juan, and Alfred Stepan. 1996. *Problems of Democratic Transition and Consolidation*. Baltimore, MD: John Hopkins University Press.

Marsh, Christopher. 2002. *Russia at the Polls: Voters, Elections and Democratization*. Washington, DC: CQ Press.

McRoberts, Kenneth. 1997. *Misconceiving Canada: The Struggle for National Unity*. Toronto: Oxford University Press.

Monière, Denis, and Jean H. Guay. 1996. *La bataille du Québec: Troisième épisode*. Québec: Fides.

Nadeau, Richard, Pierre Martin, and André Blais. 1999. "Attitudes toward Risk Taking and Individual Choice in the Quebec Referendum on Sovereignty," *British Journal of Political Science* 29: 523-39.

Noel, S.J.R. 1971. *Politics in Newfoundland*. Toronto: University of Toronto Press.

Pammett, Jon H., Harold D. Clarke, Jane Jenson, and Lawrence LeDuc. 1983. "Political Support and Voting Behaviour in the Quebec Referendum," in Allan Kornberg and Harold D. Clarke, *Political Support in Canada: The Crisis Years*. Durham, NC: Duke University Press.

Pammett, Jon H., and Lawrence LeDuc. 2001. "Sovereignty, Leadership and Voting in the Quebec Referendums," *Electoral Studies* 20: 265-80.

Pinard, Maurice, and Richard Hamilton. 1977. "The Independence Issue and the Polarization of the Electorate: The 1973 Quebec Election," *Canadian Journal of Political Science* 10: 215-59.

———. 1978. "The Parti Québécois Comes to Power: An Analysis of the

1976 Quebec Election," *Canadian Journal of Political Science* 11: 739-775.

———. 1984. "Les québécois votent Non: Le sens et la portée du vote," in Jean Crête, ed., *Le comportement électoral au Québec*. Chicoutimi, QC: Gaetan Morin.

Pinard, Maurice, Robert Bernier, and Vincent Lemieux. 1997. *Un combat inachevé*. Sainte-Foy, QC: Presses de l'Université du Québec.

Saint-Germain, Maurice, and Gilles Grenier. 1994. "Le parti québécois, le 'Non' à Charlottetown et le bloc québécois: Est-ce le même électorat?" *Revue québécoise de science politique* 26: 161-78.

Timson, Annis Mae. 1994. "To Be or Not to Be: A Sovereign Quebec?" *The World Today* 50: 202-3.

Trent, John E., Robert Young, and Guy Lachapelle, eds. 1996. *Québec-Canada: What is the Path Ahead?* Ottawa: University of Ottawa Press.

Turcotte, André. 1996. "A la prochaine ... again: The Quebec Referendum of 1995," *Electoral Studies* 15: 399-402.

Young, Robert A. 1994a. *The Breakup of Czechoslovakia*. Kingston, ON: Queen's University, Institute of Intergovernmental Relations.

———. 1994b. "How Do Secessions Happen?" *Canadian Journal of Political Science* 27: 773-92.

———. 1999. *The Struggle for Quebec*. Montreal: McGill-Queen's University Press.

UKRAINE

Birch, Sarah. 1995. "The Ukrainian Parliamentary and Presidential Elections of 1994," *Electoral Studies* 14: 93-99.

———. 2000. *Elections and Democratization in Ukraine*. New York: St. Martin's.

Brady, Henry and Cynthia Kaplan. 1994. "Eastern Europe and the Former Soviet Union," in David Butler and Austin Ranney, eds., *Referendums around the World: The Growing Use of Direct Democracy*. London: Macmillan.

D'Anieri, Paul, Robert Kravchuk, and Taras Kuzio. 1999. *Politics and Society in Ukraine*. Boulder, CO: Westview Press.

Kubicek, Paul. 2000. *Unbroken Ties: The State, Interest Associations, and Corporatism in Ukraine*. Ann Arbor, MI: University of Michigan Press.

Kuzio, Taras, ed. 1998. *Contemporary Ukraine: Dynamics of Post-Soviet Transformation*. Armonk, NY: M.E. Sharpe.

Kuzio, Taras and Andrew Wilson. 1994. *Ukraine: Perestroika to Independence*. New York: St. Martin's.

Kuzio, Taras, Robert Kravchuk, and Paul D'Anieri. 1999. *State and Institution Building in Ukraine*. New York: St. Martin's.

Linz, Juan, and Alfred Stepan. 1996. *Problems of Democratic Transition and Consolidation*. Baltimore, MD: Johns Hopkins University Press.

Tolz, Vera, and Melanie Newton, eds. 1993. *The USSR in 1991: A Record of Events*. Boulder, CO: Westview Press.

White, Stephen, and Ronald Hill. 1996. "Russia, the Former Soviet Union, and Eastern Europe: The Referendum as a Flexible Political Instrument," in Michael Gallagher and Pier Vincenzi Uleri, eds., *The Referendum Experience in Europe*. London: Macmillan.

SCOTLAND AND WALES

Balsom, Denis. 1996. "The United Kingdom: Constitutional Pragmatism and the Adoption of the Referendum," in Michael Gallagher and Pier Vincenzi Uleri, eds., *The Referendum Experience in Europe*. London: Macmillan.

Balsom, Denis, and Ian McAllister. 1979. "The Welsh and Scottish Devolution Referenda," *Parliamentary Affairs* 32: 394-409.

Bochel, John, David Denver, and Allan MacCartney. 1981. *The Referendum Experience: Scotland, 1979*. Aberdeen: Aberdeen University Press.

Bogdanor, Vernon. 1981. *The People and the Party System: The Referendum and Electoral Reform in British Politics*. Cambridge: Cambridge University Press.

———. 1996. *Politics and the Constitution*. Aldershot, England: Dartmouth.

Broughton, David. 1998. "The Welsh Devolution Referendum of 1997," *Representation* 35: 200-09.

Denver, David. 2002. "Voting in the 1997 Scottish and Welsh Devolution Referendums: Information, Interests and Opinions," *European Journal of Political Research* 41: 827-43.

Denver, David, James Mitchell, Charles Pattie, and Hugh Bochel. 2000. *Scotland Decides*. London: Frank Cass.

Denver, David, Charles Pattie, Hugh Bochel, and James Mitchell. 1998. "The Devolution Referendums in Scotland," *Representation* 35: 210-18.

Foulkes, David, J. Barry Jones, and Rick Wilford, eds. 1983. *The Welsh Veto: The Wales Act 1978 and the Referendum*. Cardiff: University of Wales Press.

Luke, Paul, and David Johnson. 1976. "Devolution by Referendum," *Parliamentary Affairs* 29: 332-39.

McAllister, Laura. 1998. "The Welsh Devolution Referendum: Definitely Maybe," *Parliamentary Affairs* 51: 149-65.

Miller, William L. 1998. "The Periphery and Its Paradoxes," *West European Politics* 21: 167-96.

Mitchell, James, David Denver, Charles Pattie, and Hugh Bochel. 1998. "The 1997 Devolution Referendum in Scotland," *Parliamentary Affairs* 51: 166-81.

Taylor, Bridget, and Katerina Thomson, eds. 1999. *Scotland and Wales: Nations Again?* Cardiff: University of Wales Press.

PUERTO RICO

Álvarez Rivera, Manuel. *Elections in Puerto Rico*. http://ElectionsPuertoRico.org/home_en.html.

Anderson, Robert. 1988. "Political Parties in Puerto Rico and the Politics of Status," *Caribbean Studies* 21: 1-43.

Berríos Martínez, Rubén. 1997. "Puerto Rico's Decolonization," *Foreign Affairs* 76: 100-14.

Falk, Pamela, ed. 1986. *The Political Status of Puerto Rico*. Lexington, MA: D.C. Heath.

García Passalacqua, Juan. 1994. "The Grand Dilemma: Viability and Sovereignty for Puerto Rico," *Annals of the American Academy of Political and Social Science* 94: 151-64.

Heine, Jorge, ed. 1983. *Time for Decision: The United States and Puerto Rico*. Lanham, MD: North-South Publishing.

Morales Carrión, Arturo. 1983. *Puerto Rico: A Political and Cultural History*. New York: Norton.

Puerto Rico. Commonwealth of Puerto Rico Elections Commission. http://www.ceepur.net/?en.

———. Office of the Governor. *The Self Determination Process for Puerto Rico* http://www.prfaa-govpr.org/sdp_contents.htm.

Rivera, Angel and Aaron Ramos. 1997. "The Quest for a New Political Arrangement in Puerto Rico," *Caribbean Studies* 26: 265-92.

University of Geneva. Center for the Study of Direct Democracy. http://c2d.unige.ch/start.en.msql.

Chapter 6

Kesselman, Mark and Joel Krieger. 1992. *European Politics in Transition.* 2d ed. Lexington, MA: D.C. Heath.

Parkinson, John. 2001. "Who Knows Best? The Creation of the Citizen-Initiated Referendum in New Zealand," *Government and Opposition* 36: 403-21.

Rourke, John T., Richard P. Hiskes, and Cyrus Zirakzadeh. 1992. *Direct Democracy and International Politics: Deciding International Issues through Referendums.* Boulder, CO: Lynne Rienner.

Setälä, Maija. 1999. *Referendums and Democratic Government.* New York: St. Martin's.

SWEDEN

Arter, David. 1999. *Scandinavian Politics Today.* Manchester: Manchester University Press.

Bennulf, Martin, and Sören Holmberg. 1990. "The Green Breakthrough in Sweden," *Scandinavian Political Studies* 13: 165-84.

Gramberg, Donald and Sören Holmberg. 1988. "Preferences, Expectations and Voting in Sweden's Referendum on Nuclear Power," *Social Science Quarterly* 67: 379-91.

Knutsen, Oddbjørn. 1990. "The Materialist/Postmaterialist Value Dimension in the Nordic Countries," *West European Politics* 13: 258-74.

Lane, Jan-Erik, ed. 1991. *Understanding the Swedish Model.* London: Frank Cass.

Lindström, Ulf. 1982. "The Changing Scandinavian Voter: When, Where, Who, Why," *European Journal of Political Research* 10.

Pontusson, Jonas. 1992. "Sweden," in Mark Kesselman and Joel Krieger, *European Politics in Transition.* 2d ed. Lexington, MA: D.C. Heath.

Ruin, Olof. 1996. "Sweden: The Referendum as an Instrument for Defusing Political Issues," in Michael Gallagher and Pier Vincenzi Uleri, eds., *The Referendum Experience in Europe.* London: Macmillan.

Sainsbury, Diane. 1986. "The Electoral Difficulty of the Scandinavian Social Democrats in the 1970s," *Comparative Politics* 18: 1-19.

———. 1992. "The 1991 Swedish Elections: Protest, Fragmentation and a Shift to the Right," *West European Politics* 15: 160-6.

Setälä, Maija. 1999. *Referendums and Democratic Government.* New York: St. Martin's.

IRELAND

Adshead, Maura. 1996. "Sea Change on the Isle of Saints and Scholars: The 1995 Irish Referendum on the Introduction of Divorce," *Electoral Studies* 15: 138-42.

Collins, Neil, and Terry Cradden. 1997. *Irish Politics Today.* Manchester: Manchester University Press.

Darcy, Robert, and Michael Laver. 1990. "Referendum Dynamics and the Irish Divorce Amendment," *Public Opinion Quarterly* 54: 4-20.

Gallagher, Michael. 1996. "Ireland: the Referendum as a Conservative Device," in Michael Gallagher and Pier Vincenzo Uleri, eds., *The Referendum Experience in Europe.* London: Macmillan.

Gilland, Karin. 1999. "Referenda in the Republic of Ireland," *Electoral Studies* 18: 430-9.

Girvin, Brian. 1993. "The Referendums on Abortion," *Irish Political Studies* 8: 118-24.

———. 1996. "The Irish Divorce Referendum of November 1995," *Irish Political Studies* 11.

O'Leary, Cornelius, and Tom Hesketh. 1988. "The Irish Abortion and Divorce Referendum Campaigns," *Irish Political Studies* 3: 43-62.

O'Mahony, Jane. 1998. "The Irish Referendum Experience," *Representation* 35: 225-36.

Sinnott, Richard. 1995. *Irish Voters Decide: Voting Behaviour in Elections and Referendums since 1918*. Manchester: Manchester University Press.

CALIFORNIA

Allswang, John M. 2000. *The Initiative and Referendum in California, 1898-1998*. Stanford, CA: Stanford University Press.

Banducci, Susan. 1998. "Direct Legislation: When Is It Used and When Does It Pass?" in Shaun Bowler, Todd Donovan and Caroline J. Tolbert, eds., *Citizens as Legislators: Direct Democracy in the United States*. Columbus, OH: Ohio State University Press.

Bowler, Shaun, and Todd Donovan. 1998a. *Demanding Choices: Opinion, Voting, and Direct Democracy*. Ann Arbor, MI: University of Michigan Press.

———. 1998b. "Two Cheers for Direct Democracy, or Who's Afraid of the Initiative Process," *Representation* 35: 247-54.

———. 2000. "California's Experience with Direct Democracy," *Parliamentary Affairs* 53: 644-56.

Bowler, Shaun, Todd Donovan, and Caroline J. Tolbert, eds. 1998. *Citizens as Legislators: Direct Democracy in the United States*. Columbus, OH: Ohio State University Press.

Broder, David. 2000. *Democracy Derailed*. New York: Harcourt.

California Ballot Propositions Database. http://www.uchastings.edu/library/ballotprops.htm.

Collins, Richard B.. 2001. "How Democratic Are Initiatives?" *University of Colorado Law Review* 72: 983-1003.

Cronin, Thomas. 1989. *Direct Democracy: The Politics of Initiative, Referendum and Recall*. Cambridge, MA: Harvard University Press.

Donovan, Todd, Shaun Bowler, and David McCuan. 2001. "Political Consultants and the Initiative Industrial Complex," in Larry Sabato, Howard Ernst and Bruce Larson, eds., *Dangerous Democracy: The Battle over Ballot Initiatives in America*. Lanham, MD: Rowan and Littlefield.

Dougherty, Regina, Everett C. Ladd, David Wilber and Lynn Zayachkiwsky, eds. 1997. *America at the Polls*. Storrs, CT: University of Connecticut, Roper Center.

Gamble Barbara. 1997. "Putting Civil Rights to a Popular Vote," *American Political ScienceReview* 91: 245-69.

Gerber, Elisabeth. 1999. *The Populist Paradox*. Princeton, NJ: Princeton University Press.

Haskell, John. 2001. *Direct Democracy or Representative Government?* Boulder, CO: Westview Press.

Initiative and Referendum Institute. United States. http://www.iandrinstitute.org.

Lupia, Arthur. 1992. "Busy Voters, Agenda Control, and the Power of Information," *American Political Science Review* 86: 390-403.

———. 1994. "Shortcuts vs. Encyclopedias: Information and Voting Behavior in California's Insurance Reform Elections," *American Political Science Review* 88: 63-76.

Lupia, Arthur, and Matthew McCubbins. 1998. *The Democratic Dilemma: Can Citizens Learn What They Need To Know?* New York: Cambridge University Press.

Magleby, David. 1984. *Direct Legislation: Voting on Ballot Propositions in the United States.* Baltimore, MD: Johns Hopkins University Press.

———. 1988. "Taking the Initiative: Direct Legislation and Direct Democracy in the 1980s," *PS* 21: 601-11

———. 1994. "Direct Legislation in the American States," in David Butler and Austin Ranney, *Referendums around the World: The Growing Use of Referendums.* London: Macmillan.

———. 1995. "Let the Voters Decide? An Assessment of the Initiative and Referendum Process," *University of Colorado Law Review* 66: 13-46

Sabato, Larry, Howard Ernst, and Bruce Larson, eds. 2001. *Dangerous Democracy: The Battle Over Ballot Initiatives in America.* Lanham, MD: Rowan & Littlefield.

Schmidt, David. 1989. *Citizen Lawmakers: The Ballot Initiative Revolution.* Philadelphia, PA: Temple University Press.

Schrag, Peter. 1998. *Paradise Lost: California's Experience, America's Future.* New York: New Press.

SWITZERLAND

Christin, Thomas, Simon Hug, and Pascal Sciarini. 2002. "Interests and Information in Referendum Voting: An Analysis of Swiss Voters," *European Journal of Political Research* 41: 759-76.

Franklin, Mark. 1996. "Electoral Participation," in Lawrence LeDuc, Richard G. Niemi, and Pippa Norris, *Comparing Democracies: Elections and Voting in Global Perspective.* Beverly Hills, CA: Sage Publications.

Geneva, University of. Center for the Study of Direct Democracy. http://c2d.unige.ch/start.en.msql.

Kobach, Kris. 1993a. *The Referendum: Direct Democracy in Switzerland.* Dartmouth, England: Aldershot.

———. 1993b. "Recent Developments in Swiss Direct Democracy," *Electoral Studies* 12:342-65.

———. 1994. "Switzerland," in David Butler and Austin Ranney, *Referendums around the World: The Growing Use of Direct Democracy.* London: Macmillan.

———. 1997. "Direct Democracy and Swiss Isolationism," *West European Politics* 20: 185-211.

Kriesi, Hanspeter. 1993. *Citoyenneté et démocratie directe.* Zürich: Seismo.

Kriesi, Hanspeter, and Dominique Wisler. 1996. "Social Movements and Direct Democracy in Switzerland," *European Journal of Political Research* 30: 19-40.

Qvortrup, Mads. 1998. "Voter Knowledge and Participation: A Comparative Study of Referendums in Denmark and Switzerland," *Representation* 35: 255-64.

Setälä, Maija. 1999. *Referendums and Democratic Government.* New York: St. Martin's.

Switzerland, Government of. http://193.5.216.31/ch/f/pore/va/19990613/index.html.

Treschel, Alexander, and Hanspeter Kriesi. 1996. "Switzerland: The Referendum and Initiative as a Centerpiece of the Political System," in Michael Gallagher and Pier Vincenzo

Uleri, eds., *The Referendum Experience in Europe*. London: Macmillan.

Treschel, Alexander, and Pascal Sciarini. 1998. "Direct Democracy in Switzerland: Do Elites Matter?" *European Journal of Political Research* 33: 99-124.

Chapter 7

Aardal, Bernt, Anders Todal Jenssen, Henrik Oscarsson, Risto Sänkiaho, and Erika Säynässalo. 1998. "Can Ideology Explain the EU Vote?" in Anders Todal Jenssen, Pertti Pesonen, and Mikael Gilljam, eds., *To Join or Not to Join: Three Nordic Referendums on Membership in the European Union*. Oslo: Scandinavian University Press.

Bowler, Shaun, and Todd Donovan. 1998. *Demanding Choices: Opinion, Voting, and Direct Democracy*. Ann Arbor, MI: University of Michigan Press.

Budge, Ian. 1996. *The New Challenge of Direct Democracy*. Cambridge: Polity Press.

Butler, David, and Austin Ranney, eds., 1994. *Referendums Around the World: The Growing Use of Direct Democracy*. London: Macmillan.

Christin, Thomas, Simon Hug, and Pascal Sciarini. 2002. "Interests and Information in Referendum Voting: An Analysis of Swiss Voters," *European Journal of Political Research* 41: 759-76.

Cronin, Thomas. 1989. *Direct Democracy: The Politics of Initiative, Referendum and Recall*. Cambridge, MA: Harvard University Press.

Darcy, Robert, and Michael Laver. 1990. "Referendum Dynamics and the Irish Divorce Amendment," *Public Opinion Quarterly* 54: 4-20.

Franklin, Mark, Cees van der Eijk, and Michael Marsh. 1995. "Referendum Outcomes and Trust in Government: Public Support for Europe in the Wake of Maastricht," *West European Politics* 18:101-17.

Franklin, Mark, Michael Marsh, and Christopher Wlezien. 1994. "Attitudes toward Europe and Referendum Votes: A Response to Siune and Svensson," *Electoral Studies* 13: 117-21.

Gallagher, Michael and Pier Vincenzo Uleri, eds. 1996. *The Referendum Experience in Europe*. London: Macmillan.

Gundelach, Peter, and Karen Siune, eds. 1992. *From Voters to Participants*. Aarhus, Denmark: Institute for Political Science, University of Aarhus.

Heath, Anthony, and Bridget Taylor. 1999. "Were the Scottish and Welsh Referendums Second Order Elections?" in Bridget Taylor and Katarina Thomson, eds., *Scotland and Wales: Nations Again?* Cardiff: University of Wales Press.

Jenssen, Anders Todal, Pertti Pesonen, and Mikael Gilljam, eds. 1998. *To Join or Not to Join: Three Nordic Referendums on Membership in the European Union*. Oslo: Scandinavian University Press.

Johnston, Richard, André Blais, Elisabeth Gidengil, and Neil Nevitte. 1996. *The Challenge of Direct Democracy: The 1992 Canadian Referendum*. Montreal: McGill-Queen's University Press.

LeDuc, Lawrence. 2001a. "What Can Comparative Research Tell Us about the *Next* Quebec Referendum?" Paper presented to the annual meeting of the Canadian Political Science Association, Québec.

———. 2001b. "Opinion Formation and Reversal in Referendum Campaigns." Paper presented to the annual meeting of the American Political Science Association, San Francisco, CA.

———. 2002. "Referendums and Elections: How Do Campaigns Differ?" in David Farrell and Rüdiger Schmitt-Beck, eds., *Do Political Campaigns Matter? Campaign Effects in Elections and Referendums*. London: Routledge.

LeDuc, Lawrence, and Jon H. Pammett. 1995. "Referendum Voting: Attitudes and Behaviour in the 1992 Constitutional Referendum," *Canadian Journal of Political Science* 28: 3-33.

———. 2001. "Sovereignty, Leadership and Voting in the Quebec Referendums," *Electoral Studies* 20: 265-80.

LeDuc, Lawrence, and Palle Svensson, eds. 2002. *Interests, Information and Voting in Referendums*. Special issue of the *European Journal of Political Research* 41, no. 6.

Listhaug, Ola, Sören Holmberg and Risto Sänkiaho. 1998. "Partisanship and EU Choice," in Anders Todal Jenssen, Pertti Pesonen, and Mikael Gilljam, eds., *To Join or Not to Join: Three Nordic Referendums on Membership in the European Union*. Oslo: Scandinavian University Press.

Lupia, Arthur. 1992. "Busy Voters, Agenda Control, and the Power of Information," *American Political Science Review* 86: 390-403.

———. 1994. "Shortcuts vs. Encyclopedias: Information and Voting Behavior in California's Insurance Reform Elections," *American Political Science Review* 88: 63-76.

Lupia, Arthur, and Matthew McCubbins. 1998. *The Democratic Dilemma: Can Citizens Learn What They Need To Know?* Cambridge: Cambridge University Press.

Luskin, Robert C., James S. Fishkin, Ian McAllister, John Higley, and Pamela Ryan. 2000. "Information Effects in Referendum Voting: Evidence from the Australian Deliberative Poll." Paper presented to the World Congress of the International Political Science Association, Québec.

McAllister, Ian. 2000. "Elections without Cues: The 1999 Australian Republic Referendum." Paper, Research School of Social Sciences, Australian National University.

Morel, Laurence. 1993. "Party Attitudes toward Referendums in Western Europe," *West European Politics* 16: 225-43.

Pesonen, Pertti. 1998. "Voting Decisions," in Anders Todal Jenssen, Pertti Pesonen, and Mikael Gilljam, eds., *To Join or Not to Join: Three Nordic Referendums on Membership in the European Union*. Oslo: Scandinavian University Press.

Qvortrup, Mads. 1998. "Voter Knowledge and Participation: A Comparative Study of Referendums in Denmark and Switzerland," *Representation* 35:255-64.

Siune, Karen, Palle Svensson, and Ole Tonsgaard. 1994. "The European Union: Why the Danes said No in 1992 but Yes in 1993," *Electoral Studies* 13:107-15.

Taylor, Bridget, and Katerina Thompson, eds. 1999. *Scotland and Wales: Nations Again?* Cardiff: University of Wales Press.

Tonsgaard, Ole. 1992. "A Theoretical Model of Referendum Behaviour," in Peter Gundelach and Karen Siune, eds., *From Voters to Participants*. Aarhus, Denmark: Institute for Political Science, University of Aarhus.

Zaller, John R. 1992. *The Nature and Origins of Mass Opinion*. New York: Cambridge University Press.

Chapter 8

Banducci, Susan. 1998. "Direct Legislation: When Is It Used and When Does It Pass?" in Shaun Bowler, Todd Donovan and Caroline J. Tolbert, eds., *Citizens as Legislators: Direct Democracy in the United States.* Columbus, OH: Ohio State University Press.

Bowler, Shaun, and Todd Donovan. 1998. "Two Cheers for Direct Democracy, or Who's Afraid of the Initiative Process?" *Representation* 35: 247-54.

Bowler, Shaun, Todd Donovan, and Caroline J. Tolbert, eds. 1998. *Citizens as Legislators: Direct Democracy in the United States.* Columbus, Ohio: Ohio State University Press.

Broder, David. 2000. *Democracy Derailed.* New York: Harcourt.

Budge, Ian. 1996. *The New Challenge of Direct Democracy.* Cambridge: Polity Press.

Donovan, Todd, and Shaun Bowler. 1998. "Responsive or Responsible Government?" in Shaun Bowler, Todd Donovan and Caroline J. Tolbert, eds., *Citizens as Legislators: Direct Democracy in the United States.* Columbus, OH: Ohio State University Press.

Gamble, Barbara. 1997. "Putting Civil Rights to a Popular Vote," *American Journal of Political Science* 91: 245-69.

Gerber, Elisabeth. 1999. *The Populist Paradox.* Princeton, NJ: Princeton University Press.

Haskell, John. 2001. *Direct Democracy or Representative Government?* Boulder, CO: Westview Press.

Hamon, Francis. 1995. *Le référendum: Étude comparative.* Paris: LGDJ.

Kobach, Kris. 1993. *The Referendum: Direct Democracy in Switzerland.* Dartmouth, England: Aldershot.

Mendelsohn, Matthew, and Andrew Parkin, eds. 2001. *Referendum Democracy: Citizens, Elites, and Deliberation in Referendum Campaigns.* London: Palgrave.

Sabato, Larry, Howard Ernst, and Bruce Larson, eds. 2001. *Dangerous Democracy: The Battle over Ballot Initiatives in America.* Lanham, MD: Rowan & Littlefield.

Setälä, Maija. 1999. *Referendums and Democratic Government.* New York: St. Martin's.

Seyd, Patrick. 1998. "In Praise of Party," *Parliamentary Affairs* 51: 198-208.

Index